PRIVATIZING A PROVINCE

PRIVATIZING A PROVINCE

THE NEW RIGHT IN SASKATCHEWAN

JAMES M. PITSULA
Department of History, University of Regina

&

KENNETH A. RASMUSSEN
Faculty of Administration, University of Regina

1990
New Star Books
Vancouver

Printed and bound in Canada
1 2 3 4 5   94 93 92 91 90
First printing May 1990

The publisher is grateful for assistance provided by the Canada Council

New Star Books Ltd.
2504 York Avenue
Vancouver, B.C.
V6K 1E3

F
1034
.P57
1990

Canadian Cataloguing in Publication Data
Pitsula, James Michael.
Privatizing a province

ISBN 0-921586-10-8 (bound). – ISBN 0-921586-09-4 (pbk.)

1. Conservatism – Saskatchewan.   2. Saskatchewan – Politics and government –
1982-   3. Privatization – Saskatchewan.   4. Progressive Conservative Party of
Saskatchewan.   I. Rasmussen, Kenneth A., 1957- II. Title.
FC3527.2.P57 1990   320.97124   C90-091091-7
F1072.P57 1990

To the memory of
Tommy Douglas

ACKNOWLEDGMENTS

Many people assisted us in preparing this book, but the main debt is owed to our research assistant Linda Sarafinchan. She dug out and brought order to large amounts of information, and helped us sort out the issues and develop our interpretation of the new right in Saskatchewan.

We would also like to thank Helen Yum, whose red pen brought clarity and precision to the manuscript. We are grateful to Marilyn Bickford, who did most of the typing, sometimes under severe time constraints; Susane Sorochan, who gave extra secretarial help; and Paula Rein, who proofread portions of the manuscript.

Thanks are also due to the staff of the Government Publications Section of the University of Regina Library for their efforts in locating materials, and to Rolf Maurer and Audrey McClellan of New Star Books.

Finally, we wish to acknowledge the financial assistance for the project from: the Canadian Studies Program of the Department of the Secretary of State; the Faculty of Administration, University of Regina, Research Fund; and the Social Sciences and Humanities Research Council General Research Fund.

The contents of the book are the sole responsibility of the authors.

CONTENTS

◇ ───────────────── ◇

INTRODUCTION

T he purpose of this book is to describe and analyze the impact of the new right upon Saskatchewan since 1982. The term "new right" refers to the political movement that seeks to implement neo-conservative ideology. At the heart of the ideology is a profound aversion to government intervention in the economy, the welfare state, and collectivist values in general, combined with an equally profound admiration for private enterprise and the free market system. The new right works in close alliance with the new Christian right, sometimes known as the "moral majority," a movement dedicated to using the state to enforce its own particular moral code. Since the late 1970s the new right has been a force to be reckoned with in the United States, Great Britain, and elsewhere. In Canada, too, the impact has been felt. Although the Mulroney government has displayed many of the symptoms, the most extreme manifestations have occurred at the provincial level. The spearheads of the new right in Canada have been Bill Vander Zalm's British Columbia and Grant Devine's Saskatchewan.

Since the Tories took power in 1982, Saskatchewan, long regarded as a laboratory for social democracy, has been a hotbed for neo-conservatism. Grant Devine and key players in his government belong to the same ideological family as Margaret Thatcher, Ronald Reagan, and other apostles of the new right. The Saskatchewan Tories are genuine neo-conservatives. Their belief that the role of government must be reduced led to the announcement of the biggest sell-off of publicly owned assets in the history of the province; under them, privatization became a veritable crusade.

But the impact of the new right on Saskatchewan is not limited to the sale of Crown corporations and the contracting out of government services. It encompasses an attack on all institutions except those based upon private decision-making in the marketplace. The welfare state is held in deep suspicion because it is seen as both anti-family and detrimental to individual initiative. The result in Saskatchewan has been the erosion of social services and the virtual breakdown of the public welfare system. The new right also directs its fire against labour unions, who are blamed for interfering with the workings of the market and for restricting the freedom of individual employees and employers. The Saskatchewan government has accordingly moved to weaken the labour movement and reduce union rights.

In a more general way, the impact of the new right includes a denigration of the role of government in society. It is simply assumed that government bureaucracy will do things badly and that the private sector can always do a better job. Devine and his colleagues have made known their disregard for government as an institution in a number of ways. Firings, forced early retirements, and political witch hunts have left a civil service that was once regarded as one of the finest in Canada in a state of demoralized disarray. The Devine government has flouted the conventions of parliamentary democracy, failed to be properly accountable for the spending of public money, meddled with the independence of the judiciary, indulged in outrageous patronage, and demonstrated a level of incompetence that can only be described as astounding. This pattern of mismanagement can be linked, at least partly, to the new right's disdain for the institution of government, which they regard as an irksome burden rather than a valuable instrument for collective action and social betterment.

Although it is an international movement with a common ideological core, neo-conservatism does not express itself in precisely the same way in every country or province. Thatcherism, for example, places much more emphasis on privatization than does Reaganism, which emphasizes deregulation. The reason for the difference is that the British government had, over the years, set up a large number of public sector corporations; the American government, by contrast, had established relatively few and chose to regulate instead. Margaret Thatcher had considerably more publicly owned property to dispose of than did Ronald Reagan, with the result that privatization figured more prominently in Britain. Local conditions and circumstances invariably modify the way neo-conservative principles are applied in a particular country. The new right is an international phenomenon with local variants.

It is not surprising, therefore, to find that Saskatchewan has developed its own distinctive brand of neo-conservatism. The two main factors influencing the new right in Saskatchewan are the province's strong, well-entrenched social democratic tradition, and the hinterland nature of the economy. The former requires the Tory government to package its ideology carefully so as not to offend large sections of the electorate; the latter makes it necessary to compromise neo-conservative free market principles.

When elected in 1982, the Tories inherited a substantial Crown corporation sector, the very size of which provided ample opportunities for privatization. At the same time, the Devine government had to contend with the fact that most people in Saskatchewan liked their Crown corporations, which were by and large perceived as having served the province well. And while the NDP had been defeated in 1982, the CCF/NDP social democratic legacy had not been entirely discredited. The significance of this point becomes clearer when the Saskatchewan election in 1982 is compared with the British election of 1979. When the Tories under Margaret Thatcher took power in Britain, the economy was a mess, government debt was huge, and trade unions were believed to be dictating to the Labour government. When the Tories took power in Saskatchewan, the economy was in fairly good shape, the budget had been balanced eleven years in a row, and the labour unions were accusing the NDP government of not listening to them. Thatcher had no difficulty boldly proclaiming a neo-conservative revolution. If Devine had done the same in Saskatchewan, he would have been perceived as too right-wing and would have lost the 1982 election.

Through most of his years in office, Devine has not made a habit of denouncing Saskatchewan's social democratic heritage. Indeed, his fanciful claim to be the natural heir to Tommy Douglas suggests the opposite. Devine has been particularly non-ideological around election time. Neither the 1982 nor the 1986 campaign was fought by the Tories on clear right-versus-left lines. In its first term, the government carried out a few privatizations, but all the while publicly denied any grand strategy to privatize everything. Not until 1987 was the government entirely frank about its new right agenda. At that time, Devine, in Maggie Thatcher-style, announced the death of socialism, the "Waterloo of the NDP," and the privatization of all Crown corporations except utilities (later it turned out that not even utilities were exempt). This was Devine's clearest declaration of his neo-conservative principles. As the government's second term wound down and the inevitable election began to loom, he backtracked, confessing that he had perhaps "gotten too far ahead" of public opinion. The ideology was consistent, but for tactical reasons it had to be held in abeyance for a while. The continuing strength of social democratic values has prevented the Tory government from privatizing Saskatchewan as quickly as it would like.

The other major factor that has put a damper on the new right is the nature of the prairie economy. When they first took power, the Tories believed that all they needed to do was declare the province "open for business" and entrepreneurs and investors would rush in. It didn't happen for the simple reason that Saskatchewan has a small, scattered population located a long distance from the major markets and concentrations of capital in Canada. Historically, economic development in the province has been facilitated by government because the free market by itself has not done the job. Even the Tories were forced to recognize that "open for business" pronouncements were not enough. The free market had judged Saskatchewan, and found it wanting on its terms.

Devine's next strategy was to use government to intervene aggressively in the economy, putting taxpayers' money at risk to prop up private businesses in a manner that would have made a neo-conservative purist blush. Paradoxically, the Tories continued to insist that they believed in the free market, though their actions proved otherwise. Devine gave assurances that as soon as a venture became profitable, the government would withdraw its interest. In other words, the taxpayers assumed the risks of investment but were denied the rewards.

Since the 1982 election, the new right has dominated in Saskatchewan. What was once considered Canada's most progressive province has become one of the most right wing. The Devine government has launched a massive program of privatization, weakened the welfare state, promoted the values of the new Christian right, attacked labour unions, and downgraded the role of government. These initiatives were entirely in keeping with the goals of the new right in other parts of the world. Saskatchewan, however, has its own particular historical traditions, its own economic opportunities and problems, and its own political culture. The new right has necessarily had to take these into account. The following chapters are the record of the unique version of the new right that has evolved in Saskatchewan.

1

THE NEW RIGHT
IN SASKATCHEWAN

> Any emphasis on economic activity at the
> expense of working people, consumers, and the
> environment is a classic move to the right.
> — ALLAN BLAKENEY, *Leader-Post,*
> *22 October 1982.*

The 1982 election of the Progressive Conservatives under Grant Devine marked a significant turning point in Saskatchewan history.

Since 1944, the province had been a stronghold for the CCF/NDP and social democracy. The governments of Tommy Douglas, Woodrow Lloyd, and Allan Blakeney pioneered social legislation, most notably medicare; established progressive labour standards; showed leadership in protecting human rights; and created many profitable Crown corporations. The CCF/NDP vision was that government had an important role in developing the economy and advancing the welfare of the community.

Since 1982, the Tories have taken the province in a dramatically different direction. They have undermined the programs of the welfare state, weakened trade unions, neglected human rights, and privatized Crown corporations. They saw government not as an instrument for the betterment of society, but as an oppressive burden on the backs of the people.

At the heart of the Progressive Conservative attempt to transform Saskatchewan lies the ideology of neo-conservatism. It marks a distinct break with traditional Canadian conservatism. The older conservatism maintained a paternal concern for the "condition of the people," which came from a strong sense of community. In fact, its claim to the concept of community gave it something in common with social democracy – hence the term "red Tory," which describes a conservative who accepts some socialist ideas.[1] This type of conservatism willingly used the state to help create a political community, and Tory politicians in this mold were champions of the people and welfare state policies. They were also the creators of the Canadian National Railway, the Canadian Broadcasting Corporation, and a host of other intrusive economic policies that would horrify the conservative politicians of today.[2]

The new right in Saskatchewan has broken with this tradition and accepted the superiority of the market over democratic government. In most respects, it borrows its ideas from American and British neo-conservatives. Devine's outspoken moralizing and promotion of family values have an affinity with Jerry Falwell, Pat Robertson and the Moral Majority. His admiration of the American economic system, his eager endorsement of free trade with the United States, his tendency to adopt the style of an American governor, and his disdain for the traditions of parliamentary government all testify to the strength of the American influence. The Devine government's strident denunciations of public ownership and avid commitment to privatization are reminiscent of Thatcherism. Indeed, this British policy import quickly became the ideological marker flag of the Saskatchewan Tories.

The only aspect of old Canadian conservatism they've kept is a populist streak inherited from leaders like John Diefenbaker and Alvin Hamilton. Otherwise, the new conservatism in Saskatchewan imitates ideological movements in other countries, while also developing its own distinct identity. This chapter seeks to define the Saskatchewan variant of the new right. Before doing that, however, it is well to outline some of the main elements that constitute the ideology of neo-conservatism and the political movement known as the new right.

Neo-conservatism and the new right

The new right is the name given to the political movement that
emerged from the ideas associated with American neo-conservatism.[3] Generally speaking, neo-conservatism extols the private
sector and denigrates the public sector. It condemns government
for interfering with the ability of individuals to make and spend
money as they please. Neo-conservatives reject all forms of col-
lectivism, and thus have little or no use for trade unions, the
social programs of the welfare state, government-owned companies, or state agencies to protect human rights. Their agenda
implies not just tolerance for, but also acceptance of, social and
economic inequality, justified on the grounds that this will lead to
greater economic performance. Only the competitive marketplace can be trusted to sort out the winners and the losers, and if
people want to be their brother's keeper they can do so on their
own time on a volunteer or charitable basis. Neo-conservatives
minimize the role of government as an instrument of collective
responsibility, co-operation, community interest, or social
solidarity. These concepts simply have no place in the lexicon of
neo-conservatism.

Some of these ideas go back a long way. That the market should
be sovereign and that the best government is the least government are not new beliefs. What, then, is "new" about "neo"-con-
servatism? Its newness comes from its challenge of the political
consensus that emerged in most western nations after the Second
World War.

This consensus was founded upon the acceptance, to one
degree or another, of certain basic principles. First among these
was the adoption of Keynesian-type economic policies after the
disaster of the Great Depression, capitalism's greatest crisis to
date. The English economist John Maynard Keynes founded a
school of economic theory centered on the idea that government
intervention in the economy, if correctly and skilfully done,
could smooth out the ups and downs in the business cycle and
help avoid the periodic depressions that plagued capitalism.
Keynes thought the Great Depression was caused by a lack of

investment and a falling level of demand. He argued that in times of heavy unemployment, the greatest danger lay in the reduction of spending by governments and the general public, resulting in a decrease in the general level of income. To overcome this, Keynes recommended that in times of recession, a government should have a deficit budget to stimulate the economy, while in times of inflation induced by an overheated economy a surplus budget was called for. Government policy-makers did not always implement or even understand the finer points of Keynes's theory, but the important point is that they unanimously accepted his central premise, that governments have a role in guiding the economy.

Although Keynesian economics and the welfare state might appear to be two separate issues, they are, in fact, closely intertwined. Keynes maintained that for a capitalist economy to function well, a high level of consumer demand has to be sustained. This is not easy when wealth and income are poorly distributed. For a capitalist economy to avoid recession, it has to get money into the hands of people who will spend it. Paradoxical as it sounded, Keynes viewed the welfare state not as the end of free-market capitalism, but as its salvation. He can therefore be credited with creating a non-socialist response to the crisis of capitalism at the end of the Second World War.

Keynes heralded the abandonment of the old-style laissez-faire liberalism and its replacement by the modern welfare state. The old liberalism did not give government a role in either controlling economic growth or providing welfare policies. In fact, it discouraged both. Before the "Keynesian revolution," governments could perhaps justify limited social welfare on the basis of charitable or democratic principles, and could play a limited role in the reorganization of industry when it was in the interests of business. Yet these types of actions were always viewed as exceptions to the laissez-faire model rather than as a systematic challenge to it. After Keynes, the economic and social role of the state was completely transformed. It now had a justification for providing a wide array of welfare policies. Not surprisingly, neither business nor labour objected to these new policies. State intervention helped reduce the uncertainties which large corporations face in the market, and labour welcomed government policies aimed at full employment and programs to protect workers from the ill effects of temporary job loss.[4]

The creation of the Keynesian welfare state ensured a significant role for government in society. After World War II and up to the mid-1970s, virtually all political commentators and policy makers assumed that governments should intervene in the economy and should guarantee a minimum standard of living for all. This meant public education, medicare, unemployment insurance, old age pensions, social assistance, and trade union rights. It also meant a reasonably high level of taxation to pay for all these programs, based on the principle that the rich should pay more. As it turned out, the rich were often able to evade paying their share of taxes, but nonetheless, the principle that guided government economic policy was that it is unfair for wealth to be concentrated among those who had amassed property or who had high-paying jobs. Even if the market dictated that one person be paid well and another person poorly or not at all, the decree of the market was not necessarily regarded as a just decree. The fortunate were expected to help out the less fortunate, not as a matter of charity, but as a matter of responsibility, a responsibility ordained by the community and enforced by the government.

For nearly 30 years after the end of the war, the western world enjoyed almost uninterrupted prosperity. Then, in the 1970s, the system began to break down. The strain imposed by the Vietnam War on the American economy, the quadrupling of the price of oil as the result of OPEC, stagflation (the combination of high unemployment and high inflation), new demands by a variety of social groups, and the ever-increasing burden of government debt shook the post-war consensus.[5] Neo-conservatives saw the stability of the capitalist system threatened. They saw the welfare state as overburdening democracy and feared the consequences. And, unlike the old Keynesian politicians and policy makers, who seemed helpless in the face of these new developments, neo-conservatives believed they had a remedy.

There had been critics of the welfare state ever since its inception in the mid-1940s. Until the mid-1970s, however, they had largely been seen as cranks who wanted to turn back the clock and return to the old discredited system of laissez-faire liberalism. But by this time many disillusioned liberals and conservatives began to rediscover the writings of these previously ignored economists. The theories of Friedrich A. Hayek and Milton Friedman were eagerly embraced as offering the only viable solution to the continuing crisis that faced capitalist societies.

The founding father of neo-conservative economic philosophy was unquestionably Hayek, whose 1944 classic *The Road to Serfdom* was a blistering attack on interventionist economic policies and egalitarian attempts to regulate social life and redistribute income.[6] Hayek feared the interventionist model. He believed that it would lead to socialism and central planning, which would produce a society ruled by a planning elite, leaving no room for entrepreneurship, individual initiative or the market. State socialism, defined as any large scale interference with the market, was, in his view, impossible in principle and totalitarian in practice. In place of the interventionist model, Hayek reasserted the pre-eminence of the individual in the marketplace and the paramount need for individual freedom to be protected from an expansive state. For Hayek, any erosion of the right of the individual to buy and sell in the market was a gradual erosion of his freedom. Thus, any attempt to protect the individual from the injustice of the market had to be staunchly resisted. Hayek's central point was that tampering with the perfect equilibrium of the market could lead only to unbridled socialist tyranny.

The other leading intellectual figure of the new right was Milton Friedman, who also insisted that freedom could be guaranteed only by the operation of the market.[7] Friedman, however, went a step further than Hayek in asserting, almost as a matter of faith, that government is always a less efficient producer of goods and service than is the market. He struck a responsive chord with disillusioned Keynesians when he argued that all welfare measures constitute an unjustifiable burden on society because they depress economic growth without ever achieving their stated objectives.

Both Hayek and Friedman had been saying for a long time that government activity should be cut to a bare minimum and that the market should rule. Now, in the context of economic recession and growing debt, their ideas moved from the fringe to the mainstream. Monetarism and supply-side economics displaced

Keynesianism. It became fashionable to talk about the theory of incentives and to deplore government assistance for the poor. It was good for people to be poor; being poor made them work hard to lift themselves out of poverty. It was good for people to be rich; the existence of rich people encouraged others to think that if they took risks, were innovative and worked hard, they too could be rich and not have to worry about the government taking the fruits of their entrepreneurship away from them. A less secure social safety net would sharpen the survival instincts of a citizenry too long pampered by affluence and welfare. According to the neo-conservatives, government interference in the economy was a kind of sickness; the free market was hailed as a miracle worker.

Neo-conservatives also took exception to the utopianism of the postwar approach to social policy which was based on the assumption that human happiness and progress could be advanced through political action and government policy. They argued that many of these problems were ultimately unsolvable because human nature can't really be changed. Underlying neo-conservative ideology was the belief that people are not naturally inclined to altruism, but rather are strongly motivated by self-interest. Thus, any improvements in the human condition could only come about through individual struggle in the market. Furthermore, they bitterly accused Keynesians, whether they were politicians seeking votes, bureaucrats seeking budgets, or interest groups seeking benefits, of unreasonably raising people's expectations. When governments failed to deliver on promises of fairness and equality, a decline in confidence and a distrust of political institutions emerged.[8]

Implicated in this assault on social policy was the vast government bureaucracy. Neo-conservatives viewed it as a vested interest because civil servants, who formed a large part of the middle class, had a substantial interest in keeping government growing. To the neo-conservatives, the fact that much of the money spent on welfare went to well-paid bureaucrats, rather than to the people whom it was intended to help, was reason enough to seek better solutions to social problems. The power, status and wealth of these bureaucrats depended upon active governments promoting new programs and protecting old ones. Their education, their professional commitment and their access to centres of decision-making made bureaucrats highly successful in defending their interests to the detriment of those in the private sector who paid taxes to support them.[9] Neo-conservatives and government bureaucrats were natural enemies.

Adding to the fury of the neo-conservative attack on the welfare state is an alliance forged with the new Christian right, which has become a force to be reckoned with in American politics. The Christian right claims to have Biblical sanction for free market economics, and prescribes moral solutions for the problems afflicting society. Poverty, unemployment, family breakdown, crime, drug addiction, pornography, sexual permissiveness would all end if people were "born again." Because the new Christian right is profoundly anti-government, it is compatible with secular neo-conservatism. Government social programs and anti-poverty campaigns are judged to be useless because all social problems are simply questions of individual morality. Indeed, the welfare state is worse than useless because it takes the onus off individuals and families. The family teaches children individual self-worth and moral responsibility, and prepares young people for the battle of life in a sternly competitive world. Socialism and feminism are the twin enemies of the family, one because it allegedly robs families of their rightful role, the other because it takes mothers out of the home.

Although the Christian right is anti-government in that it opposes the welfare state, it heartily approves of some types of government activity. The power of the state can legitimately be used to curtail individual liberty as long as the purpose is the enforcement of Christian morality, as defined by the Bible and authoritatively interpreted by the new Christian right. Values such as tolerance, pluralism, and freedom of choice are rejected in the name of a higher morality, one that "would make America great again." For the Christian right, morality is not a private but a public matter. On these grounds, it campaigns for coercive state action on such issues as abortion, homosexuality, and school prayer.

Neo-conservative economics merged with moral majority values to create a potent political movement. This movement was based on a consensus concerning moral and political values, the use of the market as a mechanism for the promotion of social ends, the restoration of the family, church and volunteerism, and the defence of the old-fashioned virtues of hard work and self-reliance. The election of Margaret Thatcher in 1979 and Ronald Reagan in 1980 confirmed that, armed with neo-conservative ideas, the new right was on the march. What had formerly been an untried ideology became government policy.

Grant Devine and the new right

The high tide of the new right hit Saskatchewan in 1982 with the election of Grant Devine and the Progressive Conservatives. Devine in many ways typifies the new right in the province. He was born July 5, 1944 in Regina, and was raised on a farm that his grandfather had homesteaded near Lake Valley, not far from Moose Jaw. His was a seemingly idyllic rural upbringing in a close-knit family. He went to school in winter by horse and sleigh, and in summer rode his pony, Sparky. Sparky, Devine later reminisced, "was the best horse in the world. I could round up a hundred head of cattle on him without any trouble and just to prove how well he knew cattle I'd do it with just a saddle, no bridle."[10] Though short, Devine was a good athlete. He also took piano lessons, won an award for being the best camper at church camp, and was elected president of the high school student council.[11]

After high school, he enrolled at the University of Saskatchewan where he earned a Bachelor of Science degree in agriculture. He then took a job as a marketing specialist with the Department of Agriculture in Ottawa. His duties included assisting with agricultural commodity legislation and acting as an advisor to the Food Prices Review Board. Not happy with his lowly rank in the bureaucracy, Devine quit his job and moved back to the west.[12] He returned to school, graduating from the University of Alberta with two Masters degrees, one in agricultural economics, the other in business administration. In 1972, he began work on a PhD in agricultural economics at Ohio State University. Completing his degree in 1976, he joined the University of Saskatchewan, teaching courses in agricultural marketing and consumer economics.

The catalyst for Devine's move into politics was Dick Collver, the man who brought the Progressive Conservative party of Saskatchewan out of the wilderness to the point where it offered a real challenge to the incumbent NDP. In the 1978 general election, Devine ran as a Tory in the riding of Saskatoon Nutana, where he was soundly defeated. This setback did not discourage him from contesting the Tory party leadership in November 1979. His flashy campaign, complete with brass band and balloons, won him the leadership on the first ballot. As leader he failed in his first attempt to win a seat in the legislature. When victory finally came, it was sweet. Devine swept to power in the 1982 election with 55 of 64 seats in the legislature.

Devine has summed up his personal and political philosophy as "God first, family second, the Conservative party third, and the NDP under my thumb." This motto is adapted from the slogan of the Mary Kay Cosmetic Company, for whom Devine's wife once worked. The Mary Kay credo – "God first, family second, and business third" – is entirely compatible with the Amway-style thinking of the new right in the United States. Devine maintains that politicians have both a right and a responsibility to provide moral guidance: "I think one of the biggest challenges we face in this country and North America is one of morals."[13] Though raised in the United Church, Devine converted to Roman Catholicism at the age of 22 when he married Chantal Guillaume. He makes no apologies for his plain-spokenness on matters of religion and morality.[14] His views on this subject were highlighted in an interview with Peter Gzowski, who chided Devine for his public pronouncements on personal moral issues: "That's a handy little sermon you gave me about how to live my life inside the home, but you're a politician!" Devine retorted that many politicians, including Tommy Douglas, had once been preachers.[15]

According to Devine, the family comes next in importance after God. Indeed, the two are closely connected, because a secure family life provides children with a good religious upbringing. References to the importance of the family crop up repeatedly in Devine's public statements. During the 1982 election campaign, he promised that a Conservative government would reunite families whose children had been forced to leave the province to find work. He brought tears to the eyes of listeners as he told how a lonely, elderly couple circled the date on the calendar when their children and grandchildren would be coming home from Alberta to visit.[16] In 1984, he gave a televised province-wide speech dwelling on the themes of God, family, and "the spirit of Saskatchewan." At the end of the speech, his wife and children walked on stage, presenting a family tableau as the credits rolled.[17] To a much greater extent than Premier Blakeney had done, Devine was willing to put his family on display. Chantal Devine explained that she and her husband wanted their family to serve as a role model: "We're out to build a better society. That's a hefty job, but that's the way it is."[18]

Devine has used the family metaphor in a variety of contexts. When questioned about his unwavering support for Brian Mulroney even when federal policies were not beneficial to Saskatchewan, Devine replied, "I have no hesitation in being loyal. I believe in what he's doing. It's fundamental. It's like a team . . . like a family."[19] The Premier employed the same figure of speech in describing Canadian-American relations: "We are, frankly, family. We're your best customers and you are ours."[20] And when apologizing for a backbencher's racist comments, he said, "When you're leader of a party or a government it's not unlike being a father figure in a big family. Your children make contributions and sometimes they trip. But they're your family and you pick them up and carry on together."[21]

Devine has gone as far as to claim that New Democrats are anti-family and don't love their children: "The Marxist philosophy is give them [children] whatever they want. They don't love their children, they're afraid of their children."[22] He has further suggested that rural families are superior to urban families. During the 1988 by-election in Regina Elphinstone, an inner-city riding, Devine observed that family structure and a sense of caring seemed to break down in urban areas: "When you move into cities, you become anonymous. You don't know your neighbour, you don't know the people, you don't know the people next door." Being anonymous, "people say we'll have to have someone take care of you. It will have to be big government, it will have to be the mayor, it's going to have to be someone else."[23] In a manner consistent with the Christian right, Devine uses his support for the family as a base from which to attack the welfare state.

His opinions about the family are personal and subjective. He offers no evidence that government social programs hurt families, or that rural families are better than urban families, or that New Democrats are against families. Allan Blakeney mildly observes that, contrary to what Devine might think, the Conservative party does not have a monopoly on basic human values like love, God, and family,[24] but Devine either believes, or finds it politically expedient to believe, that the PC party and moral virtue are synonymous.

Devine's religious convictions have led him to oppose abortion. His views are shared by his wife: "I would venture to say that 98 per cent of the women that you find out peace-marching or against nuclear energy are pro-choice. They haven't got their objectives straight. They are living in the 'I'-centred egotistical society. They don't have God as their focus. Very selfish."[25] On another controversial moral issue, Devine took an equally strong stand. When Svend Robinson, NDP MP for Burnaby, told the public he was gay, Devine harshly condemned him. He was afraid, he said, that Robinson's statement might cause other people to become gay: "I don't want my children thinking that this is a reasonable, normal thing to do." Devine went on to equate homosexuality with crime: "You love the sinner, but you hate the sin. I feel the same about bank robbers – for whatever reason, they have to take from people, which is illegal and in my view immoral."[26]

Like others in the Christian right, Devine believes that moral tolerance is dangerous: "If you make a sieve too tolerant, the holes in the sieve are so large that the seed falls through with the chaff. It can't be so tolerant that it doesn't do anything. You have to separate the wheat from the chaff. That's what life is about."[27] According to the Tory leader, the clamor for human rights is unhealthy: "If you have all the rights and no responsibilities, it's anarchy." People were "sick of legislated rights. . . We have become so tolerant, there are hardly any rules left."[28]

"God first, family second, and business third" – so says Mary

Kay Cosmetics. Business, in the sense of free market economics, is also at the core of Devine's political philosophy. In this respect, he identifies with Reaganism and Thatcherism, particularly with their contempt for government and their deification of the market. Devine declared himself a "market-oriented free enterpriser": "I can tolerate a lot of government in health and education, but I can't tolerate government running farms or building new businesses, pumping oil, mining, or in the forestry business."[29] His faith in the free market and his admiration for the American economic system came out in an interview with the western Canadian Roman Catholic newspaper *Prairie Messenger*. The reporter asked Devine for his thoughts on the Christian dictum "love one another" and the need to help people who are marginalized in a "survival of the fittest culture." Did the Premier "ever experience conflict in being a Christian leader of a government that is perceived as favouring those who are capable, accomplished, or privileged?" The Premier replied that a market system produced more jobs, wealth, and opportunity than did a non-market system, and, therefore, there was no conflict in being a free-enterpriser and wanting to help your fellow man. He praised the American economy as a model worthy of emulation.[30]

Devine's neo-conservative commitment to competitive capitalism has made him suspicious of government social programs. He wants families and volunteers to assume some of the burden of the welfare state. Once, after meeting with a diverse group of religious leaders, Devine commented: "One of the people summed it up well. He said we shouldn't have government replace God. It gets to the point where everyone expects everything from government. I believe there is a good role for religious life and volunteer support. Because it comes from the heart, there is something magic about it."[31] Devine holds these views in the face of a brief prepared by officials of the United, Catholic, Anglican, Presbyterian, and Lutheran churches rejecting the idea that they should take over the delivery of social services. "We see this as a dangerous assumption," their brief states. "The non-governmental agencies simply don't have the skills, time, or money to replace trained professionals or to supply enough material aid."[32]

Devine's belief in the free market led him to support the Canada-U.S. free trade deal negotiated by the Mulroney and Reagan governments. When New Democrats questioned the terms of the deal, Devine branded them "economic cowards" and part of the "Castro culture." "Cuba is under a socialist government – their view of the United States and their view of Canada is exactly what the NDP are trying to perpetrate on the people of this country."[33] Devine has always had, or pretended to have, trouble telling the difference between the NDP and godless Marxist-Leninists: "This beautiful country of Canada was not founded by Marx, not founded by Lenin and it wasn't founded by Chairman Mao. And today, these great people are not going to bend, or bow or be broken by new Marxist zealots."[34]

Although Devine is ideologically committed to a more limited role for government, he is enough of a political pragmatist to allow his agenda to unfold gradually. Because Crown corporations were popular in Saskatchewan, he did not immediately begin his campaign to privatize them. In fact, shortly after being elected, he spoke in praise of government-owned companies: "Crown corporations can do a very, very effective job if they are run properly. There are two areas where they need caution. One is the rapid expansion in the private sector. It's made people afraid to invest in Saskatchewan. The other is the high degree of influence and impact of a great deal of political pressure brought to bear on professionals. Let's keep those Crown corporations officers operating like the true professionals they can be."[35] During the Tory government's first term in office, it nibbled at the Crown sector, but refrained from massive sell-offs. The full scope of the new right's economic program was not disclosed until the second term. At that time, Devine boldly proclaimed that the neo-conservative revolution had arrived.

As ideologically motivated as Grant Devine is, he has had to face the fact that the free market does not always work in Saskatchewan's favour. The hinterland nature of the provincial economy means that government participation is often needed to stimulate development. Applying pure neo-conservative doctrine to Saskatchewan is a prescription for depression. Although Devine does not admit that there is anything wrong with market-oriented free enterprise, his government has repeatedly intervened in the economy to assist private corporations with public funds. In a free market, if a venture is likely to be profitable, private investors risk their capital. If the venture were to succeed, the investors earn a profit. Devine's approach has been to risk taxpayers' money to assist private investors to undertake a project not otherwise viable by the standards of the market. If the venture succeeds, he promises, the government will withdraw, leaving the private investors to garner the profits. In theory, Devine believes in free enterprise and wants the government out of the economy. In practice, however, Devine's actions show he believes not in pure free enterprise, but in government-subsidized free enterprise.

Grant Devine is the most visible symbol of the new aggressive brand of conservatism that has emerged in Saskatchewan, but he is by no means a voice in the wilderness. His views parallel those of the entire new right coalition, whether it be the Chamber of Commerce, REAL Women, the Institute for Saskatchewan Enterprise, or Campaign Life. These various organizations, each with its own agenda, have rallied around Grant Devine and the PC party. Their various positions are distilled into a virulent attack on socialism that is expressed most forcefully in the PC party newspaper, *Saskatchewan Viewpoint*.

This newspaper is a vehicle for the dissemination of neo-conservatism in Saskatchewan, and has published many articles that reflect Devine's brand of conservatism, usually in a much more strident tone. Articles have appeared under such headlines as "The Tide of Socialism is Running Out" or "The Now Dead Party." They joyfully announced the decline of socialism and central planning, while at the same time praising the dawn of a new capitalism with a strong and vigorous market protecting one and all from NDP-inspired tyranny. Typically, the newspaper explained: "People have discovered that socialism and big government don't work. They have found that what Adam Smith said two centuries ago about the natural order of economic affairs is true. Let businessmen, industrialists and entrepreneurs run their own affairs with as little state intervention as possible and you will create wealth for both the rich and the poor, the powerful and the weak. All will be enhanced."[36] The paper also published articles calling attention to past Communist atrocities such as the

10 million Ukrainians murdered in Stalin's terror state, or the "chilling conformity" and the "suppression of individuality" that supposedly characterize Sweden. The message is that socialism leads to centralization, which leads to despotism in which individuality, freedom, and initiative are all crushed.

While party newspapers tend to be polemical and vehemently partisan, *Saskatchewan Viewpoint* appears to be a fairly accurate representation of the views of the rank and file Progressive Conservatives in Saskatchewan. Tory conventions are marked by a similar brand of posturing about less government and the need to follow the discipline of the market. There are endless complaints about the horrors of bureaucracy, the generosity of social programs, the meddlesome Human Rights Commission, and the under-worked, over-paid civil service.[37] Indeed, compared to the delegates, cabinet ministers often sound like the voice of moderation. Delegates have demanded the abolition of the metric system, the end of rent controls, the sale of all Crown corporations, support for Star Wars, a return to capital punishment, forced labour for welfare recipients, and the employment of prisoners on road construction. The CBC has been denounced as "fairly left-leaning, watched by left-leaning people . . . [therefore] it should be paid for by left-leaning people."[38] It is a vision of Saskatchewan totally opposed to social democracy as represented by the NDP.

After 1982, the Tories under Grant Devine had a chance to make their imprint on the province. Step-by-step the neo-conservative program unfolded: the promotion of Christian right moral values, the experiments with supply-side economics, the touting of free enterprise, the reining in of the Crown corporations, the attacks on the civil service, social programs and trade unions, and the massive push towards privatization. The first step toward achieving these goals was the defeat of the NDP government.

Notes for Chapter 1

1. Gad Horowitz, "Conservatism, Liberalism and Socialism: An Interpretation," *Canadian Journal of Economics and Political Science* 32, May 1966, pp. 143-171. 2. W. Christian and C. Campbell, *Political Parties and Ideologies in Canada*, second edition (Toronto: McGraw Hill-Ryerson, 1983), p. 90.

3. Gillian Peele, *Revival and Reaction: The Right in Contemporary America* (Oxford: Clarendon Press, 1984). 4. David A. Wolfe, "Mercantilism, Liberalism and Keynesianism: Changing Forms of State Intervention In Capitalist Economies," *Canadian Journal of Political and Social Theory* 5, Winter/Spring 1981. 5. Philip Resnick, "The Ideology of Neo-Conservatism", Warren Magnusson *et al.*, eds., *The New Reality: The Politics of Restraint in British Columbia* (Vancouver: New Star Books, 1984). 6. Friedrich A. Hayek, *The Road to Serfdom* (Chicago: University of Chicago Press, 1944). 7. Milton Friedman, *Capitalism and Freedom* (Chicago: University of Chicago Press, 1962). 8. Nigel Ashford, "New Conservatism and Old Socialism," *Government and Opposition* 16, Summer 1981, pp. 352-369, 360. 9. *Ibid.*, 359.

10. *Star-Phoenix*, 30 November 1982. 11. *Leader-Post*, 8 May 1982. 12. *Ibid.*, 9 February 1985. 13. *Ibid.*, Dale Eisler, 3 March 1988. 14. *Globe and Mail*, 13 May 1988. 15. Susan Swedburg-Kohli, "Devine Shows Tougher Side," *Saskatchewan Report*, May 1988. 16. *Leader-Post*, Eisler, 27 January 1983. 17. *Ibid.*, 10 November 1984. 18. *Ibid.*, 9 February 1985. 19. *Globe and Mail*, 21 December 1987. 20. *Leader-Post*, 30 June 1989. 21. *Ibid.*, 21 December 1982. 22. *Ibid.*, Eisler, 16 November 1987. 23. *Ibid.*, 30 March 1988. 24. *Ibid.*, 10 November 1984. 25. Sherry Holenski, "Is There Life After Mary Kay?" *The Font*, April 1988. 26. *Leader-Post*, 2 March 1988. 27. *Globe and Mail*, 13 May 1988. 28. *Ibid.* 29. *Globe and Mail*, 23 June 1986. 30. *Prairie Messenger*, 28 January 1985. 31. *Leader-Post*, Eisler, 12 May 1987. 32. *Ibid.* 33. *Ibid.*, 16 October 1987. 34. *Ibid.*, Eisler, 16 November 1987. 35. *Globe and Mail*, 29 June 1982. 36. "Worldwide Change Occurring," *Saskatchewan Viewpoint*, Winter Edition 1984. 37. J.F. Conway, "We've only just begun," *Briarpatch*, January/February 1983. 38. *Leader-Post*, 9 November 1985.

2

ELECTION 1982

◇ ─────────────────────────────── ◇

THE MONDAY NIGHT MASSACRE

> Saskatchewan has so much going for it that you
> can afford to mismanage it and still break even.
> — GRANT DEVINE, *Leader-Post*,
> 19 January 1983.

Prior to the 1980s, the provincial Progressive Conservative
party had never been much of a force in Saskatchewan politics. The closest the party had come to forming a government was
in 1929, when it was the senior partner in a coalition that also
included independents and Progressives. The government was
thrown out of office after one term, a victim of the general misery
caused by the Great Depression. From the time of the defeat of the
Tory-led coalition in 1934 until 1982, Saskatchewan politics was
dominated by the Liberal party (1934-44 and 1964-71), the CCF
(1944-64), or the NDP (1971-82).

The rise of the provincial Tories really began in the mid-1970s.
Although they won only 15 seats in the 1978 election, they began
to be perceived as the real alternative to the governing party. The
groundwork had been laid for the stunning success of the Conservatives in 1982.

The Tories' spectacular rise to power was directly linked to the
collapse of the Liberal party in Western Canada.[1] Westerners

perceived the Trudeau government as insensitive to their needs and interests, and many traditional Liberal voters found Trudeau too left-wing for their taste. As a result, the core anti-socialist vote moved away from the Liberals to the Tories. One might say that the rise of the Tories in Saskatchewan can be laid at the door of that notorious "socialist," Pierre Trudeau.

Another reason for the improved fortunes of the Conservative party was growing disenchantment with the bureaucratic style of government offered by Allan Blakeney's NDP. After many years in power, left-wing movements can become the status quo that they once fought to change, and lose touch with the concerns and opinions of ordinary citizens. This happened to the Saskatchewan NDP. In the course of the 1970s, the NDP government shifted its focus from social issues to economic ones. There was much suspicion that the expansion of public ownership in the natural resource sector was being financed at the expense of social spending.[2] The preoccupation with negotiating the patriation and amendment of the constitution, the priority given to the management of Crown corporations, and a penchant for bureaucratic responses to social and economic problems all distanced the government from the people. Even traditional NDP supporters became alienated from the NDP establishment.

This alienation was evident among the rural and farm population. Agrarian distrust of bureaucracy and officialdom, which had contributed to the defeat of the CCF in 1964, returned to haunt the NDP.[3] In addition, the economic position of farmers was changing in a way that bolstered Conservative and diminished NDP support. As a rule of thumb, the more land a farmer has and the wealthier he is, the more likely he will vote PC. The large, prosperous farmer tends to see himself more as a businessman than as a worker. Since the trend in Saskatchewan was towards larger, more capital-intensive farms, the old farmer-worker alliance that lay at the heart of the CCF became increasingly difficult to hold intact. Ironically, the very success of the Blakeney government's programs to strengthen the agricultural economy undermined the NDP's rural support. The more financially secure farmers became, the less they wanted to make common cause with the workers in the cities.

The changing values of rural Saskatchewan were also related to a generational change, as the men and women who had immigrated to the prairies during the early part of the century and who had lived through the Great Depression of the 1930s were replaced by their less radical children and grandchildren. The older generation of farmers tended to be hostile towards "big business" and "vested interests," and saw the grain companies, Eastern banks, and the CPR as nefarious forces and class enemies. To assert some control over their economic destiny, farmers had organized their own producers' and consumers' co-operatives and credit unions. They became politically sophisticated and forged a populist brand of socialism in the Co-operative Commonwealth Federation. But their sons and daughters tended to be less hostile towards big business. In fact, many of them were substantial capitalists themselves, owning several sections of land and hundreds of thousands of dollars worth of machinery.

The CCF had been an authentic grassroots movement. Its success was based on its ability to mobilize people and get them directly involved in the political process. Even today, the CCF legacy can be detected in the passionate commitment so many Saskatchewan people bring to their politics. The grassroots involvement of CCFers emerged from a shared sense of class and community. Urban and rural, workers and farmers, they saw themselves as the "people" engaged in a common struggle to build a "co-operative commonwealth." The struggle was not only against harsh physical conditions and an unforgiving climate, it was against the "rich and powerful," the "profiteers," and the "parasites on society." As a new generation of farmers took over from their parents and grandparents in the 1960s and 1970s, this kind of radical talk seemed more and more dated. In rural Saskatchewan, class homogeneity broke down. The big farmers had less in common with small farmers and even less in common with urban workers.

Replacing Dick Collver as leader with Grant Devine in 1979 also helped the Saskatchewan Tories. While not without political skills, Collver was a maverick tinged with scandal. Grant Devine combined his predecessor's folksy style and populist appeal with respectability. A PhD in agricultural economics, a professor at the

University of Saskatchewan, a family man, a farmer, Devine was a credible candidate for premier.

By 1982, the Conservatives had emerged as the real alternative to the NDP in Saskatchewan as Liberals disgusted with Trudeau moved in droves to the Tories. NDP strength was waning in rural areas because of changes in the agricultural economy and population. The Blakeney government seemed so preoccupied with bureaucratic management and constitutional negotiations that it was remote from the people. And the Conservatives had a leader who was not conspicuously disqualified to lead a government. The stage was set for a political upset.

The NDP's tactical blunders

Premier Blakeney did not have to call an election until October 1983, when his five-year term would be up, but the decision was taken to have an election on Monday, April 26, 1982. April was not a good month for the NDP. It was an April election in 1964 that felled Woodrow Lloyd and brought Liberal Ross Thatcher to power. Nonetheless, the NDP strategists in 1982 saw an advantage in holding the election sooner rather than later. The Canadian economy was heading into a serious recession, and the political prospects for incumbent governments were likely to get worse rather than better. Furthermore, the polls looked good. Obviously, the NDP pollsters were not asking the right questions. They failed to detect the underlying discontent or the readiness of the public for a change.[4]

The signs of a spring election were evident everywhere in 1982. The calling of the session of the legislature was delayed, the Crown corporations issued annual reports announcing profits and plans to extend service, and $100,000 was spent on pamphlets explaining the NDP's position on the Crow Rate, the guaranteed low freight rates for Western farmers which the federal government was in the process of dismantling. The final signal that an election was imminent came with the delivery of the budget on March 19. It was loaded with a wide assortment of handouts for almost every interest in the NDP coalition, and was described by one political commentator as "an undisguised bribe for the voters of Saskatchewan."[5] At the same time, the budget was balanced, as had been the previous eleven budgets. The Blakeney government wished to convey the message that it had administered the affairs of the province so well that it could significantly increase spending on health, education, and social services, and still balance the books.

The budget was delivered the same night that Prime Minister Trudeau was in Regina addressing a fund-raising dinner for the Liberal party. The timing of the two events was perhaps not a co-incidence, in light of the NDP strategy to fight the election against Ottawa, particularly the federal government's plans to do away with the Crow Rate. The Crow issue was regarded by the NDP as a heaven-sent opportunity to pose as the defenders of Saskatchewan people against the assaults of the federal government. This strategy had worked very well for the NDP in the past: Blakeney's triumph over the Thatcher Liberals in 1971 was partly due to the attack on the Trudeau government's unpopular agricultural policies, and NDP victories in 1975 and 1978 were assisted by the battles for provincial control of natural resources. The NDP thought the fight to retain the Crow Rate would pull the same levers and rally support for the Blakeney government.

The only problem with this strategy was that both the provincial Tories and the provincial Liberals agreed that the Crow Rate should be kept. Nor was it helpful for the NDP to claim that the provincial Liberals secretly approved of what the federal Liberal government was doing, since the main threat was not coming from the Liberals anyway. The NDP tried to paint Grant Devine as being anti-Crow Rate by dredging up some articles he had written as a professor of agricultural economics, but this tactic failed. The arguments were somewhat arcane, and, moreover, Devine could not be convincingly blamed for what Pierre Trudeau was doing. Thus, the fight for the Crow Rate, which the NDP had counted upon as a centrepiece of their campaign, fizzled.

Once it became clear that the Crow issue was not going to fly, the NDP was at a loss because it had no back-up policy aimed specifically at the rural vote.[6] Worse, with the exception of the beef stabilization program, a $10 million support measure for the depressed cattle industry, the NDP had not come up with a popular new agricultural policy in years. The government Land Bank, which purchased land from retiring farmers and then leased it to young farmers, had come under heavy attack. The Conservatives accused the NDP of setting up Soviet-style collective farms. In place of the Land Bank, they promised to give farmers low-interest loans to buy their own land, a promise that was immensely popular.

The NDP pre-election budget also proved to be a blunder. There had been an intensive debate in cabinet and caucus as to whether it should be a "tax relief" budget or a "more money for services" budget.[7] Eventually, the government decided to increase spending rather than cut taxes. It was a disastrous choice. Although the budget concentrated on traditional NDP issues – increased spending on health care, more money for housing for the elderly, renters' rebates, more low-income housing and so on – it did almost nothing for middle-income people who were beginning to feel the pinch of the recession of the early 1980s and who were looking for some relief from extremely high interest rates. The central problem with the budget was that the government turned its back on the middle class. The Saskatchewan NDP traditionally had strong support among middle-income earners, but in 1982 the Tories' pocketbook campaign attracted these voters. By offering substantial tax cuts and subsidizing home mortgage interest rates at 13.75 percent when the going rate was 18 percent, the Tories captured the middle class.

Ironically, the fact that the budget was balanced worked against, not for, the NDP. Voters were looking for some help in tough times. They felt that if the government was in such good financial shape, why wasn't it decreasing taxes or spending money to give some relief to people? In that sense, the NDP's financial responsibility did them a lot of harm. In financial matters, the Tories were more in tune with what the people were thinking and what they were looking for. The NDP was not only out-maneuvered, it gave the Tories the weapon they needed to overturn the government – a full treasury. Without that, the Tories' expensive campaign promises would not have been plausible. In addition, there was a widespread, false perception of the Heritage Fund, the province's portfolio of investments in Saskatchewan's natural resource corporations. Many people believed the Heritage Fund to be a pile of money lying around waiting to be spent. The illusion that the province owned a large amount of surplus cash made Tory tax cut promises appear more responsible than they really were.

With its ill-conceived 1982 budget, the NDP lost the support of the middle class. Equally worrisome, its trade union support slipped away. A social democratic government inevitably has problems with its labour allies. If it gives labour everything it wants, it is accused of being a pawn of the unions. If it denies trade union requests, it is pilloried as a traitor to the workers. The Blakeney government faced this dilemma just before the election when nearly 5000 non-medical hospital staff workers went on strike. The day before the election was announced, the government legislated the strikers back to work, ending the sixteen-day-old legal work stoppage. The Canadian Union of Public Employees (CUPE), the union representing the workers, maintained that the government had acted hastily and that the two sides were close to a negotiated settlement. Blakeney disagreed, suggesting that the union had been planning to escalate the strike. The back-to-work legislation also prohibited strikes in all essential services for the duration of the election campaign.[8]

The Conservatives were quick to point out that ten years earlier, the NDP had taken great pride in repealing the law that had been enacted by Ross Thatcher's government to prevent strikes in essential services. Although Thatcher's bill was far more sweeping – it was not restricted to the period of election campaigns, as Blakeney's bill was – labour saw the new bill as similar in principle. The NDP seemed to be reneging on its commitment to free collective bargaining. The most curious aspect of this whole episode was the spectacle of the Tories posing as the defenders of union rights, while portraying the NDP as union bashers. The Tories were notorious for their anti-union attitudes, especially their hostility to public sector unions, but on this occasion they embraced labour as a long-lost friend.

The NDP claimed that the back-to-work legislation had nothing to do with the election, a statement only a die-hard NDP partisan could believe. The government had obviously decided that it was better to alienate the labour movement than risk having the public angry about interrupted health service. The cost to the NDP campaign was high. Many trade unionists who in past elections had canvassed, put up signs, and did other kinds of volunteer work for the NDP, this time stayed home. In one Saskatoon riding, an independent labour candidate was fielded to run against an incumbent NDP cabinet minister. CUPE supported the Aboriginal Peoples Party in the ten ridings where it nominated candidates, and, in the other ridings, advised its members to spoil their ballots to show their displeasure with the government.[9] Even the Catholic newspaper *Prairie Messenger*, taking its cue from Pope John Paul II's support of Solidarity in Poland, denounced the NDP's anti-union action.[10] The decision to force the hospital employees back to work cast a shadow over the whole NDP campaign. Blakeney was dogged by union protesters, and, at one rally, during an exchange with a local CUPE official, angrily ripped the microphone out of the hand of a reporter.[11]

The NDP campaign was in deep trouble even before the election started. Organized labour was unhappy with the government, the pre-election budget did not go far enough in appealing to the middle-class pocketbook, and the Crow Rate issue had flopped. The NDP adopted the slogans, "Tested and Trusted" and "The People Who Care," implying that they had provided competent and compassionate government – in effect, saying "elect us and we'll give you more of the same."

The PCs and the pocketbook issues

As it turned out, the campaign themes selected by the NDP were largely irrelevant because as soon as the election was called, the PCs took the initiative, set the tone, and dictated the pace. The NDP spent most of their time responding or attempting to respond to the themes set forth by their opponents. The Tories were in a fighting mood. Their polls told them they had a real chance to knock off the Blakeney government. An astonishing 70 percent of people surveyed said that they felt the NDP no longer cared about the average person. Fortified by this poll, Devine vigorously challenged the NDP claim to be the "people who care." On the contrary, Devine said, the NDP did not care about the needs and the interests of the ordinary people. He claimed that all the Blakeney government cared about was building up a larger government bureaucracy, establishing more Crown corporations, and buying greater amounts of land to lease back to farmers. The Tories skillfully blended a populist theme ("we need a government that cares about the people") with a neo-conservative theme ("the government is too big"). These two themes were rolled together in one emotive slogan: "There's so much more we can be." Devine took aim at a series of NDP ads praising Saskatchewan's "family of Crown corporations." He claimed that people wanted a government that cared about real families, not a phony family of government-owned companies. There again, he struck a rhetorical chord that was both populist and neo-conservative.

The first Tory promise, dramatically delivered at Devine's news conference opening the campaign, was the elimination of the 20 percent tax on gasoline. This bold move immediately caught the attention of the voters. As one farmer at a PC rally said, "Hit 'em with that 40 cents; that's what makes the cash register ring."[12] It turned out that Devine had all the details wrong. He told his audiences that gasoline in Saskatchewan cost $1.95 a gallon, while south of the border in North Dakota, it was only 95 cents. He failed to take into account the difference in the value of the dollar, the larger Imperial gallon, the fact that gas actually sold for $1.28 in North Dakota, and the fact that the provincial tax was only 26 cents per gallon, not the 40 cents he claimed.[13] The promised tax reduction was also flawed in that it would benefit many out-of-province drivers and truckers who would be using Saskatchewan's highways free of charge. But none of this seemed to matter. The important thing was that the Tories were talking the simple pocketbook language people wanted to hear. Gas would go down 26 cents per gallon. End of discussion.

The second popular promise made by the Tories early in the campaign was the Mortgage Interest Reduction Plan. It provided $100 million to guarantee a ceiling of 13.75 percent on home mortgages up to a value of $50,000 for a three-year period. The plan was available to all home-owners regardless of their income. The NDP reasonably argued that it made no sense for the government to subsidize those who could easily afford to pay for their own homes. Furthermore, the program amounted to a subsidy to the banks who were in no need of financial assistance. The NDP offered a more complicated plan, targeting assistance to new home buyers, seniors, and renters. Once again, however, all criticisms of the PC proposal were brushed aside. What mattered was that interest rates were outrageously high, and families were losing their homes. Devine offered a clear-cut and easy-to-understand solution, and people liked it.

These two major promises were accompanied by others, including a pledge to phase out the 5 percent sales tax and a commitment to reduce the provincial income tax by 10 percent. Tax cuts were central to the Tory platform.

A week into the campaign, the NDP knew it was in serious trouble. A strategic decision had to be made: should it attack the Tories or imitate them? The latter course was chosen. Out came a stream of expensive promises: Denticare, the elimination of school taxes, vision care for children and senior citizens, doubling the mortgage interest rate tax credit, a $2000 grant for first-time home buyers, and reduced insurance premiums for good drivers. Some of these had been part of the original NDP platform, scheduled for announcement; others were brand new. In any event, the attempt to copy rather than condemn the lavish Tory promises was futile. The Tories had beaten the NDP to the public trough and, in some perverse fashion, were seen as more honourable for having done so. When the NDP pointed out that their promises were much less expensive than the Tory promises, most voters were not listening.

Devine's credibility was key to the success of the Tory campaign, and for him it was a make-or-break election. He had already failed twice to win a seat in the legislature. His leadership was on the line, and he had narrowly escaped being dumped by the Tory caucus.[14] Once the election was called, his considerable political gifts came to the fore. His down-home, farm-boy style was in marked contrast to Blakeney's formal, reserved manner. Devine appeared in TV commercials without a jacket or tie; he could be found mainstreeting with a toothpick in his mouth or snapping a wad of chewing gum. He refused staged meetings with "passers-by" who had been hand-picked by campaign organizers, preferring instead to talk to anyone who happened to be walking by. Devine's folksy conversation, sprinkled with "you betcha" and "nice talkin' to ya," had great appeal. The fact that he could boast of being the "only political leader in the country who holds a permit book"[15] was an asset in rural areas. Blakeney, by contrast, looked and acted like a high-level bureaucrat or a Bay Street banker. The two leaders seemed to reflect the two campaigns – one distant and out-of-touch, the other close to the people and in tune with their thinking.

As the election campaign unfolded, the Tories gained momentum, while the NDP floundered. Near the end of the campaign, the Tories drew 3,200 cheering supporters to a rally in Regina. In the same building the previous night the NDP was able to attract only a dispirited crowd of 1,700. Although Devine confidently predicted the Tories would win 50 seats, even he underestimated the size of the victory.[16] The key was the large number of undecided voters, most of whom voted Tory. On April 26, the Tories received 54.1 percent of the popular vote and 55 out of 64 seats in the legislature, the largest majority in Saskatchewan political history. The NDP was humiliated with 9 seats and 37.6 percent of the popular vote.

The ideological significance of the 1982 election

The loss of the election was a signal that the NDP government's policies and methods had alienated many of the party's most trusted supporters. Many began pointing an accusing finger at Allan Blakeney, who was not a grassroots politician or a party builder. His approach was criticized as being technocratic, because he tended to look for bureaucratic rather than political solutions. He was blamed for the disillusionment in the party. Trade unionists were shocked at his support of federal wage and price controls and his ordering strikers back to work; feminists were dismayed at his refusal to ensure full access to abortion and his failure to spend more money on child care; socialists were offended by his attempt to promote public ownership as a non-ideological issue; and environmentalists and peace activists felt betrayed by his eagerness to support uranium development.[17] The core leadership of the NDP was guilty of arrogance, losing touch, and failing to listen, all of which marked a growing separation between the people and the party. As Blakeney himself admitted, "It is very clear from the results, that we were not responding to the aspirations and expectations of the people of Saskatchewan."[18]

The Tories had a much better grasp of popular opinion. They ran a slick, modern campaign based on state-of-the-art polling. Long before the election was called, Decima, the Conservative party polling firm, did a major attitudinal survey to discern the mood of the electorate. How did people feel about their situation in general? What were the sources of their dissatisfaction, and what were they looking for? Decima found that the people felt that their government did not care about them. They were worried about inflation, interest rates, and high taxes. They felt frustrated because they did not think they were sharing in the great resource wealth and Crown corporation profits that the government was always talking about. The Tories tailored their campaign to speak to these concerns. They promised to abolish the gas tax, subsidize mortgage payments, and, in general, make the government responsive to the little guy. Devine managed to portray the NDP as power-hungry bureaucrats who would not lift a finger to help people stung by high prices and impossible mortgage payments.

While the populist theme was dominant, the neo-conservative theme was not altogether absent. Devine accused the NDP socialists of having smothered the free spirit and private initiative of the people: "Profit has become a dirty word in Saskatchewan...We have to become proud of profit."[19] Alleging that the NDP wanted to hold on to power so that it "can own more of the farms and more of the businesses and more of your life,"[20] the Tories offered freedom from "socialist tyranny." Devine promised to restore "personal ambition, aspiration, and competition that the NDP has replaced with mediocrity." The NDP's reply to these charges was to call attention to the record. The Crown corporations were well-managed and making profits. In 1981, Saskatchewan had the lowest unemployment rate in the country and the best job creation rate per capita. At the same time, Saskatchewan's economy, with a net growth rate of 8 percent, outperformed the rest of the country.[21]

Devine effectively combined his offensive against Blakeney government socialism with an attack on Trudeau government socialism. The Saskatchewan NDP and the federal Liberals were said to be united in a left-wing cabal.[22] For example, the 1982 provincial budget was dismissed as "Trudeauism at its best." At a dramatic point in his election speeches, Devine never failed to rip up a piece of paper, saying that was exactly what he would do with the oil agreement the Saskatchewan government had signed with Ottawa. This was a good tactic, given the low esteem in which Trudeau was held in the West. By making Blakeney and Trudeau ideological bedfellows, Devine was able to do what Blakeney had tried and failed to do with the Crow Rate. Devine, not Blakeney, was able to present himself as the true defender of Saskatchewan against the federal government.

Echoes of Ronald Reagan were sometimes detectable in Devine's campaign rhetoric, such as when he explained how low taxes raised more money than high taxes: "When you drop the burden of tax, people go to work and they pay more taxes because they're working."[23] The NDP suggested that the Tories had modelled their philosophy on American neo-conservatism. They accused the Tories of trying to "make an evil out of helping your neighbour" and preaching "selfishness as a basic doctrine."[24] One NDP ad consisted of a series of Tory quotes expressing glowing admiration for Reagan and neo-conservative economics. Reagan's tax cuts had disproportionately benefited wealthy Americans. The same thing would happen in Saskatchewan, the NDP warned, if the Tories gained power and implemented their program of tax cuts.

In the main, however, Devine did not present the Tory party as the embodiment of neo-conservatism. Those affiliated with the radical right, whether of the unfettered free enterprise variety or the moral fundamentalist variety, were certainly welcome in the Conservative party. They were given comfort and enough nods and winks to make them feel at home, but when Devine went out to the electorate at large, he played down neo-conservatism and played up populism. For example, he did not go overboard in promoting free enterprise and the private sector. He did not promise to privatize anything, except the Land Bank. Devine seemed to be saying to the Saskatchewan people, "you can continue to have everything you had under the NDP, plus more money in your pocket." Expressive of his muted neo-conservatism was his use of the slogan "compassion and competition." A Tory government would not be so devoted to the principles of free enterprise that it would fail to give help to those who needed it.

At times, Devine attacked the NDP government for not being interventionist enough. When homeowners were suffering from unbearable interest rates, the Blakeney government had not intervened with across-the-board subsidies. Despite the Tories' faith in the free market, they refused to allow the market to set interest rates. Devine also attacked the NDP's inadequate spending on health care, saying that it was eighth in the nation in per capita terms. In the 1978 election, the NDP had pummeled the Tories for being less than fully supportive of medicare. Now the shoe was on the other foot. Devine took the NDP to task for betraying their own legacy: "We are proud of the tradition of Tommy Douglas, who brought it [medicare] in here, and John Diefenbaker, who extended it across the country."[25] Leaving aside the fact that it was Lester Pearson, not John Diefenbaker, who extended medicare across the country, Devine's statement was revealing. The Tories were portraying themselves as cofounders of medicare and better friends of socialized medicine than the NDP. The Tories even claimed to be friends of the labour movement, denouncing the Blakeney government's decision to legislate the hospital workers back to work just before the election.

In summary, the Tories were the populists of 1982. They hammered home the point that the NDP government, pursuing its own bureaucratic goals, was out of touch with the people. Devine also struck the themes of the new right – that government was too big, that state socialism was strangling initiative, that there had to be more room for free enterprise and private wealth – but, in general, populism overshadowed neo-conservatism in the Tory campaign. Devine managed to hint to his extremist followers that he was on the same wavelength as Ronald Reagan and Margaret Thatcher, without coming across to the general public as an ideologue. For the most part, his new right agenda remained hidden, and Devine's 1982 victory could not be interpreted as a mandate for neo-conservative policies. Indeed, upon taking power the Tories initially emphasized their populism. But the longer they stayed in power, the more they revealed their neo-conservative convictions.

Notes for Chapter 2

1. David E. Smith, *The Regional Decline of a National Party: Liberals on the Prairies* (Toronto: University of Toronto Press, 1981). 2. *Briarpatch*, June 1982. 3. S.M. Lipset, *Agrarian Socialism*, second edition (Berkeley: The University of California Press, 1971).

4. Interview, Elwood Cowley, 31 July 1989. 5. *Leader-Post*, 19 March 1982. 6. Keith Brown, "Crow Issue Didn't Sell in Rural Saskatchewan Ridings," *Briarpatch*, June 1982. 7. Interview, Elwood Cowley, 31 July 1989. 8. *Leader-Post*, 26 March 1982. 9. *Ibid.*, 16 April 1982. 10. Editorial, *Prairie Messenger*, 4 April 1982. 11. *Leader-Post*, 31 March 1982.

12. *Ibid.*, 6 April 1982. 13. *Ibid.*, 10 April 1982. 14. Colin Thatcher, *Backrooms: A Story of Politics* (Saskatoon: Western Producer Prairie Books, 1985). 15. *Leader-Post*, 31 March 1982. 16. *Ibid.*, 23 April 1982.

17. J. F. Conway, "The End of the Blakeney Era: An Assessment," *NeWest Review*, November 1987. 18. *Leader-Post*, 27 April 1982. 19. *Ibid.*, 24 April 1982. 20. *Ibid.*, 20 April 1982. 21. *Ibid.*, 22 April 1982. 22. *Ibid.*, 31 March 1982. 23. *Ibid.*, 6 April 1982. 24. *Ibid.*, 30 March 1982. 25. *Ibid.*, 8 April 1982.

3

THE TORIES
TAKE CHARGE

There's no damn difference between selling cars
and selling Saskatchewan.
– PAUL ROUSSEAU, *Financial Post*,
6 November 1982

Grant Devine's first task after the election was to select his cabinet. The clear choice for Deputy-Premier was Eric Berntson, a husky farmer from Carievale, a small town in southeastern Saskatchewan. Born in 1941, Berntson had a varied and unconventional background. He quit school in grade nine because, as he later recalled, "I'd had enough of that silliness."[1] He later finished his grade 12 at night school in Halifax so that he could join the Royal Canadian Air Force. After spending eight years in the navy and air force, he moved to Calgary where he worked nights in electronic data processing for National Cash Register. During the day, he attended university: "I took truckloads of classes. Pre-law, pre-med, lots of political science. Seven years – but I never did finish a degree."[2]

Berntson later joked that he was "railroaded" into politics because he had been "the most vocal guy in the local coffee shop."[3] In 1975 he was elected as the MLA for the traditionally Conservative rural riding of Souris-Cannington. Possessed of a keen political brain, he emerged as a dominant figure in the Tory party and Grant Devine's right-hand man. Devine acknowledged Berntson's contribution to the 1982 election victory by giving him three key responsibilities: Deputy Premier, Minister of Agriculture, and Government House Leader. Some political commentators suggested that Berntson was the de facto administrative head of the government.[4] While Devine was on the road giving speeches, attending conferences, and talking to the media, Berntson handled day-to-day decision-making. Devine presented the government's public image; Berntson concentrated on the daily grind of governing.

Another major figure in the government was Bob Andrew, who was appointed Minister of Finance. He had practised law in Kindersley, the rural constituency where he was first elected in 1978. A long-time party activist who had supported both Robert Stanfield and Joe Clark, Andrew had a reputation as a "red Tory." He believed that the left-versus-right polarity in politics had become irrelevant: "The political left or right is not going to solve economic problems in this country."[5] Andrew let it be known from time to time that he was familiar with the latest trends in economic thought in the United States and elsewhere. This habit of referring knowingly to current economic theory resulted in a sarcastic jibe from NDP finance critic Ned Shillington who remarked, "Bob Andrew is the sort of guy who reads one non-fiction book a year and then considers himself a towering intellectual."[6] Ignoring the criticism directed his way, Andrew worked diligently as finance minister during a difficult economic period. He was unabashedly pleased with his own work, matter-of-factly describing one of his budgets as "the best budget to be brought down in the country in the last five years."[7]

Other cabinet heavyweights included Gary Lane and Colin Thatcher. Lane, the senior partner in the Regina law firm of Lane and Whitmore, was first elected as a Liberal in 1971. In 1976, he decided that the provincial Liberal party was going nowhere and that the resurgent Tories under Dick Collver had the best chance to dethrone the NDP. His conversion was rewarded in 1982 when Devine made him Minister of Justice and minister responsible for SaskTel. The mercurial Colin Thatcher, son of a former Liberal premier, joined the Tories soon after Lane made his move. He apparently had his eyes on the agriculture portfolio, but that went to Berntson. Thatcher had to be content with Energy and Mines as well as responsibility for Saskoil and the Saskatchewan Mining Development Corporation. His political career was cut short in 1984 when he was charged with the murder of his former wife.

Paul Rousseau, MLA for Regina South, was one of the few cabinet members who represented an urban riding. A former car dealer who described himself as an "entrepreneur," Rousseau was touted as bringing business expertise to a government otherwise lacking in that area. He became Minister of Industry as well as minister responsible for Saskatchewan Government Insurance, the Saskatchewan Economic Development Corporation, and the Crown Investment Corporation. The last was a holding company that supervised the affairs of the province's 24 Crown corporations. Rousseau's lacklustre ministerial career ended in 1986 when he accepted a patronage plum and went off to London, England to serve as Saskatchewan's Agent-General.

One of the biggest cabinet jobs was health. It was given to Graham Taylor, the operator of a mixed farm and former principal of Wolseley High School. Taylor was first elected in 1978 and ran second to Devine in the leadership race in 1979. Devine did not seem to hold this against him, giving him a portfolio that was of the first rank, especially in Saskatchewan where health issues are always paramount.

Devine's government was notable for having the first two women cabinet ministers in the history of the province. Joan Duncan, the member for Maple Creek, was the co-owner and operator, with her husband, of a drug store. She viewed herself as a politician, not as a spokesperson for "so-called women's issues."[8] Her first portfolios were Supply and Services, and Revenue and Financial Services. Duncan's female colleague was Patricia Smith, the manager of a small business in Swift Current, who became Social Services Minister. She had made her mark as the first woman in the province to be elected chairperson of a board of education, and the first woman president of the Saskatchewan School Trustees' Association. Like Duncan, Smith was unenthusiastic about the feminist movement: "Although radicals get a lot of press and attention, much of that is negative attention. The very radical ones open themselves to ridicule because they are not very realistic. They seem to feel that if something is good for women, it's good period."[9]

The cabinet had a definite rural bias, twelve of its seventeen members representing rural areas. By occupation, there were six farmers, four business people, four teachers, two lawyers, and a public relations manager. The business people could not be described as leading lights of the private sector: a car dealer, a co-proprietor of a drug store, a manager of a small business, and the president of a farm implements manufacturing firm. The collective mind of the cabinet had a very limited sense of what government was capable of doing. Unlike the NDP, which saw government as an agent of economic and social development, the Tory cabinet tended to be suspicious of government as an institution. What held the cabinet together was a common hatred of "state socialism" and a determination to move Saskatchewan's political culture to the right.

The assault on the civil service

To do this, the cabinet believed it was necessary to weed out the NDP sympathizers from the civil service and put a Tory stamp on the bureaucracy. This task was entrusted to a transition team headed by the triumvirate of Eric Berntson, Bob Andrew, and Gary Lane. Terry Leier, a defeated Conservative candidate in the 1979 federal election, provided legal advice.

It did not take long for the blood to spill. Within a month of the election, political commentator Dale Eisler wrote: "We are now in the midst of a full-scale purge of the civil service, one that is shaking the bureaucracy to its core and filling the hallways of government with fear and that has all but ground the process of administration to a halt."[10] The Tories fervently believed that the civil service was peopled with NDP subversives who would go to any length to wreck the PC policy agenda. Another important goal of the Conservatives was to create job openings for hundreds of patronage seekers. The extent of the purge was unprecedented in post-war political history in Canada. When the NDP came into office in 1971, they fired 69 people. With the Tories, the numbers stretched into the hundreds.

The purge extended from senior officials all the way down the administrative ladder. Throughout much of the spring and summer of 1982, the transition team operated like a latter-day Committee of Public Safety, made infamous during the French Revolution for its guillotining of all those suspected of being disloyal to the revolution. They closely scrutinized personnel files, got copies of NDP membership lists, and proceeded to fire as many "socialist sympathizers" as could be identified. Deputy ministers and presidents of Crown corporations were among the first targets. Next came Order-in-Council appointees – that is, the people who had been appointed by cabinet. These people were not necessarily partisan; some had been hired for their special expertise or because their functions did not fit into regular departments. The Tories showed their inexperience by assuming that all cabinet appointments were NDP-tainted.

Grant Devine personally displayed ignorance about the rights of civil servants in Saskatchewan. He inflamed the entire bureaucracy when he suggested that it should be "thoroughly professional and entirely loyal at all times, and to that end, we want to ensure that no civil servants hold membership cards in any political party."[11] This threat contravened the Charter of Rights and Freedoms, the Saskatchewan Human Rights Code, and the collective agreement between the government and the unions. Saskatchewan had traditionally been a leader among the provinces in extending political rights to public servants, and until the election of the Tories, the right to hold a membership in a political party had been regarded as a basic right of citizenship. Devine was forced to retract his statement when it was pointed out to him that he did not have the right to dictate the political activity of civil servants. However, despite the formal retraction, the real message got through. Many public servants drew the obvious inference that if they were going to support any political party, it had better be the Tories.

As the weeks passed the firings continued, with everyone from assistant deputy ministers to secretaries living in the fear that they might be the next to go. Stories began to appear in the newspapers of fired civil servants forming support groups, being afraid to be seen talking in public with known New Democrats, and complaining that prospective employers were afraid to hire them for fear that they would lose government contracts.[12] Parents gave up NDP memberships out of a desire to protect their children's jobs. Government workers who wished to make a financial contribution to the NDP did so on a strictly cash basis for fear that cheques could be traced. The attacks, the emotional aftermath, and the "reign of terror" atmosphere all contributed to a steep decline in the morale of the civil service.

A revealing aspect of this process was that many of the firings were done at the behest of external constituencies, such as the provincial Chamber of Commerce. One prominent victim was Bob Sass, the executive director of the Occupational Health and Safety Branch of the Department of Labour. Sass was a nationally recognized expert; his firing was perceived as being motivated by his strong stand in defence of workers. Labour unions across the country protested the dismissal as "a frontal attack on working people in Saskatchewan and a declaration of war on the trade union movement."[13] A similar case was the firing of Dr. Hugh Walker, the executive director of the Community Health Branch in the Department of Health. The NDP charged that he was removed from his job because he would not go along with Tory plans to downgrade health services.[14] Other agencies, such as the Saskatchewan Housing Corporation, lost many employees simply because their mandates were not a priority for the new government.[15]

Throughout this period, the Tories appeared high-handed and arbitrary, showing little of the compassion they had talked about during the election. In fact, Devine absurdly called the dismissals "extremely constructive leading to increased productivity in the public sector."[16] In his televised address at the close of 1982, he made the unconvincing claim that "I've never seen such optimism and heard of such optimism in the civil service for years."

One of the more distressing aspects of this episode was that no one was told why they were fired. They were only informed that three criteria were being used: their political activity; their relationship to other civil servants; and their job performance. Many were turfed out primarily to make room for Tory appointments. Not surprisingly, many of these people sought redress either through the Public Service Commission appeal board, or through the courts. Numerous cases ended in large cash settlements, such as the $57,000 awarded to Doug Archer, later elected mayor of Regina. On the other hand, Order-in-Council appointments were usually treated differently. The government was deemed to have the right to fire these people because they had no protection under the Labour Standards Act or the collective agreement with the Saskatchewan Government Employees Union.[17]

On purely administrative grounds, the Tory attack on the civil service was unwise because it destroyed the sense of professionalism and responsibility that had been built up over the years. The province lost some of its best administrative talent. There was an exodus of top-flight managers and their families, an ironic sequel to the Tory election promise to "bring the children home."

This attack on the traditions, values and professionalism of the civil service was a natural outcome of neo-conservative ideology. The Tories resented the provincial bureaucracy, which they believed had been built up by the NDP to administer a whole range of "socialist" policies. Bureaucracy was not a neutral instrument to the Tories, but rather a symbol of the NDP's unwarranted tampering with the economic and social life of the province. The PCs came to office with the goal, not to make government more efficient, but rather to reduce its role. They were not interested in improving the civil service or making it more professional, because to do so would make it more influential.

Abolishing the Land Bank

After the cabinet had been installed and the civil service purged, the new government was ready to implement its open-for-business policies. For the Tories, the Land Bank was the most blatant intrusion of the state in the operations of the private enterprise economy. The ten-year-old Land Bank had been established by the NDP as a way of dealing with the problem of intergenerational land transfer. The problem was that older farmers, who needed a retirement income, wanted to sell their land, but young people, who wished to establish family farms, could not afford to buy. Land that was put on the market was often sold to well-established farmers who already owned large acreages. This reinforced the trend toward the concentration of land in fewer hands and the decline of the family farm.

The NDP solution was to allow retiring farmers the option of selling their land to the government, which in turn leased it to young farmers. The Land Bank helped prospective farmers get established in the business because renting land was less expensive than buying. Struggling farmers who did not own a large enough farm to have an economically viable unit also found it advantageous to lease additional acreage. After a five-year period, Land Bank tenants had an option to buy the land they rented from the government. The aim of the program was to increase the number of family farms or, at least, slow down their disappearance.

As of December 1982, the Land Bank had acquired ownership of some 1.195 million acres, for which it had paid about $150 million. Because of the rise in land values in the 1970s, the market value had grown to $500 million. The capital gain had gone to the government rather than to farmers or land speculators. The Tories found insupportable the idea that the government should own farmland. Eric Berntson likened the Land Bank to Stalin's policy of forced collectivization, in which farmers were shot if they refused to turn their land over to the state.[18] The Land Bank, he said, was nothing short of an NDP plot to make "sharecroppers" out of the farmers of Saskatchewan. The Tories declared that they had an entirely different policy: farmers should be owners, not tenants.

In support of the policy, the government introduced the Farm Purchase Program to replace the Land Bank. The new program provided financial assistance to farmers who were borrowing money through the federal Farm Credit Corporation to purchase farmland. Farmers received rebates equal to the difference between their loan payments and what the payments would have been at a fixed interest rate of 8 percent. In other words, the lending institution collected interest at the going rate, but the farmer paid only 8 percent, the difference being made up by the provincial treasury. Interest rate protection under the Farm Purchase Program lasted ten years. For the first five years, the guaranteed interest rate was 8 percent, and for the final five years, 12 percent. After that, the farmer was on his own.

The Tories were extremely proud of the plan. Berntson called it "one of the most imaginative, innovative, and far-reaching pieces of legislation ever presented in any legislative assembly in North America."[19] However, the program had its limitations. It did little for the aspiring farmer who lacked the capital for security on a loan because the Farm Credit Corporation required as security two acres for every acre borrowed against. Moreover, the only true measure of the success or failure of the program was whether it met its stated objective: to turn farm renters into farm owners. Census Canada figures showed that between 1981 and 1986, approximately 2.5 million acres of land in Saskatchewan changed from "ownership" to "rented" status. This was two and one half times the holdings of the Land Bank prior to 1982. Farm foreclosures resulted in more and more land ending up in the hands of the chartered banks. The Royal Bank alone was estimated to hold 120,000 acres. Thus, the Farm Purchase Program, which was finally terminated in 1987, did not arrest the trend towards increasing amounts of farmland rented, rather than owned, by the person doing the farming. The abolition of the Land Bank had not resulted in less tenancy and more ownership.

Open for Business

Nonetheless, the decision to bring government acquisition of farmland to a halt was a victory for neo-conservative ideology, because it represented government withdrawal from the economy. It was, in fact, an early example of the transfer of assets from the public to the private domain – in other words, privatization. But the Devine government was initially unwilling to put privatization at the centre of its economic development strategy. It preferred a less radical approach. Instead of being drastically reduced, the public sector would be kept at about the same size or modestly trimmed. Meanwhile, the private sector would be encouraged to grow to fill the space in the economy that would otherwise have been occupied by an expanding government sector.

The Tories were convinced that international business was shunning Saskatchewan because it was seen as the most socialistic jurisdiction in North America. A new image was needed; Saskatchewan had to be presented to the businessmen of the world as an exciting hotbed of capitalism. Devine appeared to honestly believe that once investors and entrepreneurs knew that the long, dark reign of socialism was over, they would flock to Saskatchewan.

This was the main idea behind the "Open for Business" conference hosted by the government of Saskatchewan and the *Financial Post* on October 19 and 20, 1982. It showcased the new government's economic policy based on restricting the Crown corporations and letting the competitive market be the engine of growth. The event was essentially part of the Tories' public relations campaign, designed to get the message out that the new government of Saskatchewan liked businessmen, and wanted them to invest in the province. More than anything else, the conference was about attitude, particularly the development of a neo-conservative attitude north of the U.S. border. Simultaneously, the Chamber of Commerce, naturally ecstatic about this whole turn of events, held its own "Business Week" with the theme "Profit, the root of all jobs." The Open for Business conference was a moment of triumph and glory for the new right, celebrating its achievement of finally taking power in Saskatchewan.

Among the businessmen who attended the conference were Grant Reuber, deputy chairman of the Bank of Montreal, and a leading ideologue for the new right in Canada; Matteaus Balz-Wieland, first vice-president for Credit Suisse; Donald Lenz, vice-president of Goldman Sachs of New York; and Gary Piddy, production co-ordinator of Getty Oil of Los Angeles. The Tories were determined that from now on, all new jobs would come from the private sector. This was a wildly optimistic assessment of the abilities and willingness of the private sector to help out Saskatchewan, and in the end, it proved naive. Later, the Devine government would be forced to reverse its position and throw millions of dollars at businesses to help them create jobs, but, at this point, they believed that the private sector would succeed on its own.

The advertised highlight of the conference was a speech by

Grant Devine in which he outlined the Tories' new industrial strategy. He promised to bring together what he called the "four solitudes" of business, government, labour and education. This commitment was belied by how the conference had been organized. While a steady stream of businessmen, consultants and others with a vested interest in pro-private industry policies had filed through the Premier's office, no representatives from the labour movement or the academic community had been asked for advice. [20]

When Devine delivered his speech on the last night of the conference, his audience must have felt they had stumbled into an election rally. The speech had the flavour of a warmed-over entree from the spring campaign. Devine spoke in vague generalities about the new "positive attitude" in the province and joked that Saskatchewan had decided "not to participate" in the worldwide economic recession. What Devine wanted more than anything else was enthusiasm, which, he contended, had been drained away by high taxes, excessive regulation, and undue nationalization. He interpreted his huge election victory as a mandate to make fundamental changes in the direction of the province. He even declared that the size of his win put him above politics, placing him at the head of "an alliance of confident thinking people from all political parties and all walks of life." This was typical of Devine. Whenever he wanted to push the province to the right, he claimed to be motivated by "common sense" or to be doing something "no reasonable person could object to." It was a technique for softening his hard ideological edges.

As to the specifics of economic strategy, Devine committed his government to deregulation, one of the central features of the agenda of the new right. He announced that the Tories would vigorously proceed with regulatory reform. During its first year, the government rescinded 750 regulations and developed a system called zero-based regulatory review in which all existing regulations were reviewed in consultation with those affected. The government also eased the environmental regulation review process.

Devine's speech touched on other ways of promoting economic

growth. He took the opportunity to cancel the back-in rights of the Saskatchewan Mining and Development Corporation. Until this time, SMDC had enjoyed the option of participating in any new mineral exploration or development in northern Saskatchewan. Under the new rules, private companies were no longer forced to accept the public corporation as a joint venture partner.

Much of Devine's industrial strategy was symbolic and repeated announcements that had already been made. All the same, it was warmly received by those attending the conference, who rarely heard politicians talk so enthusiastically about the virtues of corporate capitalism, rugged individualism, and business culture.

The Tories made it clear that they were committed to the principles that profits were good and that taxes were the mortal enemy of the business class. The government's role would be to support private business, not replace it. It would be appropriate for the government to provide infrastructure, for example, roads and electric power, and to improve educational facilities, especially technical schools, but not to go into business for itself. The Tories promised to work closely with the business community, making sure it got the information needed to help it prosper. Above all, Devine pledged never to forget why businessmen were in business – to make money.[21]

The NDP could not resist raining on the Tory parade. In the days leading up to the conference, the opposition announced their intention to buy back or expropriate any Crown corporations or government assets sold by the Tories. This statement enraged the conference organizer, Minister of Industry Paul Rousseau, who nonetheless wisely decided not to engage in a debate with the NDP while the conference was under way. Despite his efforts to downplay the incident, businessmen grilled both Rousseau and Devine on the consequences of a return to power by the NDP. The only assurance the Tories could offer was that the private sector would perform so well that the NDP would not dare touch it. An even weaker response was that because of the Tories' vast majority, the NDP would be out of power for a very long time.

The Open for Business conference was basically an exercise in attitude-building. The Tories thought that if they talked enough about private enterprise, a vibrant, private sector would spring into existence. In the heady months following the toppling of the seemingly rock-solid NDP government, they felt the entire world would share their exhilaration at having "liberated" Saskatchewan. Tory policy-makers turned their gaze southward, hoping to find inspiration in the powerful neo-conservative current blowing across the United States. Their preferred model was the southern state of Georgia, which had been able to transform itself from an agricultural to a manufacturing economy in relatively short time. This had been accomplished through the passage of repressive labour legislation, most notoriously the so-called right-to-work laws. Such laws banned the closed shop and gave all employees union benefits whether they belonged to the union or not. This meant there was no advantage to joining a union, effectively eroding the union's effectiveness. In the long run, workers were left defenceless and forced to deal with their employers on an individual basis. Saskatchewan Tories were also impressed with the Georgia Developers Association, a government-appointed economic advisory body that was intended to attract investment to the state. A similar body was created in Saskatchewan and was formally announced at the Open for Business conference.

The other aspect of Georgia's development strategy which appealed to the Tories was the role taken by Governor George Busbee, who actively solicited private enterprise and relentlessly extolled the virtues of his state to national and international investors. It was a role that suited Devine perfectly. He believed that the first and most important step in creating a private enterprise utopia on the prairies was getting the message out. He hit the road, talking to any group that would give him a hearing, tirelessly repeating that Saskatchewan was "Open for Business." Devine was not much interested in day-to-day administration. Unlike Blakeney, who had kept informed of the detailed operations of government departments and Crown corporations, Devine saw himself less as an administrator than as a front man pitching the Conservative vision for the future. He considered himself Saskatchewan's number one salesman. His folksy sayings became a trademark: "There's so much more we can be;" "Give'er snoose, Bruce;" "Don't say whoa in a mud hole;" "Saskatchewan is the best kept secret in the world;" "We're world-class;" "Saskatchewan has decided not to participate in the world-wide recession," and so on.

If nothing else, Devine embedded his sayings in the public consciousness. Whether his boosterism helped the Saskatchewan economy was another question. The downside of Devine's informal, cheerleading style was that he came across as unsophisticated, if not downright foolish. A cartoon in the Regina *Leader-Post* alluded to this by depicting a Japanese businessman with a puzzled expression on his face, meditating on a newspaper headline reading "Give'er snoose Bruce." At times, Devine seemed to revel in his countrified image. At the first ministers' conference held shortly after the election of Brian Mulroney, the Premier complimented the Prime Minister: "I give you 'A' marks for givin' 'er snoose right off the bat. You are wisely using and spending a big batch of money that hasn't been spent that wisely before." As for Canada's attitude to foreign investors, Devine recommended a policy based on "Come on over to my house because I've got the coffee pot on."[22] This was a clear departure from the low-key style of former premier Blakeney.

Devine's salesmanship was also marred by a tendency to attack, in a hysterical manner, those he perceived as enemies. When Premier David Peterson of Ontario expressed concern about the future of his province's wine industry under free trade with the United States, Devine incoherently raved: "I think people are making a silk purse out of a sow's ear blowing it way out of context. Some people might rattle sabres and say I'm not going to play with you, with my grapes. Well, I say go play with your grapes at home."[23]

For better or worse, Devine cast himself in the role of image-maker for the province. He was not alone, of course. In the wake of the Open for Business conference, various cabinet ministers fanned out across the country and, indeed, around the world, telling business people that the government of Saskatchewan really cared about them. Cabinet ministers jetted to London, Vienna, Hong Kong, Australia, Bulgaria, Brazil, and many other places, telling potential investors of the new "pro-business attitude" in Saskatchewan. They cited the removal of the gas tax, mortgage interest reduction plans, deregulation, and resource royalty holidays as examples of the new outlook. As Eric Berntson put it, "The words 'foreign investment', like profit, are not dirty words to us. When we talk economic development, we recognize friends, not passports." While many cabinet ministers pitched in and contributed to the sales effort, none ever achieved the same media profile as the Premier. Devine and "open for business" were inseparably linked.

Pragmatism versus ideology

The "Open for Business" philosophy was entirely consistent with the economics of the new right. Government interventionism and state socialism were decried; the free market was exalted. At the same time, however, the "Open for Business" initiative concentrated more on the expansion of private enterprise than on the reduction of the public sector. Devine promised that Crown corporations would not be allowed to grow, but he did not say they would be sold. This was not altogether satisfactory to the Tory party rank and file and to certain members of the business community. They thought the election of 1982 signalled a more profound neo-conservative revolution than the cabinet initially seemed willing to undertake.

The split between the cabinet and the grassroots of the party broke open at the Tory convention in November 1982. The delegates passed resolutions calling for right-to-work legislation, an immediate freeze on the minimum wage, and other attacks on labour.[24] At later conventions, the party pushed even further, advocating the sale of "all Crown Corporations which are not providing essential services".[25] They even passed a resolution opposing the redistribution of wealth.[26]

During the government's first term, most cabinet ministers tried to dissuade the delegates from adopting far right policies by warning that an open war with the labour movement would poison the investment climate in the province.[27] Finance Minister Bob Andrew supported a moderate approach, suggesting that right-to-work legislation would destroy the co-operative spirit the Tories were trying to build among business, labour and government. He advised caution, musing that as one "continues in power, one tends to move towards a more moderate position."[28] Justice Minister Gary Lane ruminated along similar lines: "If one is talking philosophically, the Conservative Party has always been in the middle of the road."[29] The government wanted to be perceived as pragmatic, not ideologically driven or extremist.

Symptomatic of the government's moderation was its failure to slash the size of the bureaucracy. Neo-conservative doctrine dictates that the role of the government should decrease and the number of people working for the government should decline. Devine showed no interest in aggressively trimming the public service. If anything, he sent out the opposite signal by expanding his cabinet, making it the largest in Saskatchewan's history. He rationalized the move by arguing that reduced workloads would give ministers more time to talk to their constituents. The Tories also created a whole new layer of political bureaucrats, a veritable army of special assistants, executive assistants, press secretaries, and communications advisors. Handing out government jobs rewarded a large number of party faithful, but it directly flouted neo-conservative philosophy.

Elements of the business community were also disappointed with the government's failure to be more right-wing. Some business people had greeted the election of the Tories with enthusiasm, if not rapture. Within a month of the change of government, the executive director of the Saskatchewan Chamber of Commerce effused, "State capitalism was a major concern of ours. We now feel we have a government in power that has sympathy with that concern."[30] The government certainly wanted to be viewed as a businessman's government. One sign was the abandonment of the NDP practice of not showing legislation to private firms until it had been presented in the legislature. The Tories willingly granted companies access to proposed bills and sought their recommendations.

Some business leaders hoped that the Devine government would speedily usher in a neo-conservative revolution. No one expressed this attitude more directly than Roger Phillips, the president of Interprovincial Steel Company (Ipsco). A few days after the election, in a speech to the Regina Chamber of Commerce, he put forward the idea that business had no responsibility to society except to create wealth. This idea was straight out of Milton Friedman. Phillips later headed the Institute for Saskatchewan Enterprise, a right-wing think tank whose purpose was to provide an "unbiased" defence of the government's plans to privatize Crown corporations. In the early years, however, the Devine government shied away from the extreme conservatism favoured by Phillips and others.

The government's moderate course disillusioned some top-level Tories. One unnamed government member stated that he felt that the Devine government was merely marking time "while the NDP are on a holiday."[31] This contained a grain of truth. At first, the cabinet appeared in no hurry to proclaim a right-wing revolution. For the time being, it was enough to extend hospitality to capitalists. The cabinet resisted calls by the Chamber of Commerce and Tory party conventions to privatize everything in sight. More than once, Devine said he had no intention of engaging in a sell-off of public corporations, adding, the "government's job is to manage them the best we can while gradually moving towards privatizing some of the Crowns." The economic plan was to rein in the Crown corporations and to encourage private investors to take up the slack.

The problem with this "Open for Business" approach was that it was based on false assumptions. The NDP had not chased away businesses in the manner alleged by Tory partisans. Although the Blakeney government had seen a role for public corporations in the development of natural resources like uranium, potash, and oil, it had encouraged the private sector, too. The NDP had favoured a mixed economy, giving the Crown corporations, private companies, and co-operatives an opportunity to grow. Contrary to Devine's supercharged rhetoric, it had been possible for businesses to make a profit in NDP Saskatchewan. The Tories wrongly believed that as soon as Blakeney's government was defeated, business would rush in to take advantage of previously untapped profit-making opportunities. Not so. As a matter of fact, the Open for Business conference coincided with a sharp downturn in the provincial economy. The Tories quickly learned that making speeches about the wonders of private enterprise did little but raise expectations that were not fulfilled. Some concrete measures were urgently required to stimulate a faltering economy.

Notes for Chapter 3

1. *Business Review*, Fall 1983. 2. *Ibid.* 3. *Ibid.* 4. *Leader-Post*, 11 July 1989. 5. *Ibid.*, 23 May 1984. 6. *Ibid.*, Eisler, 31 May 1989. 7. *Business Review*, Summer 1984. 8. *CitiView*, April 1987. 9. *Business Review*, Spring 1985.

10. *Leader-Post*, 13 May 1982. 11. *Ibid.*, 27 May 1982. 12. *Ibid.*, 6 July 1982. 13. *Ibid.*, 23 August 1982. 14. *Ibid.*, 5 June 1983. 15. *Ibid.*, 9 September 1983. 16. *Ibid.*, 14 August 1982. 17. *Ibid.*, 14 April 1984.

18. *Ibid.*, 7 December 1982. 19. *Ibid.*, 2 December 1982.

20. *Ibid.*, 15 November 1982. 21. *Ibid.*, 3 November 1982. 22. *Ibid.*, 15 February 1985. 23. *Ibid.*, Eisler, 21 May 1988.

24. *Star-Phoenix*, 13 November 1982. 25. *Leader-Post*, 22 January 1985. 26. *Star-Phoenix*, 9 November 1985. 27. *Leader-Post*, 15 November 1982. 28. *Ibid.* 29. *Ibid.*, 5 November 1985. 30. *Ibid.*, 11 May 1982. 31. Prince Albert *Herald*, 18 January 1984.

4

◊ ──────────────────── ◊

THE FREE MARKET JUDGES SASKATCHEWAN

> Saskatchewan has decided not to participate
> in the recession.
> — GRANT DEVINE, *October 1982.*

Saskatchewan's new Conservative government wanted to give the market a greater role in the province's economy, but was not entirely sure how to do it. One of the first attempts was an experiment with supply-side economics.

According to this theory, progressive taxation destroys incentive by robbing high-income earners of the fruits of their effort and initiative. Lowering taxes produces the opposite result and generates enough incremental economic activity to compensate for the revenues lost because of lower tax rates. The government deficit is predicted to shrink, rather than grow, when taxes are decreased. Although George Bush denounced supply-side theory as "voodoo economics," Ronald Reagan embraced it in 1980, when he began slashing billions of dollars in personal and corporate income taxes, while increasing military spending. The unfortunate result was a huge deficit, quickly making the United States the largest debtor nation in the world.[1]

Although supply-side economics failed south of the border, the

Tory government was eager to apply it to Saskatchewan. The first major initiative in tax reduction was the elimination of the gasoline tax, which put an average $200 a year into the pocket of every citizen who owned a car. It was hoped that people would spend this money, thereby giving a boost to the economy. The problem was that most of the extra cash was spent on consumer goods, which may have stimulated the retail trade, but did little to create new jobs or new wealth. Much of the money was used to buy goods manufactured in central Canada or elsewhere, but not in Saskatchewan.

Recognizing that abolishing the gas tax was an efficient way to win votes, but an inefficient way to stimulate economic growth, the government became more selective by targeting tax cuts to certain sectors of the economy. The most conspicuous example was a major tax break for the oil industry, featuring a one-year royalty and tax holiday for wells drilled from 1 June 1982 until the end of 1983. The policy also included a 30 percent reduction in royalties for some old wells drilled since 1974, a reduction from 40 to 50 percent of the provincial share of future price increases, and a royalty reduction of between 10 and 20 percent on light and medium oil depending on when the well was drilled. All of this was expected to cost the province $35 million, but the lost revenue would be recovered from the increased exploration and drilling stimulated by the tax breaks.

The policy was tied to another Tory economic goal, the development of local entrepreneurial talent. To encourage independent oil producers, local oilmen were invited to Grant Devine's office shortly after the election and promised "special considerations," the implication being that they would be treated differently from the multinationals. Devine advised them to form their own association, separate from the Canadian Petroleum Association, which would become a lobby group that would have the ear of the government.[2]

Responding enthusiastically to the tax breaks, producers began almost immediately to increase their activity in the oil patch. Neither declining world prices nor the federal government's revenue grab in the National Energy Program deterred them. A record amount of exploration was recorded in the first year of the tax holiday.[3] Oil companies were often able to remake their entire investment before they paid one penny in taxes.[4]

However, one important reason for the vitality of the industry was the increase in drilling for natural gas, a development that had less to do with tax breaks than with the government's election promise to extend gas service to rural areas. Interest in natural gas continued to increase with the deregulation of gas markets in Canada, and the growing demand for natural gas in the United States. The industry boomed in Alberta and Manitoba, as well as Saskatchewan.

The Devine government was extremely pleased with its oil and gas policy and offered it to the Macdonald Commission on free trade, and anyone else who would listen, as a model for the revitalization of a wide variety of industries in the country. The policy was based on allowing the free market to work without being discouraged by burdensome taxation. The concept of maximizing the government's take through royalties was abandoned in favour of accelerated economic activity. This intensified development came at a price. Since oil is a finite resource, the government sacrificed permanently its ability to obtain a larger share of the value of the resource. If the royalties had not been cancelled, development would have taken place over a longer time period with more of the wealth captured through taxes, and less to the owners of the oil companies.

On the heels of the oil policy, other tax incentives were announced. Corporate income tax for small manufacturing and processing businesses was eliminated. At the same time, the government tried to promote manufacturing and processing by offering business tax credits and by awarding grants as an incentive for creating a job that lasted at least one year. These industrial incentive grants were later phased out when it became evident that many of these jobs would have been created with or without the grant.

In March 1984, the government introduced Venture Capital Corporations. Designed to provide risk capital for small businesses worth up to $5 million, VCCs permitted investors to put money in "risky" enterprises while receiving a tax credit which, in effect, substantially limited the risk. People could invest up to

$10,000 in an approved VCC, which allowed them to claim a 30 percent provincial tax credit. The Tories hoped that this policy would develop the entrepreneurial instincts of the cautious Saskatchewan investor.

Pleased with the benefits and popularity of these types of policies, the Tories continued to tinker with the tax system. In 1985, the government proudly unveiled Canada's first flat tax. It was based on the principle that one should pay a fixed percentage of one's income in taxes regardless of income level, and was fundamentally opposed to the concept of progressive taxation. The flat tax was tied to supply-side economics in that providing a tax break to the wealthy was supposed to encourage them to be more productive. Knowing that their gains would not be taxed away, they would have a stronger incentive to work hard, be innovative, and invest their money. Finance Minister Bob Andrew asserted the flat tax "would allow the free market to play its hand and in the end, if you allow the free market to play its hand, it is going to be a benefit." To strengthen the argument for his proposed tax "reform," Andrew cited the United States: "The flat tax is an issue endorsed by both the Democrats and the Republicans. Now if that doesn't tell people something, I don't know what does."[5]

Andrew maintained that low income earners would like the flat tax because it would mean that everybody would pay income tax. Here he had a point. It was well known that the progressive character of the tax system had been eroded by a multiplicity of deductions, exemptions, tax shelters, and quick write-off schemes. High income earners, with the aid of professional tax advisors, readily found ways to avoid taxes. Accordingly, the flat tax seemed to be a step in the direction of fairness.

The fatal flaw in Andrew's argument was that his flat tax was designed to enable high income earners to protect a substantial portion of their income by investing in various types of housing projects, frontier oil exploration, VCCs, and other easily accessible tax shelters. The 1 percent tax (later increased to 2 percent) was levied on net income, that is, income after deductions for such items as investments, health club memberships, retirement plan contributions, and car expenses. On the other hand, deductions for dependent children, contributions to churches, and charities were not allowed. The deductions favoured by the wealthy still applied, while those for the average worker did not. The Tories ignored the obvious reality that the wealthy could afford to pay more taxes. As Frances Russell, a Winnipeg political columnist, observed, "A flat tax with loopholes is not reform, it is a further repudiation of the ability-to-pay principle, a new ploy to skin the middle class for the benefit of the wealthy."[6] One of the proponents of the flat tax had been Peter Pocklington, who championed the idea during his bid for the leadership of the federal Conservative party in 1983. Even Pocklington, who was on the far right of the Tory party, admitted that a flat tax with loopholes was not fair. The Devine government's tax was not perceived by the public as a "reform," but as an inequitable tax grab.

The unpopularity of the flat tax added to the generally disappointing results of the government's economic development policies. The theory of supply-side economics and economic reality proved to be two different things. Tax incentives and so-called tax reforms failed to provide Saskatchewan with the prosperity promised by the Tories. Bankruptcies climbed from 458 in 1981 to 901 in 1983, unemployment went from 4.8 percent to 7.4 percent, and Saskatchewan's job creation rate was half that of Manitoba.[7] The province's gross domestic product did not keep pace with the national average, and Saskatchewan continued to have the lowest manufacturing capacity per capita in the country after Prince Edward Island and Newfoundland.[8] Although Devine had declared in 1982 that Saskatchewan was not going to participate in the recession, he had been proven wrong.

The provincial debt

Meanwhile, Saskatchewan's ballooning provincial debt testified to the worsening economic situation. The debt also pointed out the contradiction between neo-conservative antipathy to Keynesian deficit spending and the necessities imposed by economic reality. The first sign of trouble appeared in 1982. The new government's first budget was essentially the NDP's pre-election budget warmed over, with one glaring difference: for the first time since the early 1960s Saskatchewan's budget showed a deficit. And whereas no previous shortfall had been much more than $3 million dollars, the deficit forecast in the 1982 budget was a startling $227 million, an amount the government called "minimum and manageable."[9] The Tories blamed the debt on exaggerated projections of natural resource revenues by the NDP. Resource revenues had indeed fallen and continued to fall, but not by $227 million. The bulk of the debt was caused by the Tories' election promises, especially the elimination of the gas tax, which cost $120 million, and the mortgage interest reduction plan, which was budgeted for $40 million.

While the size of the 1982 debt was a shock, it was but a faint hint of what was to come. The deficit for 1983 was $331 million; for 1984, $379 million; and 1985, $584 million, leaving an accumulated debt after four years of Tory rule of more than $1.7 billion. By 1989 the debt exceeded $4 billion. The government, awash in a sea of red ink, offered a series of explanations and rationalizations. At the time of the 1983 budget, Finance Minister Bob Andrew tried to sound optimistic: "I am convinced that our course is the correct one, and that we will succeed in returning to a balanced budget position when our economy improves."[10] The following year he made no apology for an even larger deficit: "My view is that it doesn't make a lot of sense for us to balance our budget or to bring our deficit down significantly if the other provinces are going in the other direction. We can balance ours ... but the net result is we're going to end up losing in [federal] transfer adjustments."[11] By that line of reasoning, deficits should be as large as possible in order to improve the financial position of the province. Devine alleged that "the public endorsed the fact that the province was bearing the brunt of the difficult international time rather than imposing it on people by raising taxes to protect Crown corporations or a government department."[12] Thus, the Tories began to make a virtue of the size of the debt, citing it as proof of their dedication to basic health and education programs.

The mounting deficits, of course, put an end to all talk of tax cuts. The 1982 election promises to eliminate the 5 percent sales tax and reduce the provincial income tax by 10 points were quietly dropped. Far from fulfilling commitments to decrease taxes, the government had to increase them. The 1985 budget imposed the new flat tax, an unprecedented tax on the sale of used vehicles, and abolished property improvement grants and renters' rebates. With these tax increases, the government moved in a direction exactly opposite from the one it had promised in 1982. The elimination of the gas tax had been advertised as the largest tax reduction in Saskatchewan history. The sequel to this accomplishment was the 1985 budget, which contained the largest tax increase in Saskatchewan history. There was no doubt that the Tories were off-track. What made matters worse for the government was the loss of its populist image. The tax holidays for the oil companies contrasted with heavier burdens for the middle class and the poor. The tax on used cars appeared particularly harsh since it was paid by people who could not afford to buy a new car.

The 1985 budget was a political disaster, and the government moved immediately to make amends. Andrew, who had been condemned publicly by his own cabinet colleagues for the tax increases, admitted that his budget had been less than perfect: "In the process of taking bold steps sometimes you can lose what you're trying to accomplish. I think what people are saying is that we're prepared to pay our fair share, but it must be a fair share."[13] Devine, too, sounded contrite, advising his cabinet to rethink future policy proposals with the aim of reducing the burden of tax.[14] He also shuffled the cabinet, partly in a manoeuvre to get Bob Andrew out of finance. The new minister, Gary Lane, stressed that he was not happy with the 1985 budget and favoured more tax cuts like those given to the oil industry. His 1986 budget repealed the odious used cars tax and was generally more palatable to the public. However, it masked rather than addressed the government's financial problems. It was based on erroneous figures and understated the deficit by $800 million, an awkward fact the government chose to suppress until after the 1986 election.

But the economic problems were very real and the true state of the province's finances could not be concealed forever. The simple-minded open-for-business sloganeering had not averted recession. Tax cuts had created some activity in the oil industry, but cuts had been superseded by tax increases in an effort to control the deficit. Neo-conservativism decreed that the market was supreme and that its judgments had to be accepted. The trouble was that the free market had pronounced a negative judgment on Saskatchewan. Capital flows to where it can make the greatest return, and that place wasn't Saskatchewan. The province had too small a local market and was too far away from other markets to support an indigenous manufacturing base of any size. It was the old Canadian story of hinterland underdevelopment. The Tories could not complain that the market system was not working. It was working all too well and allocating investment dollars to the industrial heartland of Ontario and Quebec. The problem was not the failure of free market forces to operate; the problem was that when they operated, they produced a recession in Saskatchewan.

Government support for free enterprise

The Tories were forced to compromise their ideology, and the Devine government was obliged to become a partner in development. However, unlike the NDP, who wanted to be both an active partner in enterprise and an outright owner, the Tories were content to be a silent partner and a temporary and reluctant owner. They put up the cash, guaranteed the loans, and took much, if not all, of the risk, while the "entrepreneur" managed the company. If the venture succeeded, the government pulled out, leaving the private partner to reap the profits. If the venture faltered, the government stayed in to prop it up.

By 1984, the Tories had increased the budgets of the economic departments by 32.9 percent and were busy handing out money to the private sector. One example was Char Inc., established to manufacture barbecue briquettes in Grant Devine's own riding of Estevan. The government managed to lure a Quebec businessman to the province with a $220,000 loan from the Saskatchewan Economic Development Corporation (SEDCO), an additional

$145,000 from the provincial government, and a $182,413 grant from the federal Department of Regional Economic Expansion. Yet, even with all this assistance, the business closed after only three weeks and laid off all but three employees, who remained to make kitty litter.

A more successful venture was Canapharm Industries, a manufacturer and distributor of pharmaceutical supplies. The plant was located in Wolseley, a small town in Health Minister Graham Taylor's constituency. Canapharm received a mortgage from SEDCO and was financed through a tax credit scheme involving 40 local residents who created a venture capital corporation. While Wolseley residents were delighted and the government glowing with pride, Canapharm was not an example of the free market operating in Saskatchewan. It exemplified government-assisted economic development, something all hinterland governments are forced into in one form or another.

According to Grant Devine, the "perfect example" of economic diversification was Supercart International, a Regina manufacturer of plastic shopping carts.[15] By the time it declared bankruptcy, the company had received $366,000 from the federal government, $250,000 from the provincial government, $400,000 from SEDCO, $65,000 from the City of Regina, and $1 million through the provincial Venture Capital Corporation scheme. Robert Silzer, the entrepreneur behind the plan, boasted his new factory would put Regina on the map as the shopping cart capital of the world, but by January 1987 he was being sued for fraud by the Canadian Imperial Bank of Commerce, the federal government, and the Supercart Venture Capital Corporation. The company never did produce any shopping carts, except for a few prototypes. In an obvious understatement, Graham Taylor, then Minister of Small Business and Tourism, reflected: "People believed it was something there would be a market for... Unfortunately, in the world of business often things don't work out."[16]

More ambitious than any of these ventures was the plan to build at least one and possibly two heavy oil upgraders. Prior to the Tories' taking power, Saskoil, a Crown-owned company, had been involved in an upgrader consortium consisting of Husky Oil,

Gulf Resources Canada, Shell, and Petro-Canada. The consortium disintegrated in September 1982, when Husky pulled out. After being frustrated by the unwillingness of the multinationals to negotiate seriously about participating in an expensive enhanced oil recovery project that would only be profitable with much higher oil prices, the Devine government began to look for another partner. It found one in Federated Co-operatives Ltd., owners of the Consumers Co-operative Refinery in Regina.

The negotiations for this heavy oil upgrader were long and difficult involving Federated Co-ops, the federal government, and the provincial government. In the end, the Saskatchewan government agreed to take a 15 percent equity and Federated Co-op a 5 percent equity with the remaining 80 percent coming from federal and provincial loan guarantees. Federated Co-op's 5 percent came from a loan provided by the provincial government. Interest on this loan was payable from the outset, but the principal was payable only after the upgrader produced dividends. For its 5 percent investment, Federated Co-op controlled 50 percent of the project, and even that 5 percent was borrowed from the province.[17]

In actual dollar terms, the province put up $120 million of the estimated $700 million startup costs. Of that, $97.5 million took the form of an investment guaranteeing provincial equity in the project, and the other $32.5 million was loaned to the company at a preferred rate. The Co-op borrowed the remaining 80 percent ($520 million) from commercial lenders, aided by federal and provincial loan guarantees. Payments on these loans began only when the upgrader started operating in 1987.[18] With all the development money coming from the federal and provincial governments, the Co-op Upgrader was hardly a shining example of private enterprise taking risks and creating wealth. It was clearly public enterprise with a private sector manager.

So great was the Devine government's desire to attract business to the province that it offered Peter Pocklington highly favourable terms to build three pork-processing plants. The deal consisted of $22 million in loans and grants from the provincial government on the condition that Pocklington invested $15 million of his own money. Gainers, the Edmonton meat packer that

Pocklington controlled, built the first stage, a $7 million bacon-processing plant in North Battleford, using government grants and low-cost loans. The City of North Battleford also paid a $3,500 subsidy for every job created that lasted three years up to a maximum of 200.[19] But the second and third plants, which were to have involved investment by Pocklington, were later cancelled because of "adverse market conditions." A Montana government official with whom Pocklington also negotiated commented that he was "shocked" that Saskatchewan would hand over millions of dollars to Pocklington without an ironclad contract for the completion of the entire project.[20]

Pocklington claimed to be unhappy about having to take money from government: "It's my personal preference not to be involved in any receipt of money from the government. In a perfect world there would be no need for grants or subsidies."[21] Until that world existed, however, Pocklington would be found with his face deep in the public trough. He explained that government mismanagement forced his businesses to pay high taxes and strapped them with regulations, literally forcing him to take government handouts. Devine justified giving the money to such a pre-eminent free-enterpriser on the grounds that he "couldn't find a socialist to give it to."

Among its many economic development initiatives, the Tory government displayed a special interest in high-tech industries. In 1983, it unveiled its high-tech plans at the Futurescan '83 Conference in Saskatoon. The government created a new Department of Science and Technology, organized a major task force on high-tech in the province, promised state-of-the-art technology centres at both universities, hired a prominent Ottawa consultant to help bring high-tech to Saskatchewan, promised a tax incentive program similar to that given to the oil industry, and created a $50-million-dollar research and development fund from the Heritage Fund.[22] Grant Devine said that his government had a "mega-commitment" to new technology, and Saskatoon, the major centre for this development, was dubbed "Silicon Flats". Much of the impetus for this push came from Bob Andrew, who was fascinated with high-tech and would spout excerpts from such popular "high-tech" books as *Megatrends* and

The Third Wave. Andrew, at one time, even promoted a computer game called *Budget Challenge*, the object of which was to devise a budget without increasing the deficit. The game was set up in shopping malls throughout the province, and Andrew enthusiastically described this as a new form of citizen participation in budget-making.

The government was openhanded in giving out money to companies working with computer technology. Develcon was given $2.1 million to develop a distributed data network system, Inventronics received $1 million to manufacture metal covers for electronics equipment in Moose Jaw, and SED Systems got $10 million to build a new facility in SEDCO's Innovation Place in Saskatoon. More than $5 million was squandered on GigaText to develop a computer-aided translation system that didn't work, and nearly $1.3 million in tax credits and a $76,000 grant were doled out to Joytec to build computerized golf simulators. Joytec was subsequently bought out by a Vancouver-based financier, Lawrence Nesis, and the company was moved to British Columbia, taking the Saskatchewan government investment with it. Nesis was later banned for eighteen months from the Vancouver Stock Exchange for issuing misleading press releases about Joytec's sales.

Even before these horror stories came to light, experts were cautioning the Devine government about its high-tech investment strategy. The noted American economist Lester Thurow suggested that a country the size of Canada could support only one major high-tech centre, and that was already designated as Kanata, just outside of Ottawa.[23] This advice disappointed the Tories, but failed to deflect them from their quest for the high-tech holy grail.

The success of this quest was tied to the fortunes of the province's three leading high-tech firms, Develcon, SED Systems, and Northern Telecom. By the late 1980s, all three of these firms were either cutting back or in serious financial difficulty. Northern Telecom pared its Saskatchewan operations in 1985 when it moved its transmission network division to Montreal, and rumours circulated that it planned to move its entire operation back to Eastern Canada.[24] Both SED Systems and Develcon expanded aggressively in the mid 1980s, which put them in serious financial difficulty and forced them to ask for government support. SED Systems received $10 million in low-interest loans from SEDCO for a new building. When it was unable to make even minimal interest payments, SEDCO had to buy back the building and give SED Systems a generous twenty-year lease. This leading resident of "Silicon Flats" was then sold to an Ontario firm and remained in precarious health.[25] Develcon, the other leading high-tech firm, was also the recipient of an $8.5 million low-interest loan from SEDCO. The money strengthened the company sufficiently for an Ontario corporation to take it over. From the optimism of the early 1980s to the despair of the late 1980s, high-tech proved an elusive dream. Despite the government's financial aid, only a fraction of 1 percent of Saskatchewan's work force found employment in high-tech industries.

The high-tech failure was part of a larger Devine government failure to diversify the economy away from natural resources and agriculture. In 1982, 6.2 percent of the work force was employed in secondary manufacturing, compared with 5.6 percent in 1986. Between these years there was a decline of approximately 2,000 manufacturing jobs in Saskatchewan. These figures paralleled the situation in Manitoba and Alberta, provinces that also experienced declines in the percentage of the labour force employed in manufacturing.[26] This seemed to be the inevitable result for the prairie hinterland economy in a free market system.

Perhaps the classic example of the Devine government's response to this dilemma was the Cargill fertilizer plant. The absurdities of the deal gave pause even to steadfast Tory supporters. It starkly revealed the contradiction between Devine's claim that his government was dedicated to free enterprise, and the fact that the same government was giving a huge subsidy to one of the world's largest multinational corporations.

The deal called for the construction of a $435 million nitrogen fertilizer plant fifteen miles from Regina. When fully operational, the plant would produce 1,500 tonnes of anhydrous ammonia daily and employ 150 people. It would also be the largest user of natural gas in the province. Cargill and the provincial government were to be partners in the project, but Devine promised that the government would sell its share as soon as the plant was operating and making money. Cargill agreed to put up $65 million in equity, while the government invested $64 million and provided a $305 million loan guarantee.

Ironically, Canadian Agri-Products, an Alberta company drawn to Saskatchewan by the open-for-business policy, was already planning to build a smaller fertilizer plant. By giving money to Cargill, the Tory government effectively terminated the smaller free enterprise project. The president of Agri-Products pointedly asked why a government dedicated to free enterprise would do this. Devine's only defence was to explain that the fertilizer plant "ha[d] to be large enough to survive the market cycles."[27]

Because of their neo-conservative beliefs, the Tories rejected public enterprise as an engine for economic growth in Saskatchewan. At the same time, they felt obliged to intervene in the economy to stimulate development and create jobs. Driven by necessity but trapped by ideology, they ended up entering into highly questionable deals that contradicted their own precepts about how the economy should work. The Tories' abhorrence of public enterprise was based on devotion to free enterprise, even though that same free enterprise had to be propped up by the government.

Of course, the Tories did have at their disposal the Crown corporations that had been created by the CCF and the NDP to build up the Saskatchewan economy and counteract its hinterland status. For the new right, however, the Crowns were part of the problem, not part of the solution.

Notes for Chapter 4

1. Michael K. Evans, *The Truth About Supply Side Economics* (New York: Basic Books, 1983) p. 20. 2. *Leader-Post*, 21 May 1983. 3. *Financial Post*, 15 October 1983. 4. *Ibid.*, 15 December 1983. 5. Paul Martin, "Flat Out Attack: Bob Andrew Challenges the Tax System," *Saskatchewan Business*, June 1985. 6. Frances Russell, *Winnipeg Free Press*, 27 April 1985. 7. *Leader-Post*, Eisler, 3 March 1984; *Globe and Mail*, 26 April 1983. 8. *The Labour Force*, Statistics Canada, 1981-86.
9. *Debates and Proceedings (Hansard)*, Legislative Assembly of Saskatchewan,

24 November 1982, p. 1055.   **10.** Estevan *Mercury*, 27 April 1983.   **11.** Prince Albert *Herald*, 16 March 1984.   **12.** *Leader-Post*, 26 April 1983.   **13.** *Star-Phoenix*, 9 December 1985.   **14.** *Leader-Post*, 21 December 1985.

15. *Ibid.*, 19 December 1986.   **16.** *Star-Phoenix*, 17 January 1987.   **17.** *Leader-Post*, 30 August 1985.   **18.** *Star-Phoenix*, 3 September 1985.   **19.** *Ibid.*, 28 August 1987.   **20.** *Globe and Mail*, 18 September 1989.   **21.** *Leader-Post*, 14 October 1989.   **22.** *Ibid.*, 9 June 1983.   **23.** *Star-Phoenix*, 27 October 1984. **24.** *Ibid.*, 20 October 1989.   **25.** Judy Haiven, "Sad But True," *Saskatchewan Business*, December 1989.   **26.** *The Labour Force*, Statistics Canada, 1982-86. **27.** *Leader-Post*, 12 July 1989.

5

OPEN FOR BUSINESS

DETHRONING
THE CROWNS

> Crown corporations are not creatures
> of exceptional nobility.
> – GRANT DEVINE, *from his speech at the*
> *Open For Business Conference, 20 October 1982.*

From the time it joined Confederation until the 1940s, Saskatchewan was hampered by its hinterland status. Its economy was based almost solely on wheat, and was controlled elsewhere – from Toronto and Montreal, where the banks, railways, and farm equipment corporations had their headquarters, and by international markets where the prices Saskatchewan farmers would get for their crops were determined. The province was desperate for such essentials as electricity and a telephone system, but private enterprise showed no real willingness to provide these to the small and predominantly rural population.

For Tommy Douglas, the CCF premier elected in 1944, Crown corporations were the policy instrument that would overcome the marketplace's failure to meet the needs of Saskatchewan's residents. The government stepped into the breach and, in so doing, helped to create employment opportunities and diversify a mainly agricultural economy.

Since the first of Saskatchewan's modern Crown corporations

were established in the 1940s, about $5 billion of the public's money has been invested in them. They were developed in two distinct phases. The first phase occurred during the period of CCF rule between 1944 and 1964 when Douglas and the CCF/NDP used Crown corporations to provide a wide array of services.[1] In this period, most of the province's Crown-owned utilities were formed. Saskatchewan Government Insurance (SGI), Sask-Power, and SaskTel were all built up in the 1940s.

The second phase in the development of the Crowns began with Allan Blakeney's ascent to power in 1971. During this period, the NDP government concentrated on using public corporations to develop Saskatchewan's natural resources. It was argued that Saskatchewan people were not receiving a fair return for their potash, oil and other minerals. The NDP believed that multinational companies developed these resources according to their own schedules and in their own interests. Crown corporations helped ensure that the people of Saskatchewan, rather than foreign or central Canadian companies, controlled and received maximum benefit from natural resources. Saskoil was created to explore and develop the province's oil and gas reserves, particularly heavy oil, which the multinationals had ignored in favour of cheaper conventional oil; the Saskatchewan Mining Development Corporation (SMDC) was founded to mine uranium and hard rock minerals; and the Potash Corporation of Saskatchewan (PCS) was set up to acquire, develop and operate potash mines.

Under the NDP, the Crown sector had four main goals: to strengthen and diversify the economy; to create jobs and assist regional development, for example, in the economically depressed northern areas of the province; to provide a vehicle for Saskatchewan control of its own economy; and to improve government programs and services with money earned by the Crown-owned companies.

Taxes, royalties, and dividends from natural resources went into the Heritage Fund. About 70 percent of this money then went into the Consolidated Fund to help pay for the ordinary expenditures of government, while the remaining 30 percent was re-invested in the Crowns to build up equity for future development and future profits. As of March 1981, the Heritage Fund had provided $628 million in equity investments and $90.5 million in loans repayable at market rates to the various commercial Crown corporations. An equity investment is akin to a share on the stock market. The investor, in this case the Heritage Fund, hopes the corporation will pay a dividend or that the value of the shares will increase. The real test of the investment comes when the company matures; at that time it becomes clear whether the dividends were high enough to justify the investment.

By the time the NDP was defeated in 1982, only PCS among the resource Crowns had paid significant dividends, amounting to a total of $100 million. But while the return had not been tremendous in the short run, the plan was long-term since, in the resource sector, return on investment is a long process. Meanwhile, the NDP measured success in terms of how the Crowns created employment. The Blakeney government boasted that public investment provided over 12,000 jobs and allowed maximum spin-off benefits to be directed to Saskatchewan businesses.

To make sure that the Crowns fulfilled their mandate under the NDP, an extremely close relationship existed between the government and the corporations. Ministers served as chairmen of the Crown corporations, and the top executives were often groomed and plucked from the ranks of the civil service. The ultimate expression of their close relationship was the Crown Investments Corporation (CIC), the holding company for the various Crowns. Created in 1978, it superseded the Government Finance Office, which had overseen the financial operations of the public sector corporations since 1947. Essentially a cabinet-level central agency, the CIC gave direction and overall guidance to the Crowns. Its board included cabinet ministers, and management personnel from CIC often sat on the boards of the individual corporations. Thus, the contacts between CIC and the Crown corporations were frequent and pervasive, although day-to-day management was generally left to the executives of the various companies. In essence, CIC "owned" the province's 24 Crown corporations, making it the fourth largest Crown corporation in the country, and the 16th largest corporation of any kind.

The Tories' initial attack on the Crowns

The Tories came into power hostile towards the Crowns, which they felt gave the government an excessively large role in the economy. On the other hand, the Tories did not seem to know what to do with the public enterprise structure they had inherited. Bob Andrew, the minister responsible for the CIC, speculated uncertainly about its future: "It could be weakened, or it could be strengthened. There really has not been a final decision as to where we're going." [2] There was, of course, an understanding that the Tories were unhappy with the NDP policy of relying on public enterprise to diversify the economy. From the very beginning, the new administration began to pick on the Crowns as a source of difficulty for the provincial economy. The Crowns were said to be loaded with incompetent managers, riddled with waste, and a net drain on the provincial treasury. [3] The Tories also alleged that constant political interference from the CIC caused the Crowns to make unbusinesslike and unprofitable decisions.

With such predetermined notions, the government was bound to stultify the Crown sector. The Tories wasted no time announcing that the Crown corporations would not be allowed to grow. Expansions planned by the NDP were cancelled. SGI's tentative plans to get into the life insurance business, to set up autobody repair shops, and to get into the hotel business were permanently scrapped. PCS International, a new offshore marketing subsidiary of the Potash Corporation, was disbanded a month before it was to start operation. SMDC lost its automatic back-in right to any uranium project in the province. SaskPower sold its extremely efficient Poplar River mine at Coronach and contracted out much of its maintenance work. SaskTel lost its monopoly on telephone sales and sold some of its assets.

Some Crown corporations were disbanded altogether. The 37-year-old Saskatchewan Fur Marketing Corporation was abolished in October 1982, even though the government had promised not to sell or close down any Crowns before a comprehensive review of the entire Crown sector had been completed. [4] SaskMedia, which had been established to produce films and other educational materials, was another casualty, dissolved in March 1983 with 24 jobs lost. In defence, Gary Lane, the minister responsible for SaskMedia, asserted that the private sector could do an equally effective job.[5]

Another Crown, the Saskatchewan Economic Development Corporation (SEDCO), suffered a major cutback. Its mandate was to help develop local industry and business. Because of the Tories' belief in the superiority of the market, they decided to curtail SEDCO's role. Sixteen people lost their jobs, mostly in the industrial property division, which the NDP had used to help local communities develop industrial parks. The Tory government, for its part, was inclined to believe that "no administration can develop land as well as the private sector."[6] The minister responsible for SEDCO, Jack Klein, asserted that the government was willing to sell the eleven industrial parks owned by SEDCO "if the price is right."[7]

The government also announced plans to sell off a portfolio of shares and partnerships held by CIC. These included Prairie Malt, Cable Com, Agra Industries, Nabu Manufacturing, and the mortgage on the Cornwall Shopping Centre in Regina. The government's shares in Intercontinental Packers were sold for $4.5 million to the controlling Mitchell family, although the NDP government had paid $10.2 million for these same shares in 1973. Shortly after, Intercon closed its Regina plant, with the loss of 120 jobs. The company, a large contributor to the Tory party, claimed the closure was an inevitable business decision, but the absence of government equity made the decision a lot easier. The Tories portrayed the sale as a "concrete example of the government's policy to return responsibility to the private sector."[8]

The Devine government also restructured the Heritage Fund. Whereas the NDP had used it to finance the growth of Crown corporations, the Tories removed the legislation which enabled the government to allocate a portion of the fund each year for Crown investments. This effectively dried up new money for public sector enterprise. As Bob Andrew explained, "Instead of being a bottomless well for Crown corporations, we believe that Heritage Fund revenues should be a positive vehicle for encouraging private sector development."[9] To this end, the government created two new divisions within the Heritage Fund, one to provide money for research and development and the other to fund the government's Farm Purchase Program (the Tory answer to the NDP's Land Bank).

Most commentators saw all this activity as something less than a no-holds-barred, all-out attack on the Crowns. The Tories, in fact, created five new Crown corporations: the Advanced Technology Training Centre, the New Careers Corporation, the Property Management Corporation, the Saskatchewan Water Corporation, and the Souris Basin Development Authority. But these Crowns were mainly set up to carry out quasi-departmental functions and were not true examples of public enterprise. The *Financial Post* commented in January of 1983 that, "In spite of restraints placed on the Crowns, so far what is emerging in Saskatchewan is not preparation for a massive assault on public enterprise, but rather an atmosphere of détente between the new free-enterprise government and the Crowns it inherited."[10] The NDP, however, did not accept this benign interpretation. It warned that the government was simply disguising its desire to scrap the Crowns, and that the real strategy was to chip away at the effectiveness of public corporations in order to turn public opinion against them.

The government cries Wolff

Whether key players in the government had this in mind is difficult to say and impossible to prove. The government's official position was to refer the entire subject of Crown corporation policy to a special review commission.[11] Headed by Regina accountant Wolfgang Wolff and composed of a panel of small-c conservatives, the commission was asked to examine the objectives, administrative structure and financial arrangements of Saskatchewan's Crowns. After six months' study, the report was presented in January 1983. It offered three major recommendations to improve the operations and control of the Crown corporations.

Wolff's first point was that the Crowns were suffering from a severe identity crisis and should be grouped into three separate categories: (1) departmental service units like the Saskatchewan Computer Utility Corporation (SaskComp); (2) non-competitive commercial enterprises like SaskPower and SaskTel; and (3) competitive commercial enterprises like Saskoil and PCS. Thus reorganized, the Crowns would perform their allotted tasks more effectively, Wolff believed; departmental service units would act more like government departments, and the commercial corporations would operate more like private businesses, concentrating on profit-making and paying regular dividends to their owner, the provincial government.

In proposing that the Crowns should pay regular dividends, the Wolff Commission was in fundamental opposition to NDP philosophy. Social democratic policy was based on the premise that Crown corporations served a useful purpose when they reinvested their earnings in improving services and in building the economy, as well as when they paid dividends to the treasury. Resource companies in particular, be they private or public, tend to reinvest profits back into development. In the words of Douglas Fullerton, a former board member of Saskoil and PCS, "The whole history of resource development in Canada is one of initially low or zero dividends. That is how the private sector operates, but the province is apparently excluded from using the same approach."[12] Under the NDP, PCS had used most of its profits to finance expansion, thereby increasing the value of the company. Had PCS been a publicly traded company, its shares would have quadrupled from the time it was established.

The second group of recommendations from Wolff's commission focused on the administrative structure of the Crowns. Wolff advised that the CIC no longer have a board made up of cabinet ministers and that cabinet ministers no longer serve as chairmen of Crown corporations or sit on their boards. He sought to diminish the power of ministers in order to enhance corporate autonomy. Cabinet ministers would be replaced by "qualified members of the general public."

He took special aim at the CIC, which he saw as a direct instrument of political control, a central committee of meddlesome cabinet ministers with nothing better to do than interfere with the autonomy of the Crowns. This hostility was based on the well-documented friction that existed between the parent body, with its army of MBAs and accountants, and the individual Crown corporations. So severe was the problem that at one point Allan Blakeney appointed himself CIC chairman to diffuse the tension. This led Wolff to conclude that the CIC was imposing its political will, forcing the individual Crowns into poor decisions. (He did not, however, identify any such instance. In fact, the type of conflict Wolff talked about is inherent in a conglomerate, whether public or private: individual corporations often feel they are not getting sufficient resources or are being discriminated against by head office.) While arguing that CIC had too much power, Wolff did not show how this adversely affected public investment or led to unbusinesslike decisions.

Finally, the Wolff report dismissed the notion that the Crowns have "socially-oriented mandates" to establish head offices within the province, reduce the province's vulnerability to foreign control, retain employment opportunities, introduce affirmative action programs and innovations in labour relations, and provide a "window" to enable the government to better understand and more effectively tax the resource industries. Wolff's narrow, bottom-line approach excluded these broader considerations. He failed to acknowledge, for example, that the creation of PCS meant that, for the first time, a Saskatchewan company was developing potash reserves in the province. He overlooked the fact that through SMDC, special policies ensured that northern people received a substantial share of the economic benefits from hard rock mining. He did not understand that Crown corporations have a dual purpose: to make money and at the same time achieve desirable social objectives. Wolff's critics could only conclude: "The Commission undertook its task with preconceived notions about Saskatchewan Crown corporations, and with a built-in political bias against them."[13]

The Devine government was so pleased with the inquiry that it later rewarded Wolff by naming him chairman of a renamed and restructured CIC. The Commission essentially gave a businessman's view of how Crown corporations should operate: establish your goals, keep politics away from the commercial corporations, get ministers off the boards, and concentrate on paying dividends.

All this was part of a first gentle step towards building a case for privatization. If the Crowns were not regarded as instruments of social and economic development, but rather that their sole purpose was to make short-term profits, part of the rationale for having Crown corporations disappeared. Although Wolff did not explicitly recommend privatization, his conclusions were headed in that direction.

The government implemented, after a fashion, most of Wolff's recommendations. The Crown Investments Corporation was renamed the Crown Management Board (CMB), but retained its co-ordinating and supervisory function. Although Wolff had wanted cabinet ministers off the CMB, the government appointed eight cabinet ministers and three "civilians". As well, the government announced that Tory backbenchers would be appointed to the boards of Crowns, partly, no doubt, to give the huge caucus something to do. Cabinet ministers were no longer to serve as chairmen of individual Crowns, and were replaced by private citizens. However, the Devine administration was unwilling to follow completely the logic of the Wolff Commission and made cabinet ministers the vice-chairmen of the Crown boards. The government was obviously reluctant to depoliticize the Crowns.

Political control of the Crowns was confirmed in November 1983, when the chairmen of the Crown boards were named. They included some of the most well-known Tory supporters in the province. George Hill, former PC party president, was appointed chairman of SaskPower; Staff Barootes, PC fundraiser and party strategist, was appointed chairman of SMDC; Al Wagar, a defeated Tory candidate, was named chairman of SGI; Herb Pinder Jr., a staunch Tory and prominent Saskatchewan businessman, was appointed chairman of Saskoil; and Harold Lane, a former Tory MLA, was put on the board of CMB. Bob Andrew had the candour to admit the obvious: "I don't think we're putting on for a minute that Harold Lane doesn't have a political element he can bring to the Crowns." He then added, "I don't apologize for that."[14] Thus the new chairmen, while not cabinet ministers, were far from being impartial or apolitical. As an added irony, the change increased the cost of operating the Crowns, because each new chairman received an average of $300 per day, plus a retainer. The cabinet ministers had not received any extra compensation.

In the end, the Tory promise to cut the apron strings binding the Crowns to the elected government went nowhere; Devine's government was simply unwilling to relinquish its control over them.

Politicizing the utility corporations

The most notorious example of the government's failure to depoliticize the Crowns centred on the creation of the Public Utilities Review Commission (PURC). Created immediately after the 1982 election, PURC was supposed to review the rate increases by the Crown-owned utilities, ensuring that the process of rate-setting was open, fair, and accountable, and that increases were in the public interest. These were worthy objectives, and, in fact, most other provinces had some type of regulatory authority that set rates for utilities, whether privately or publicly owned. Nevertheless, from the outset, the government found itself embroiled in controversy.

The bill establishing PURC gave the Commission broad powers, but no guidelines on how to use them. The legislation denied citizens a "general right of appeal" and instead allowed the Commission to decide who could and who could not appear before it. There were also suggestions that the new body would just produce another layer of bureaucracy, because the Crowns would need experts to make presentations and the Commission would need experts to interpret what they were saying. Another difficulty was the possibility that PURC would make bond buyers nervous because of their fear that the Commission would impose utility rate rollbacks. Finally, in a type of irony that would haunt the Tories, PURC could make it more difficult to attract business to the province, simply because the government could no longer guarantee favourable power rates.

Most serious of all was the fact that the attempt to depoliticize the utility companies was clouded by a very political decision by the newly-elected government to freeze utility rates for one year in order to make good on a campaign promise. The freeze led to declining profits for SGI and SaskTel and losses for SaskPower. This meant that these Crowns, in order to pay their own way, had to ask for significant rate increases in March 1983, when the first PURC hearings took place. As a result, some serious conflicts emerged among the various classes of utility users in the province, and the Devine government was put in the extremely unpleasant situation of having to overrule PURC when it made decisions that adversely affected any of its client groups, particularly farmers.

The Saskatchewan Power Corporation

The most intense battles, and the ones with the greatest consequences for the future of Saskatchewan politics, surfaced over PURC's efforts to devise a fair rate schedule for SaskPower, the provincial gas and electric utility. When the Tories came to office, SaskPower employed more than 3,000 people, controlled some $2 billion in assets, and had over $1 billion in short- and long-term debt, all of which made it a moderately efficient utility. The corporation had suffered its first loss, a minor one, of less than half a million dollars in 1981, but this loss did not mean that SaskPower's debt was out of line. The debt load was average for utilities of this size. Given the capital-intensive nature of power companies and the need to spread the repayment of loans over many years so as not to burden customers with excessively high rates, utilities, whether private or public, typically carry large debts. SaskPower's 1981 loss was due to the economic recession, high interest rates, and the higher cost of natural gas due to the National Energy Program. To make up for this loss, the corporation had planned to ask for an average 20 percent increase in utility rates in 1982, which still would have left the province with some of the lowest utility rates in the country. But the Tory government froze rates, imposing on SaskPower an even larger loss in 1982.

To mitigate the effects of the freeze, the power utility tried to streamline its operations by transferring some of its activities to the private sector. SaskPower's insurance business went to private firms, rather than to SGI, and maintenance work at various power stations was awarded to non-union companies paying lower wages. SaskPower also sold some of its assets and began giving private companies contracts to mine its coal. It sold a $45 million dragline and the Poplar River mine to the Manalta Coal Company, which was owned by a prominent Tory family from Alberta. The utility also imposed a hiring freeze, set up an early retirement program and postponed several multi-million dollar projects to prove to PURC that it was sincere in trying to cut costs.

Yet all these cost-cutting measures were confounded by the government's unwillingness to repudiate the NDP's policy of using the Crowns to develop the local economy. Despite the Tories' pledge to allow public corporations to operate more like businesses, SaskPower awarded a $12.6 million contract to build structural containers for its vast Nipawin hydro-electric project to Dominion Bridge of Regina, even though an out-of-province company submitted a bid that was 17 percent lower. Notwithstanding the proclamation that the province was open for business and that the free market would prevail, the government interfered with market decisions. On top of the added expense of the higher construction bid, the corporation faced other economic hardships: increases in the cost of natural gas, lower energy consumption due to the recession, weather fluctuations resulting in less power generation from the hydro-electric plants, and the $484 million Tory election promise to extend natural gas service to rural areas.

SaskPower was at this time facing a serious revenue shortfall. The 1982 deficit had been over $3 million, and, without substantial rate increases, the 1983 deficit would be even larger. Recognizing that high power bills were a political liability, SaskPower Minister Lorne McLaren began to paint a very gloomy picture of the corporation's profitability. He hinted that it had lost money since 1975, despite the evidence of audited financial statements to the contrary. McLaren eventually admitted that while profits from the electrical division had declined every year, increased profits from natural gas were able to cover these losses. The truth was that SaskPower's losses were not long-term in origin, but rather were caused by the political decision to freeze utility rates. Instead of raising rates as planned, SaskPower was denied any increase. This set the stage for the power utility's application to PURC in March 1983 for an increase of more than 20 percent.

At its first hearing, the Commission granted SaskPower an interim increase of 15 percent for electricity and 13 percent for natural gas; these rates would be reviewed six months later, in November 1983. The most aggressive interveners in these, and all subsequent, hearings were the industrial users. Their main complaint was against the system of cross-subsidization, by which they paid higher rates so that residential consumers could pay lower rates. By 1983 industrial users were subsidizing residential utility rates to the tune of $29 million. Residential consumers maintained that while they paid less, they also received poorer service, suffered more power outages, and waited longer for repairs. Industrial customers countered that they were staggering under the higher rates – an assertion they refused to document by opening their books to PURC officials. PURC, however, sided with industrial users and ordered an end to this form of cross-subsidization. PURC's recommendation was that SaskPower should adopt a cost-for-service principle in which utility users paid only for the service they received.

Industrial and residential users soon made common cause when they discovered that cross-subsidization was being used to finance the expensive rural gasification program. In this instance, PURC ruled that since rural gasification had been a Tory election promise, the provincial government should pay for it. The problem was that the Tories were already busy trying to find money to pay for their other election promises, such as eliminating the gasoline tax and implementing the mortgage reduction plan. The Tories worried about the growing deficit and sought to transfer as much debt to the Crowns as possible. Therefore Cabinet overruled PURC and instructed SaskPower to cover the entire cost of rural gasification through cross-subsidization.

The next controversy occurred in March 1984 when Sask-Power approached PURC for an additional hike of 14 percent for most users, but only 9.5 percent for farmers. Representatives of those on fixed incomes in urban areas such as welfare recipients, seniors and the working poor, appeared before PURC to argue that their need was equal to that of the farmers, and that the Commission should not allow SaskPower to give farmers a lower rate increase than city dwellers. SaskPower defended their proposal, arguing that farmers were suffering from a third straight summer of drought and could not afford a hefty rate increase. PURC, however, maintained that SaskPower was not a social service agency, and that if the government wanted to provide relief to farmers, it should do so by other means. Devine's government could not accept the Commission's ruling, and once again overruled PURC, prompting one of the Commissioners to resign in protest.

During these same hearings, PURC began to urge SaskPower to end its practice of having natural gas subsidize electricity. SaskPower argued strenuously against this. As corporation executive Oscar Hanson told the Commission, "It's important to understand that the poor health of the electric utility makes it all the more important that the corporation be allowed to maintain its gas revenues as generated by present rates."[15] Later, when the Conservatives divided SaskPower into two parts and made Hanson the president of the gas division, the argument changed completely – it became essential to privatize natural gas to ensure the viability of the electric utility.

This startling about-face occurred in the government's second term. For the time being, PURC demanded, and the government rejected, what was essentially a cost-for-service principle. PURC wanted the Tories to allow SaskPower to operate like a business. Gas customers should not subsidize electricity customers, industrial customers should not subsidize residential customers, and neither industrial nor urban residential customers should subsidize rural customers. The government found that it could live with some of PURC's rulings, but not with others. It accepted the Commission's decision that industrial customers should not be forced to subsidize residential customers. It also deregulated natural gas sales, allowing big industrial consumers to purchase directly from gas producers. Previously, SaskPower had enjoyed a monopoly on gas sales, and profits made on gas had been used to keep electricity rates down.

On other issues, particularly politically sensitive ones, the government failed to respect the Commission's rulings. When PURC proposed a 34 percent power rate increase for farmers over three years and a 21 percent increase for urban homeowners, Devine protested: "This is not the time, despite the principle, to be putting a higher burden on homeowners and farmers."[16] PURC continued to defend its position on the basis that SaskPower should not be involved in the redistribution of income. Eventually, the government got tired of fighting the Commission, and in 1987, abolished it. What had been established in 1982 as a vital and necessary reform to benefit the consumers of the province had become a political embarrassment.

Saskatchewan Government Insurance and SaskTel

In the case of SGI, PURC proved to be less of a thorn in the government's side, but even here the cabinet did not forego interference. PURC rolled back a proposed auto insurance premium increase of 6.5 percent to 3 percent, a reduction SGI reluctantly accepted. The major dispute broke out over the relationship between insurance premiums and the amount of money people paid for their deductible. PURC rightly saw these two items as closely linked, but the Tories disagreed. Thus, when PURC rolled back rate increases, the government allowed SGI to compensate for the revenue shortfall by increasing the deductible. This effectively limited PURC's role as a true consumers' watchdog. The government and PURC also clashed over the Auto Fund's Rate Stabilization Reserve. The Commission ruled that the reserve should not exceed $38.5 million on the grounds that "making today's driving public pay for future increases in insurance benefits is unreasonable and unfair."[17] PURC, therefore, ordered that about $50 million of the estimated $88.5 million in the reserve fund be returned to the public. Cabinet cancelled the order, to the chagrin of the Commissioners, who issued a statement complaining that their ability to fulfil their legislated mandate had been "seriously impaired, if not completely negated."[18]

On another front, the government blunted SGI's effectiveness by preventing it from expanding. SGI had planned to enter the highly profitable life insurance business, but was now denied access to this cash cow. Paul Rousseau, the minister responsible for SGI, held that "It would not make sense to go into the life insurance business regardless of the profit potential of it because what we're doing is infringing on the private sector, creating bigger government bureaucracies and discouraging the private sector from performing or doing business in Saskatchewan." He went on: "We're not interested in operating SGI to find ways to make money. It should provide only the necessary service."[19] The decision was warmly welcomed by friends of the Tory party like Will Klein, chairman of Pioneer Life, who noted that no "good purposes would be served by the government operating in the life insurance business."[20] The government was sending out mixed signals, demanding that Crown corporations pay dividends to the treasury, yet preventing them from competing with the private sector.

The Tories were eager to "streamline" the operations of SGI, and dismissed 120 people in an effort to "remove the fat." These reductions were to save $4 million, but eliminating such difficult-to-measure "soft" services as the safety, marketing and legal divisions, had hidden costs. Abolishing the safety division increased the possibility that the number of accidents would rise and more claims would have to be paid out. The firing of personnel meant that more legal work and marketing services had to be contracted out. Even the mainstream media felt that there needed to be some assurance that the government was "really intent on trimming the fat and not rolling out the pork barrel."[21]

Contracting out was the preferred method of privatization at SGI. After disposing of the legal and marketing divisions, the corporation gave contracts to private insurance agents for the right to renew driver's licences and licence plates. Inevitably, unsuccessful bidders for SGI business charged that holding a PC party membership helped in landing a contract.[22] For the government, contracting out these services also had the advantage of replacing union with non-union personnel. The union fought back and won an injunction halting contracting out until the government placed all 25 union members who lost their jobs in other positions. In general, the Tories' approach to SGI was to clip its wings, snuff out plans for expansion, reduce its size, and contract out services. PURC, which was supposed to have been the watchdog for insurance buyers, was put on a government leash.

Another Crown utility hampered by the government was Sask-Tel. Gary Lane, the minister in charge of the telephone utility, got into hot water by suggesting that the SaskTel building was up for sale, an assertion denied by Devine. It was soon clear, however, that the government wanted to curb the utility and pass the benefits to the private sector. In October 1982, SaskTel was forced to give up its monopoly on the ownership of telephones and related attachments. Until then, residential phone rates had been subsidized by the highly profitable practice of requiring businesses to rent telephone equipment owned by SaskTel. Private companies were now able to sell telephones and equipment, thereby depriving SaskTel of a secure and steady source of rental revenue.[23] There were other signs that SaskTel was being reined in. The corporation had to surrender its distributorship for Wang computers and was ordered out of the office furniture business. The utility also sold its cable TV network to a consortium of cable TV operators.

This treatment of SaskTel was typical of how the Tory government dealt with the Crown-owned utilities. They were denied the opportunity to undertake profitable projects, and lucrative units were sold off. Contracting out became common, resulting in more work being done by non-union staff. The government eventually dropped all pretence of its initial commitment to allow the utilities to operate according to market forces. Instead, the Crowns were fully exploited as sources of patronage for party supporters. Despite its promises, the government forced SaskPower, SGI, and SaskTel to operate in a highly-charged political atmosphere.

The natural resource Crowns: Headed for the auction block

Although the government harassed and checked the utilities, it repeatedly promised not to sell them. However, the Crown resource companies were more vulnerable. The Tories considered enterprises such as Saskoil, SMDC and PCS to be detrimental to the provincial economy because they supposedly chased away private investors. Finance Minister Bob Andrew signalled the new attitude: "The view of the government tends to be that the people of Saskatchewan have made significant contributions, whether it's in uranium, potash, or oil, and quite frankly, it's now time for them to stand on their own two feet."[24]

The Saskatchewan Oil and Gas Corporation

The first candidate for privatization was Saskoil. Colin Thatcher, the minister responsible for the corporation, stated that his "mandate was to whip it into shape and sell it."[25] Even though Saskoil was struggling because of the National Energy Program and falling world oil prices and had reported a loss in 1981, the government adopted a policy of extracting maximum short-run profits. In 1982, the company had to pay its entire profit as a dividend to the treasury. This fit in with the government's philosophy, as laid out in the Wolff Commission report, that the Crowns' first duty was to provide dividends for the province. The trouble was that the policy stunted Saskoil's plans for exploration and development. Leaving nothing to reinvest was not good business strategy. Nonetheless, Paul Schoenhals, the man who succeeded Thatcher as Minister for Saskoil, continued the ironhanded policy of profits at any cost.[26]

In 1983, Saskoil reported a record $30.9 million profit, more than double the combined profits in all the previous years. The success was due to several factors: stronger markets, a federal-provincial agreement that granted world prices for oil discovered in the last ten years, lower royalty rates, and most significantly, reduced exploration expenditures. This last point was directly related to the Tory policy of "profits now". As Saskoil President Bill Douglas acknowledged: "Our concentration in the last year and perhaps in 1984 is to take advantage of higher yielding prospects that will give us a fairly quick pay-off, but won't add substantially to reserves."[27]

Saskoil was no longer discovering enough oil to replace what it was pumping out of the ground. The former NDP government's policy of investing in the acquisition and exploration of land, which in fact made the profits of the mid-1980s possible, was being ignored.

Having drained Saskoil of all profits, the government began to consider privatization. In preparation, the Corporation was stripped of its unprofitable assets. The research and development office and the heavy oil research lab were transferred to the Saskatchewan Research Council; other activities were shifted to the Department of Energy. The Calgary office was closed, and a large number of employees fired. The government then proceeded with phase one of privatization, the sale of participation bonds. Placed on the market in 1984, the bonds were worth a modest $15 million and paid a minimum 10 percent interest, plus an additional .03 percent on each full million dollars of net revenue earned by Saskoil. Because of the healthy profits made in 1984, the bonds paid a very generous 13.3 percent return.

The decision to sell participation bonds came as a big surprise to the company's chief financial officer, Harold Johnson, and company president Bill Douglas. What was so unusual about the announcement, aside from the fact that the financial officer and the president had not been informed, was that Saskoil was awash with cash. It had just recorded a profit of over $30 million and did not need the money the bonds provided. Johnson observed that "there was nowhere we could invest the money that would give us a return equal to what we had to pay out in interest to bond holders."[28] The sale of the bonds was motivated solely by the desire to soften people up for privatization.

Following the success of the participation bonds, which Schoenhals called "a very good investment for those who took advantage of it,"[29] the Tories grew bolder. After declaring as late as April 1985 that it had no intention of privatizing Saskoil, the government announced in October of the same year that $100 million worth of shares, 33 percent of the company, was to be sold. The shares were to be sold in packages of one $9 common share and two $10 preferred shares. The preferred shares had a guaranteed interest rate; the common shares did not. The government was leading cautious Saskatchewan investors by the hand, easing them into the purchase of higher risk investments. The share issue was greeted with delight by representatives of the Saskatchewan business community, many of whom believed the government had erred only in retaining too much of the company.

The sale of shares was accompanied by a lavish advertising program that cost between $1 and $2 million. Townhall meetings were held in 25 communities. Three teams, each consisting of a cabinet minister, an executive from Saskoil and a representative from the underwriter, Wood Gundy, blanketed the province touting the benefits of the sale to a doubtful population. This skepticism was typified by a farmer from Wynyard, who bluntly informed the stock promoters: "I have a problem with selling something we already own. The revenues go into the coffers of the provincial government right now. But once it [Saskoil] goes on the market we're going to lose control, we're going to be taxed where we're not taxed right now."[30] There was also considerable suspicion that high-income urban professionals would be the major beneficiaries, while farmers in the midst of a financial crunch, and small-town business owners, dependent on farmers for their livelihood, would lack the money to buy shares and benefit from the sale.

The government recognized that it had to educate the province about the benefits of privatization. To this end, shares were sold with no commissions, and purchasers of Saskoil shares who resold less than 100 units would be assessed only a minimum commission. The shares were sold through banks, credit unions, and trust companies, because the government wanted to encourage people who were not accustomed to dealing with investment companies. Many stockbrokers objected that these other financial institutions could not offer the same quality service. However, since the Saskoil sale was but a prelude to further privatizations which would bring the investment services industry new business and huge commissions, the protests were not especially vocal. For Wood Gundy, the value of privatization was readily apparent, since it received a $4 million underwriting fee for the Saskoil issue.

Saskoil was listed on the Toronto and Montreal stock exchanges on January 14, 1986. On the same day, the company lost its Crown corporation status. The share offering sold out, raising $110 million, 54 percent of which went to Saskatchewan investors and 46 percent to out-of-province purchasers. The proportion of ownership leaving the province was high, considering that Saskatchewan residents were being offered special inducements to buy. Under the Saskatchewan Stock Savings Plan, they were able to deduct from their provincial income tax 30 percent of the cost of the shares purchased. Concern about control of Saskoil leaving Saskatchewan was somewhat allayed by the government's retaining, for the time being, 66 percent ownership, and no other person or group was allowed to own more than 4 percent of the voting shares. The government, however, made it clear that it would not take advantage of its majority ownership position to influence company decisions. Those would be left to the company's management and would presumably be oriented to maximize profits.

Despite the best laid plans of the Tories, Saskoil's recent history of good profits, and the deliberate undervaluing of its shares, the stock dropped in price shortly after the privatization. Six months later, common shares traded at $5.75, down from $9, and preferred shares were down to $9 from $10. The problem was the falling price of oil, which made the shares considerably less attractive for the average investor. As one broker said of Saskoil, "Basically, it's still regarded as a good medium to long term investment for investors looking for some risk. It's not for widows and orphans. It's not for the faint-hearted." Yet it was just these people, the "widows and orphans," that the government wanted to involve. Brokers began to advise their "less sophisticated" clients to take a capital loss, particularly on the common shares, and get out of the stock market.[31]

Saskoil became, more and more, the preserve of the sophisticated investor. Further, the corporation's outlook increasingly reflected the interests of the investors, wherever they happened to live, rather than public policy goals. As a Crown corporation, Saskoil had focused on exploring and developing Saskatchewan reserves, on hiring Saskatchewan graduates, and on building a strong Saskatchewan company. As a private company, Saskoil planned to divert expenditures to Alberta and to move at least 50 percent of its activity out of the province.[32] It cut back drilling and abandoned heavy oil exploration in Saskatchewan. Ironically, the Devine government was at the same time trying to tempt other oil companies to expand in Saskatchewan. For ideological reasons, the Tories had given up one of the levers the NDP had used to achieve this very objective.

The Potash Corporation of Saskatchewan

While Saskoil was a relatively easy target for privatization, the same could not be said of the Potash Corporation. Valued at up to $2 billion, PCS stood as a potent symbol of the province's determination to gain control of its basic resource industries. It was created in 1976, at the end of a long, tough battle waged by the Blakeney government to obtain a larger share of potash revenues. The battle had been fought against both the federal government, which tried to increase its share of the taxes at the expense of the province, and the private producers, mostly foreign-owned, who had refused to pay taxes. Establishing PCS had effectively protected provincial revenues from Ottawa because Crown corporations cannot be taxed. Furthermore, placing 50 percent of production under public ownership meant that the Saskatchewan government collected not only taxes and royalties, but profits as well. For the first time a substantial portion of the potash industry was locally owned and controlled. Saskatchewan people were appointed to high-level head office jobs. The corporation cooperated with the Saskatchewan research community to develop new technology and new potash-based products. It experimented with progressive innovations in labour relations, for example, by organizing production in such a way as to avoid extended lay-offs. Furthermore, PCS under the NDP was a steady and impressive money-maker.

The Devine government did not at first talk about privatizing PCS. Instead, it concentrated on hobbling the corporation, so that its own performance suffered and the private mining sector profited. The most blatant example of this was the decision to force PCS to stay in Canpotex, the marketing organization through which Saskatchewan companies sold their potash overseas. Each member of Canpotex had one vote and an equal say in running the organization. The drawback for PCS was that, even though it supplied 60 percent of the product sold by Canpotex, it was consistently outvoted by the combination of foreign-owned private companies. PCS was continually thwarted in its effort to move the head office of Canpotex from Toronto to Saskatchewan. More importantly, PCS and the private industry had major differences over marketing strategy. Whereas the private sector favoured spot sales at good prices, PCS wanted long-term contracts so that production could expand and miners have job security. To obtain stable marketing arrangements, PCS was willing to lower the price. The private companies rejected this approach and were also reluctant to approve barters, even though this sales technique appealed to cash-poor developing nations. Finally, Canpotex could not offer government-to-government deals, an arrangement many countries preferred and a strategy the NDP administration wanted to pursue.

Because of its growing grievances with Canpotex, PCS decided to quit the organization and strike out on its own. With the approval of the Blakeney government, it set up early in 1982 its own overseas marketing agency, PCS International. The private companies lobbied long and hard to block this development, and their prayers were answered when the Devine government was elected. One of the new administration's first moves was to quash PCS International and force PCS back into Canpotex.

The repercussions of the decision were quick in coming. Because of the Canpotex policy of dealing only on a cash basis, customers went elsewhere for their product. They turned to potash-producing countries like East Germany and Israel, who were willing to barter. The shift was most startling in the case of Brazil, where Saskatchewan's share of the market declined from 38 percent to 16 percent in one year. PCS also lost a major deal with the Japanese potash importer Zen-noh, who wanted an assured supply at a fixed price. While they had negotiated such an arrangement with PCS International in anticipation of PCS's departure from Canpotex, the dismantling of PCS International caused the deal to fall through.[33] Since Canpotex would only guarantee their price for one year, the Japanese took their business elsewhere.

Another consequence of Canpotex's pricing policy was to encourage other countries, and even other parts of Canada, to expand their productive capacity or build new mines. Israel, East Germany and the Soviet Union all increased production to compete for the international market. New Brunswick opened a mine, and even Manitoba, with relatively small potash deposits, began negotiating with India to provide potash on a stable, long-term basis. Even the inefficient and expensive potash mines of New Mexico, on the verge of closing, found new markets while the Saskatchewan mines struggled to keep old customers.

PCS was beginning to suffer financially by the summer of 1982. It was forced into the unprecedented move of laying off 1,200 employees, only 1,000 of whom were eventually rehired. While the NDP government had never faced such weak markets and excess capacity, it had been willing to draw on PCS's substantial retained earnings to keep workers employed during the down cycle. The Tories abandoned such "unbusinesslike" practices,[34] and labour relations at the corporation deteriorated rapidly. Soon after taking office, the new government, without consulting the workers, scrapped the two-year-old Work Environment Board. The board, the first of its kind in North America, had offered miners a voice in management decisions that affected their health and safety. The Tories, who believed that managers manage and workers work, saw worker participation as an unproductive, foreign idea. The labour difficulties at the Lanigan mine led to a long and sometimes violent strike, in which PCS management refused to seriously negotiate until the stockpile of potash had been depleted. The bitter struggle ended in February 1987, after nearly a year of pseudo-negotiations.

Meanwhile, PCS fortunes sank lower and lower. The Crown corporation was reduced to working at 50 percent capacity, while the rest of the industry worked at 70 percent capacity or more. It was strange that the Crown corporation with the most modern mines and the largest capacity had so much trouble marketing its product. Its sales relative to capacity were lower than the industry average, and PCS's share of Canpotex's volume dropped from 60 percent to 45 percent.[35] The root of the problem was that the Devine government treated PCS like a poor sister, while the private companies were rewarded with a larger market share. As Energy and Mines Minister Colin Thatcher confessed, "We intend to give private potash corporations a larger share of the action along with the burden of risk and potential profits from expansion."[36]

PCS made a mere $600,000 profit in 1982. This was followed by a loss of $18 million in 1983 and even more staggering losses in subsequent years. At the same time, the government insisted on taking dividends out of the corporation, including a $50 million dividend in 1982 and a $62 million dividend in 1983. This forced PCS to borrow capital on the international money market. In effect, the Tories bled the corporation to make the government's own huge debt look somewhat smaller. The NDP charged that the government was running PCS into the ground so that the public would not object if it were sold.[37] As early as 1983, the Potash Corporation Act was amended to give PCS the right "to sell, lease or otherwise dispose of its real or personal property" whenever the corporation considered such action appropriate.[38] By the end of the Tories' first term, speculation was rife that the "appropriate time" had almost come.

The Saskatchewan Mining Development Corporation

Muffled hints of privatization also surrounded the Saskatchewan Mining Development Corporation. SMDC had been set up in 1974 to tap the potential of hard rock minerals in northern Saskatchewan. It owned 50 percent of the Key Lake mine, an extremely efficient uranium producer, as well as a 20 percent interest in the Cluff Lake uranium mine and a 50 percent interest in the Star Lake gold mine. As well, SMDC was the controlling partner (50.75 percent) in the fabulously rich Cigar Lake development. Scheduled to begin production in 1993, the Cigar Lake mine contained the largest, highest-grade uranium deposit in the world. If the price of uranium were to rise significantly, the owners of SMDC stood to make a fortune. Even Energy and Mines Minister Colin Thatcher admitted that SMDC's holdings represented a potential financial bonanza for the province.[39] As with the other Crowns, the Tory strategy was not to sell the corporation immediately, but to hamstring it and force it to become less effective. Exploration and development were curtailed and the compulsory back-in clause, which forced private companies to accept SMDC as a joint-venture partner, was eliminated.

The first evidence that privatization was being seriously considered came in the form of a letter dated 9 August 1983 and addressed to Devine from Latham Burns, the chairman of Burns Fry Ltd. The latter was a firm of investment brokers in the business of selling stocks and bonds. In the letter, Burns suggested that his company become the manager for a proposed sale of SMDC. His idea was to merge SMDC with the federal Crown corporation, Eldorado Nuclear, to create a giant uranium company, which would be attractive to private investors. Burns noted: "Due to the recent number of large takeovers in the Canadian stock markets, there has been a decreasing amount of high quality investment product available to the investing public."[40] The privatization of the Crown-owned uranium companies would help make up for this deficiency. It would also give Burns Fry, the underwriter of the sale, an opportunity to earn a good profit. It was probably no coincidence that Burns Fry saw fit to contribute over $65,000 to the Tory party in 1987.

When the contents of the letter were leaked to the press, Deputy Premier Eric Berntson denied that the government was contemplating the sale of SMDC.[41] The government was not "privatization oriented," he said. He did admit, however, that professional consultants had been hired "to review all possibilities with respect to SMDC."[42] One of these consultants, Dave Heron, a chartered accountant from Saskatoon and a future deputy minister of finance, accompanied the premier on his European tour in January 1985. While in Britain, they met with British government officials and were favourably impressed with Margaret Thatcher's privatization campaign. Later during the trip, Devine discussed the future of SMDC with French banking and uranium industry officials and confided that the Crown corporation might be carved up and sold.[43] A similar opinion was offered in January 1985 by Sid Dutchak, the newly appointed minister responsible for SMDC. He saw "nothing wrong" with privatization, provided that only Saskatchewan people were allowed to buy shares. Thus, the government's position shifted by stages, from denying that SMDC was for sale to admitting that the proposal was being studied, to declaring that privatization was reasonable and desirable.

The Prince Albert Pulp Company

Action on privatizing SMDC was delayed until the government's second term. Meanwhile, the Tories turned their attention to the Prince Albert Pulp Company (Papco). Opened in 1968, the Prince Albert pulp mill had been owned and operated by New York financier and industrialist Karl Landegger. According to the deal negotiated by Premier Ross Thatcher, Landegger built the mill for a fixed price of $54.8 million and paid $7 million for 70 percent ownership. The provincial government took the remaining 30 percent ownership in return for guaranteeing $50 million of Papco bonds.[44] When Landegger wanted to sell his 70 percent in the mill in 1980, the Blakeney government bought him out for $162 million in order to bring control of Papco into Saskatchewan.

Papco made profits of $23.5 million in 1980 and $24.1 million in 1981, but due to a world-wide downturn in pulp prices, it lost money in three of the next four years. Over the five-year period prior to privatization, the company lost $44 million. Most of the loss was incurred in 1985, a poor year for forest products companies. Most experts agree that privatization is best done when the company is profitable, so that the public treasury receives a maximum return. The PC government did not follow this advice. Instead, with the pulp industry at the bottom of a cycle in 1986, it sold Papco to Weyerhaeuser Corporation of Tacoma, Washington.

Weyerhaeuser is one of the largest forest products companies in the United States and among the top 100 U.S. industrial companies. Frederick Weyerhaeuser, who founded the company in 1900, adopted the slogan, "Timber is a crop," and emphasized the policies of reforestation and perpetual harvest. The company's sales in 1985 were over $5 billion and its profits over $200 million. In Canada, Weyerhaeuser operated six sawmills in the interior of British Columbia, with sales totalling $100 million annually.

The terms of the Papco sale were curious and raised eyebrows. Weyerhaeuser received the Prince Albert pulp mill, a chemical plant in Saskatoon, and a sawmill in Big River, for no cash down. The purchase price was fixed at $248 million, later lowered to $236 million because of "inventory adjustment". This was to be paid with money the company borrowed from the Government of Saskatchewan in the form of a 30-year debenture at 8.5 percent. Weyerhaeuser did not have to make any loan payments except in years when it made profits on the mill exceeding 12 percent. Any losses on the project from 1986 to 1989 up to the amount of $73 million could be deducted from the purchase price. If the government loan to Weyerhaeuser had not been repaid after 30 years, the company could issue preferred shares to the province, but these would be non-voting and would not carry rights to any dividends. Only in the year 2040, that is 55 years after the privatization, could the province get cash for the shares. Weyerhaeuser also obtained exclusive control over an estimated 7 million acres of northern forests and a government promise to build 32 kilometres of forest roads per year for the company's use. In exchange, Weyerhaeuser promised to upgrade the pulp mill and build a $250 million paper mill in Prince Albert, which would provide 215 new full-time jobs and 700 man-years of construction work. The province guaranteed $83 million of debt used to finance the mill.[45]

The NDP focused its attack not so much on privatization as on the excessively generous terms of the deal, and on the fact that the recipient was an American multinational. The Blakeney government had not believed that Papco should remain forever under public ownership. Indeed, before the 1982 election, negotiations had been under way to sell the pulp mill to a Canadian forest products company. In the case of Papco, the issue was not privatization, but whether the government was getting fair value for its assets.

The pulp mill was sold at a time when pulp prices were very low and just before they began to climb steeply. Bleached kraft softwood pulp, one of the Prince Albert mill's main products, was selling for $400 U.S. a ton in 1986. By January 1988 the price had reached $610 U.S. a ton.[46] Even Bill Gaynor, vice-president and general manager of Weyerhaeuser's Saskatchewan division, admitted his firm was "fortunate to purchase a mill for a good price just before market conditions improved."[47] A former Papco executive who spoke to the *Globe and Mail* revealed that the management of Papco had advised the government prior to the sale in 1986 that it was a "crazy time" to sell because the pulp industry was "at the bottom of the market." The unnamed executive stated that the mill was sold for at least $100 million less than it was worth.[48] Buoyed by rising pulp prices, Weyerhaeuser made profits on the mill of $78 million from September 1986 to the end of 1987. Clearly, the American multinational corporation got a very good deal. Meanwhile, the Tory party was the beneficiary of donations from Weyerhaeuser, amounting to $10,000 in 1986, $11,000 in 1987, and over $32,000 in 1988.

Privatization: The tentative first steps

Privatization was not a major economic policy of the Tories in their first term, although it now seems certain it was part of their long-range plan. But they had to move cautiously, because Crown corporations were still popular with the public. Devine's initial policy was to stop the rapid expansion of the Crown sector to make more room for the private sector. Later, he seemed to warm to the idea of privatization, suggesting in May 1984 that he would be willing to sell Crown corporations "if there's a better place to use the money."[49]

Evidence that the Tories were becoming bolder came in the 1984 budget. Saskatchewan residents were given the opportunity to invest money in two of the province's Crown corporations, SaskPower and Saskoil. SaskPower offered regular fixed-interest savings bonds, and Saskoil offered "participation bonds." At the same time, Devine carefully allayed fears that the government was embarking on a wholesale privatization of the Crowns: "We will proceed gradually so we bring people with us, both in political and educational terms. But we do not intend to make public participation an important part of our overall strategy."[50] In retrospect, it seems clear that Devine wanted to sell the Crowns sooner, but was prevented by the fear of a public backlash.

In 1986, the privatization strategy advanced a few more steps. Equity shares were sold in Saskoil, and Weyerhaeuser got control of the Prince Albert pulp mill and other assets. But neither sale was a true test of the principle of privatization. The NDP had said all along it wanted to interest a private Canadian company in the pulp mill, and the Saskatchewan government still held a controlling interest in Saskoil. Meanwhile, the Tories repeated that they were not intent on across-the-board privatization. As late as 1985, Finance Minister Bob Andrew declared, "Privatization is yesterday's theory . . . it doesn't make sense for one government to build these things and for the next one to come and sell it off."[51]

In the second term, the government made mincemeat of this declaration. Although Devine had promised the opposite, privatization moved to the centre of the government's overall strategy. The reason for the subterfuge had been the approaching 1986 election. The Devine government would have been foolish to antagonize the electorate by revealing its plans for privatization. To do so would have risked defeat and denied the Tories the opportunity to continue implementing their new right agenda.

Notes for Chapter 5

1. George MacLean, *Public Enterprise in Saskatchewan* (Regina: Crown Investments Corporation, 1981).

2. *Leader-Post,* 7 January 1984. 3. *Star-Phoenix,* 16 June 1982. 4. *Leader-Post,* 30 October 1982. 5. *Ibid.,* 31 March 1983. 6. *Financial Post,* 16 November 1983. 7. *Leader-Post,* 12 November, 1983. 8. *Ibid.,* 7 June 1983. 9. *Star-Phoenix,* 30 March 1983. 10. *Financial Post,* 1 January 1983.

11. Government of Saskatchewan, *Report of the Crown Investments Review Commission,* 1983. 12. *Star-Phoenix,* 11 February 1983. 13. *Ibid.,* 11 February 1983. 14. *Financial Post,* 12 November 1983.

15. *Leader-Post*, January 1986. **16.** *Ibid.*, 12 June 1984. **17.** *Ibid.*, 7 January 1986. **18.** *Ibid.* **19.** *Ibid.*, 12 August 1982. **20.** *Financial Post*, 6 November, 1982. **21.** *Leader-Post*, 3 March 1983. **22.** *Ibid.*, 19 January 1985. **23.** *Ibid.*, 15 February 1983.

24. *Ibid.*, 10 March 1983. **25.** Colin Thatcher, *Backrooms*, p.193. **26.** *Leader-Post*, 17 April 1985. **27.** *Financial Post*, 28 April 1984. **28.** Interview, Harold Johnson, 10 October 1989. **29.** *Leader-Post*, 20 April 1984. **30.** *Star-Phoenix*, 19 November 1983. **31.** *Leader-Post*, 14 February 1986. **32.** *Ibid.*, 29 July 1986. **33.** *Star-Phoenix*, 16 December 1982. **34.** *Leader-Post*, 22 June 1982. **35.** *Star-Phoenix*, 26 November 1985. **36.** *Leader-Post*, 20 October 1982. **37.** *Ibid.*, 22 October 1986. **38.** *Ibid.*, 9 December 1983.

39. *Ibid.*, 15 January 1983. **40.** Latham C. Burns to Devine, 9 August 1983. **41.** *Leader-Post*, 1 June 1984. **42.** *Ibid.*, 26 April 1984. **43.** *Star-Phoenix*, 29 January 1985.

44. Paul Gingrich, "A Pulp Mill for the Asking," *Briarpatch*, October 1986. **45.** "Privatization," *Commonwealth*, March 1989. **46.** *Leader-Post*, 2 January 1988. **47.** "Privatization Primer," *Commonwealth*, March 1989. **48.** *Leader-Post*, 13 February 1987.

49. *Ibid.*, 8 May 1984. **50.** Prince Albert *Herald*, 9 April 1985. **51.** Moose Jaw *Times Herald*, 29 January 1985, quoted in Maureen Appel Malot, "The Provinces and Privatization: Are the Provinces Really Getting Out of Business?" *Privatization, Public Policy and Public Corporations in Canada*, edited by Allan Tupper and G. Bruce Doern (Montreal: Institute for Research on Public Policy, 1988), p. 412.

6

MULRONEY'S DEVINE INTERVENTION

> Saskatchewan's Progressive Conservative
> government has no plans to sell SaskTel, or any
> portion of it...these rumors are totally false,
> totally unfounded.
> — GARY LANE, *minister responsible for SaskTel,*
> *ten days before the 1986 provincial election,*
> *Leader-Post, 10 October 1986.*

Saskatchewan's 1986 provincial election campaign actually began almost a year before 20 October 1986, the date eventually chosen as voting day by Premier Grant Devine.

In November 1985, the Tories suffered a crushing defeat in the Regina North East by-election. Ed Tchorzewski, a cabinet minister in Blakeney's government, took more than 70 percent of the vote in a seat the PCs had won handily in 1982.

This unexpected by-election defeat made it clear that the Tories were in big trouble, and Devine immediately began an intensive campaign to win back the hearts and minds of voters. He admitted that the government had made mistakes, showed contrition, promised to do better. The unpopular sales tax on used cars, which had been imposed in the 1985 budget, was done away with. This, Devine said, was an example of how he was listening to the people. To silence criticism that the government was top-heavy, the size of the cabinet was trimmed from 25 to 18. The ministers were shuffled to put a new face on the administration. Stricter rules were placed on cabinet ministers' use of government aircraft, a belated reaction to the improper use of a government airplane which had resulted in the forced resignation of Highways Minister Jim Garner.

The 1986 budget presented by the new Finance Minister Gary Lane painted a rosy picture. The deficit was vastly understated in the confident expectation that the truth would not come out until after the next election. The budget also provided for the creation of a Saskatchewan Pension Plan. It gave pension protection to homemakers, part-time workers, farmers, small business proprietors and their employees, and other people not already covered by a pension plan at their workplace. Those who participated made monthly contributions, which could then be matched by the provincial government.

The Tories felt that their best hope for re-election was in the rural areas. Since 1982, the government had diligently catered to the needs of farmers. The Land Bank had been abolished and replaced with low-interest loans for young farmers trying to get established. Natural gas lines and individual telephone line service (as opposed to party lines) were extended to rural homes. Rebates on farm fuels, livestock cash advances, and loans for livestock facilities were provided. The Farmland Security Act was passed to restrict farm foreclosures, and financial aid was given to farmers hit by drought.

The stage was set for the major pre-election give-away. Prior to spring seeding in 1986, farmers were given $1 billion in low-interest farm production loans. All farmers were eligible to borrow $25 an acre at 6 percent, on a no-questions-asked basis. Neither financial need nor the ability to repay the loan had to be demonstrated, and no collateral or security was required. Wealthy farmers could take the loan and simply deposit the money in an account bearing a higher interest rate, making a tidy profit at the government's expense.

To further consolidate his hold on the countryside, Devine appointed himself Minister of Agriculture. It was a signal to farmers that he was giving top priority to agricultural issues as their spokesman and advocate. In the months heading up to the October 1986 election, he missed no opportunity to make a speech or attend a conference to talk about agriculture. He repeatedly expressed concerns about low prices and unfair agricultural subsidies in the United States and European Common Market. As both Premier and Minister of Agriculture, Devine went to twice as many national conferences and received double the media exposure. Before long, he was taking credit for "pushing agriculture to the top of the national agenda."

As well, Devine travelled to Lincoln, Nebraska, Columbus, Ohio, and Hilton Head, South Carolina, among other places, to talk agriculture. Whether he had any impact on United States governors or agricultural officials was irrelevant; what counted was that Saskatchewan newspapers, television, and radio automatically covered anything the Premier said or did, and now the media were featuring Devine as the farmer's friend and advocate. The Tory leader knew exactly what he was doing in terms of media strategy. As he told the *Western Producer*: "I'm certainly recognized as the Canadian spokesman on agriculture in terms of the premiers or ministers of agriculture . . . They understand more and more about us in Ontario and Quebec and across the country."[1] This image was to prove crucial to the outcome of the election.

The government's efforts to bolster its farm support and win back the favour of the electorate began to show results. Polls showed the Tories recovering from the low point they had reached in the latter part of 1985. By March 1986, rumours that an election call was imminent reached fever pitch, as the Conservatives opened their provincial campaign headquarters in a downtown Regina office building, and campaign trailers for PC candidates sprouted in shopping malls. Newspaper ads blared the message "The NDP Haven't Changed." As well as the advertising paid for by the Conservative party, there was an enormous amount of government promotion. A series of television ads touted the theme "Saskatchewan Builds," which would mesh with what later emerged as the PC election campaign slogan, "Keep on Building Saskatchewan." The Tories' use of the provincial treasury to advance their partisan cause could only be described as masterful.

Everything seemed ready for a spring election – and then, for some reason, Devine got cold feet. Perhaps the government's pollsters were telling it the time was not yet ripe; in any case, no election call came. But election promises kept on coming. In late summer, Devine unveiled his housing policy: home mortgage rates subsidized at 9¾ percent for ten years, matching grants of $1,500 for home improvements, $10,000 home improvement loans at 6 percent, and $3,000 grants for first-time home buyers. The urban equivalent of the farm production loan program, it capped the government's pre-election campaign and made it unnecessary for the Tories to offer much in the way of expensive election promises during the campaign itself.

The election was finally called on 19 September for a vote on 20 October. The PCs entered the campaign with a slim lead over the NDP. This in itself was a considerable achievement, given the trouncing the Tories had suffered in the Regina North East by-election the previous November. Money flowed freely for the Saskatchewan Pension Plan, farm production loans, home improvement grants and loans, and for government advertising. Devine, in his new-found role as Minister of Agriculture, charged up and down the continent, portraying himself as the leading spokesman for Saskatchewan farmers. The Tories entered the election with momentum on their side.

Election themes: Jobs and bribes

When Devine opened the campaign, he declared his main themes to be economic diversification and security for families. He claimed those concerns embodied the spirit of the province which had been so "excitingly evident at our pavilion at Expo." "The new Saskatchewan spirit has momentum, the world knows we're here," he proclaimed.[2] Set to a catchy jingle, the PC slogan, "Keep on Building Saskatchewan," played over and over again on radio and television.

Devine pointed to industrial projects already underway: a paper mill in Prince Albert, a bacon processing plant in North Battleford, and a heavy oil upgrader in Regina.[3] And this was just the beginning! If the Tories were re-elected, Swift Current would get a bandage factory; Balcarres, an ethanol plant; North Battleford, a recreational vehicle manufacturing plant; Lloydminster, a heavy oil upgrader; Regina, a fertilizer plant; and more. At times the Tory campaign seemed to be all ribbon cuttings and sod turnings, designed to give the impression that the Saskatchewan economy was moving from one triumph of diversification to another. Many projects were announced several times, although some of them would never materialize. In the last week of the campaign, Devine opened with great fanfare Nardei Fabricators, a pipe welding and fabrication plant in Regina. Four days after the election, the owner admitted that in the previous two weeks, ten workers had been laid off, leaving only four or five employees in the shop.[4]

The NDP countered with the slogan "Let's Get Saskatchewan Working Again." Blakeney pointed out that much of the Tory talk about economic growth and diversification was just that — talk. Most economic indicators concurred. Unemployment in April 1986 stood at 40,000, compared with 28,000 when Devine took office in April 1982.[5] In 1985, 6040 more people left the province than arrived.[6] As for financial well-being, the province had experienced only deficit budgets in four years of Tory rule. From a surplus of more than $140 million in May 1982, the treasury had sunk to a debt of more than $2 billion. Moody's Investor Service, a well-known New York credit rating service, dropped Saskatchewan's rating a full grade from AA1 to A1.[7]

Blakeney knew he had to be careful when condemning the Tories for mismanaging the economy. He realized that the NDP could come across as the "doom and gloom" party, full of pessimism about the province's prospects. Therefore, the New Democrats fashioned a campaign around programs to stimulate economic activity. The most ambitious job-generating scheme was the so-called 7-7-7 housing program, unveiled in the spring of 1986. It was said it would create 18,000 jobs by providing $7,000 grants to first-time buyers of new homes, renovation grants of up to $7,000 for existing homes, and a guaranteed 7 percent interest rate for mortgages.[8] Not everyone in the NDP was happy with the housing program; some thought it should be targeted more specifically to middle and lower income groups.[9] The decision to adopt the policy, despite this opposition, is attributable to two things. First, the polls showed that job creation was the number one issue for voters, and second, the NDP had been somewhat spooked by the Tory tactics in the previous election. In 1982, Devine had made a direct appeal to the pocketbook by abolishing the gas tax and guaranteeing home mortgage rates at 13¼ percent. The PC victory seemed to prove that the high road of financial responsibility was for losers. The NDP did not want to be outmaneuvered again.

Another job creation strategy in the NDP platform was "Career Start." Any employer who offered a young person a job for at least twelve months would be eligible for a wage subsidy of 50 percent to a maximum $3.50 per hour.[10] This was expected to create 5,000 new jobs. An additional 6,000 jobs were to be created over five years in highway construction and maintenance work, an opportunity provided by the Devine government's neglect of the highway system. The poor condition of the roads was a standard joke at NDP rallies. Blakeney called the highways "Devine golf courses – 18 holes a mile and a red flag in every one."[11] Another 2,000 jobs were to be created in reforestation and other projects to maintain the northern forests. Finally, as an encouragement to small businesses, the NDP offered small-scale employers loans of up to $250,000 at guaranteed interest rates of 7 percent over a period of seven years.

Both the NDP and the Tories made the economy the central theme of their campaigns. Both parties were aware that in an election that lacked a sharp ideological focus or a polarizing issue, "jobs, jobs, jobs" would be the voters' main preoccupation.

The Tories adopted as a secondary theme for their campaign "security and protection for Saskatchewan's families." Devine frequently pledged his commitment to "stay close" to families and help them through difficult times. He even told one interviewer that he considered the whole of Saskatchewan to be his extended family. All social policies were explained in terms of their impact on the family unit. For example, the housing policy was promoted as helping families with their single most important investment – their home. This policy excluded families who lived in rented accommodation. Devine also linked the fight against illegal drugs to protecting the family. In the midst of the campaign the government announced the creation of a drug abuse centre that would follow a "family-oriented treatment program."

On other policy matters, the Tories affirmed their willingness to spend money on health and education. PC ads informed voters that spending on education had jumped 52 percent since 1982. Health care expenditures had risen from $742 million in 1981 to $1.2 billion in 1986. Much of the increase was artificial because it resulted from inflation, the increase in population, and the transfer of programs from the department of social services to the department of health, but the numbers suggested that the Devine government cared about health and education. The Tories, by and large, succeeded in allaying suspicions that they were contemplating cuts in these areas.

On the social policy side, the NDP had an ambitious set of proposals. Provincial residents aged 60 years and over would receive a guaranteed annual income of at least $8,300 – about equal to a gross salary based on minimum wage. This was designed particularly for the many elderly single women "struggling to get by until they turn 65 when they become eligible for Old Age Security and other benefits."[12] The NDP also promised action on pay equity for women, more child care spaces, improved benefits for part-time workers, and expansion of the Children's Dental Plan to include coverage for orthodontics. In terms of social justice, Blakeney took aim at Tory taxation policies, which he labelled as unfair to lower and middle income earners. He promised to abolish the flat tax, and to restore the property tax rebate.

In summing up the themes of the two major parties in the 1986 campaign, what was striking were the similarities, not the differences. Both talked about economic development and job creation. Both offered improved social programs. The Tories created the Saskatchewan Pension Plan; the NDP proposed a guaranteed annual income for seniors aged 60 to 65. The Tories promised home improvement grants of $1,500 as well as $10,000 loans at 6 percent; the NDP housing program was even more generous.

The similarity between the NDP and Tory campaigns was reinforced by the absence of debate over public ownership or privati-

zation. Devine mocked Blakeney for shying away from nationalizing industry: "You don't hear the NDP opposition talking about
nationalizing things in this election. For years they've said we'll
nationalize this and take over that. Now they're an imitation. We
have taken this province on a new course of building and the old
course of nationalizing and buying is no longer fashionable or
popular or makes much sense. Now they're just following us.
They've cuddled up to us, and that's exactly where we want
them."[13] But if Blakeney was not talking about bringing anything
under public ownership, it was equally true that Devine was not
talking about privatizing anything. Both parties seemed to have
the same view on Crown corporations. The New Democrats were
not planning to create more of them, and the Tories were not
planning to sell the ones that already existed.

The similarity between the two campaigns was no accident.
Both parties were trying to attract the moderate centre, those
voters with no definite party affiliation. Devine was anxious to
keep together what he had called the "coalition of common sense"
in 1982 and what he renamed the "coalition of common purpose"
in 1986. This was a fancy way of saying that he hoped everybody
who was against the NDP would vote Tory. To win, he needed
the votes of ex-CCFers and former Liberals.

Devine's eagerness to keep intact his anti-NDP coalition
accounted for a bizarre incident involving the use of Tommy
Douglas's name. When Blakeney kicked off his campaign, he
observed that the election date, 20 October, fell on what would
have been Douglas's 82nd birthday. Blakeney exhorted NDP supporters: "What better way to honour Tommy's memory and his
life work than to join together on 20 October to return to Saskatchewan a government committed to stand up and fight for
ordinary people and for the type of society Tommy dreamed of and
did so much to create."[14] Devine, who apparently had not been
aware of the significance of the election date, handled the issue by
claiming that the former CCF premier was probably now a Tory:
"I wouldn't be surprised if he's cheering for us right now."[15]

Mrs. Douglas, Tommy's widow, considered Devine's statements outlandish and said so publicly, but the Tory leader was not
deterred. Throughout the campaign, he continued to claim

Tommy Douglas's allegiance. It was a Tory strategy to help voters differentiate the NDP from the CCF. The CCF had its roots in rural Saskatchewan, unlike the NDP, which Devine stigmatized as an urban-based, labour-dominated party. "We have replaced the CCF in rural Saskatchewan," he declared.[16]

Ex-Liberals were another component of Devine's anti-NDP coalition. The Liberal party had collapsed in 1982, capturing less than 5 percent of the popular vote and winning no seats. For the Tories, it was crucial that Saskatchewan Liberals not return to their former political home. At every rural stop in the election campaign, Devine told the same little story. When he was a kid at family gatherings, his two grandfathers would sit at opposite ends of the table. One was a Tommy Douglas man, the other a Jimmy Gardiner man. "Pretty soon, the fists would hit the table, the spoons would jump and the kids would scatter . . . and they both voted for Dief."[17] Since Devine knew that a Liberal resurgence could bring him down, well-known Grits were assiduously courted. The pressure was so great that former provincial Liberal leader Davey Steuart had to write to the *Leader-Post* to deny rumours that he was supporting Tory candidates.[18]

Agriculture: The Tories' trump card

After unemployment and job creation, the issue uppermost in people's minds was agriculture. The poor state of the farm economy had a depressing effect on the whole province. On this issue, the Tories had clear superiority over the NDP. The polls showed that any time voters focused on agriculture, support for the Tories went up. When people turned their minds to other issues, support for the Tories went down. The reason for PC strength in rural Saskatchewan was the government's record since 1982. Devine had poured a lot of cash into the farm community, including the billion-dollar farm production loan program he introduced just before the election. And, as Minister of Agriculture, Devine touted himself as the foremost defender of farmers' interests.

During the election, interest focused on whether farmers would receive a special deficiency payment from the federal government to compensate for low grain prices. It was argued that since both the United States and the European community were subsidizing their grain growers, Ottawa should do the same. The difference between the NDP and Tories was not on a question of policy – both agreed that a deficiency payment was needed – but a question of who was more likely to convince Ottawa to make the funds available.

Two days before the election was called, Devine met with Prime Minister Brian Mulroney in Ottawa, and afterwards announced to the press that help was on the way. According to the Premier, Mulroney had promised that farm aid would be included in the federal government's throne speech on 1 October. When asked what form the farm aid might take, Devine talked about a hybrid scheme with various components such as an increase in the domestic price of wheat, a Western Grain Stabilization Plan pay-out, and a deficiency payment. Whatever form the aid package took, Devine insisted that farmers needed $1 billion (down from the nearly $5 billion he had lobbied for in August) to cope with low grain prices.[19]

The NDP's position was to demand more. Blakeney said he would fight for a federal grain deficiency payment based on a wheat price of $6 per bushel. "If Brian Mulroney can find $1.5 billion to cut the taxes of the 40 largest oil companies through the elimination of the Petroleum and Gas Revenue Tax this month, then he can find $2 billion to help protect 150,000 farm families in Western Canada," he declared.[20] Further, the NDP pledged to declare a one-year moratorium on the payment of principal and interest on the farm production loans. As well, farm fuel costs would be reduced by at least 32 cents a gallon, and the federal government would be pressed to allow the production and sale of low-cost generic farm chemicals.

Since the agricultural policies of the two parties differed only in detail, the fight boiled down to which party had more clout with Ottawa. Blakeney charged that Devine was too much the obedient "yes-man," afraid to "stand up for Saskatchewan." The NDP leader reminded voters that when the Mulroney government had tried to de-index senior citizens' pensions, Devine had backed the federal Tories until the prime minister himself was forced to retreat. This was just one example, Blakeney said, of Devine putting his loyalty to Mulroney ahead of the interests of Saskatchewan people.

Devine countered that Blakeney was just "posturing." What good would "pounding away" at Mulroney do? The premier maintained that a co-operative, friendly approach was much more likely to succeed.[21] He also mocked Blakeney's lack of affinity with rural Saskatchewan, deriding him as an "urban cowboy" who couldn't ride a horse and didn't understand hockey or baseball.[22] Devine further charged that the New Democratic Party itself was out of touch with the farmers. As proof, he cited its opposition to free trade with the United States. Sweeping aside many farm organizations' opposition to the trade deal, Devine insinuated that the NDP, the unions, and Ontario were all natural enemies of rural Saskatchewan: "The NDP has got the Canadian Labour Congress and Bob White and others coming out to tell us we can't trade. Well, I'll tell Bob White and the Canadian Labour Congress that there isn't a farmer in Saskatchewan who won't tell you where to go if you start telling us where we can sell our wheat or sell our cattle, or sell anything else. You can go back to Ontario."[23] The PC leader thus managed to bash the NDP, unions, and Ontario all at the same time.

In the 1986 campaign, the agricultural issue, and possibly the outcome of the election itself, came down to one thing. Would Brian Mulroney come through with a big deficiency payment for Western farmers? If yes, Devine would look like a hero; if no, he would look like a fool. Blakeney's fate also hinged on what Mulroney would do, but Blakeney was in the unenviable position of having no leverage with the prime minister.

Leadership: A contrast of styles

In agriculture, as with other issues, not much separated the NDP from the Tories. Those who were looking for differences in the two campaigns had to look elsewhere. When issues recede in importance, the question of leadership comes to the fore, and, without a doubt, Allan Blakeney and Grant Devine were very different leaders. Whereas Devine was folksy, emotional, and spontaneous, Blakeney was formal, intellectual, and disciplined. The difference was evident in how they used language. Devine was anything but precise and had little regard for factual accuracy. Nothing was ever just "very good"; it was always "world-class." Saskatchewan wasn't just a good place to live; it was "the best-kept secret in the world." He boasted at a Moose Jaw rally that the Saskatchewan pavilion at Expo 86 in Vancouver was among the ten best. By that evening, addressing a crowd in Ponteix, he raised the ante, declaring the Saskatchewan pavilion to be the best.[24] Devine used words the way his government spent money – extravagantly and imprudently.

In contrast, Blakeney had the lawyer's habit of selecting each word with due attention to its exact meaning. Again, the parallel with money seems apt. As premier, Blakeney had watched very closely the expenditures of the various government departments. Programs were designed carefully, eligibility requirements were specified, and every expenditure had a rational explanation. Neither Devine's rhetoric nor his budget figures ever quite added up. Blakeney, on the other hand, was always intellectually coherent, whether giving a speech or administering the province's finances.

At the level of emotion, Devine was better at working a crowd. At times he hardly seemed to speak in sentences. One thought tumbled into the next, with key words or phrases being repeated over and over in a tone of voice that suggested, "Why are those other guys so blind or misguided that they can't understand this?" The flow of rhetoric was spiced with snappy one-liners ("Free trade opponents are like stopped clocks – right twice a day") and down-home stories about small boys lost in wheat fields. His audiences were moved, inspired, and entertained.

Devine was equally effective with small groups. At senior citizens' homes, he played the piano and chatted about his grandmother. In a coffeeshop full of farmers, he talked knowledgeably about the harvest.[25] When mainstreeting, he was accompanied by a photographer who took a snapshot of him with his arm around every third or fourth voter. Each Polaroid photo was then autographed by Devine, placed in a card, and presented as a souvenir.[26] Warm, personable, and relaxed, Devine was superb on the campaign trail.

Blakeney was more reserved and less "hail fellow well met." Later, looking back on his political career, he commented, "I've never been 'one of the boys.' I don't know why not, but I have never been."[27] Not comfortable wearing his heart on his sleeve, he stated his convictions in a relatively low-key manner: "I entered political life because I believed in the fundamental values of Tommy Douglas, Woodrow Lloyd and the CCF – fairness, competence and compassion. Political fashions may change from time to time, but those fundamental values are never out of style."[28] He preferred understatement to overstatement, rational argument to raw emotion. To the general public, he was a less effective communicator than Devine, whom nobody could accuse of either understatement or meticulous logic.

Devine, 42, had the advantage of youth over the 61-year-old Blakeney. The Tory leader made sly allusions to Blakeney's age ("I really believe he's getting tired"), and suggested that the NDP leader should take advantage of his party's proposal for a guaranteed annual income for those aged 60 to 65. Devine pretended to believe that the NDP's real objective was to drive older people out of the workforce and mockingly prodded Blakeney to comply: "Come on, you first, out you go..."

Although the differences in style and personality between the two leaders were obvious, the NDP made the mistake of trying to change Blakeney's image. Instead of a dignified intellectual, learned in constitutional law and public administration, he was presented as a "man of the people." Ads showed him in a plaid shirt shooting the breeze with lunch bucket-toting workers, or strolling with farmers who had just climbed off their tractors after a day in the fields. This advertising strategy was a calculated risk for the NDP.[29] They were still stung by 1982, when the government and the leader had been so out of touch with the voters. They wanted to promote Blakeney, not as a remote and aloof figure, but one who listened to the people. Devine made fun of the ads, joking that the NDP was trying to make Blakeney look just like him: "He acts like me, he talks like me, he walks like me." And Blakeney admitted, "Well, yes, I guess I do walk like Devine.

First, I lift up my right foot and move it forward, then I lift up my left foot and move it forward. Then my right foot again and the left foot the same thing." Blakeney's wit deflected the barb, but the fact remained that in an election where the two campaigns already looked very similar, the NDP ads were ill-advised.

Mulroney intervenes

The election was a close, hard-fought campaign with the Tories' hopes for victory hinging on their rural support. The most dramatic moment came mid-way through the campaign. On 1 October, the federal government's throne speech included a promise of "close consultation with the provincial governments and farm organizations to help alleviate personal hardship in our farm communities." Devine emerged from his office after watching the speech on television to tell reporters that federal financial assistance was a certainty. He said he had just spoken with John Wise, the federal agriculture minister, who had assured him: "This [the throne speech] means new cash, new money, and new initiatives in Western Canada."[30] That night, polling in the thirteen rural constituencies which had been identified by NDP strategists as swing ridings showed that Tory support had increased marginally. Before the speech, the point spread between the Tories and the NDP had been 3 percent; it was now 6 percent. The actual reference to agriculture in the throne speech had been disconcertingly vague, and farmers remained unimpressed.

The clarification came two days later, when Mulroney announced that he would work closely with Grant Devine "to devise an effective financial program. The initial estimate of assistance required is $1 billion."[31] This was the first time the federal government had mentioned a specific amount of money. Then and there, the NDP lost the election. The point spread between the Tories and the NDP in the rural swing ridings immediately jumped to 13 points.

Coming almost exactly half-way in the campaign, the intervention was timed perfectly. It enabled Devine to take credit for being the saviour of the rural economy. He put his support for

Mulroney on the line, threatening, "If I lose over this, it's going to be damned tough for Mulroney next time around."[32]

Devine later played down the importance of the federal deficiency payment: "I don't think the outcome of a Saskatchewan election will be determined by a throne speech. Or else all you'd do is have a throne speech and you'd win. You wouldn't even campaign."[33] Most observers, including Don Mazankowski, the veteran Western politician who had risen to the position of Deputy Prime Minister in Mulroney's cabinet, had a different view. When asked about the $1 billion (only $457 million of which actually went to Saskatchewan farmers), Mazankowski smiled and said, "Anything to win an election."[34]

The news of the deficiency payment had an instant and disastrous effect on the NDP campaign. The damage was not permanent; as the deficiency payment became old news, normal patterns of voter preference reasserted themselves, and the momentum shifted in favour of the NDP. Blakeney drew large crowds at five major rallies staged in the final ten days of the campaign. He addressed 3,000 placard-waving supporters in Saskatoon on 16 October: "I have a little message for the PC leader. It's short. It's simple...Grant, who has the momentum now?" The hall resounded with chants of "Four more days," the time remaining, the crowd hoped, in the life of the Devine government.[35]

On election day, more people voted for the NDP (45.06 percent) than for the PCs (44.80 percent), but the Tories captured more seats (38 compared to 25 for the NDP). The Liberals had 9.93 percent, up from 4.5 percent in 1982, and elected one member in Assiniboia-Gravelbourg. Devine's coalition had weakened, but it held together well enough to assure a second term for the Tories.

The main reason the high NDP popular vote did not translate into more seats was that the NDP strength was in the cities, where the constituencies tended to have larger populations. Whereas a solid Tory rural seat like Souris-Cannington had 6,857 voters, Regina North West, which went NDP, had 13,678. Across the province, the rural/urban split was very pronounced. The NDP took 20 of the 24 seats in the larger urban centres, including 8 of

10 seats in Regina, 8 of 10 in Saskatoon, both Moose Jaw seats and both Prince Albert seats. The Tories won 7 of the 8 constituencies with the smaller urban centers of Lloydminster, Estevan, Melfort, Melville, Swift Current, The Battlefords, Weyburn, and Yorkton. As for the 30 rural seats, Saskatchewan was almost completely solid blue. Only Humboldt, the Quill Lakes, and Assiniboia-Gravelbourg did not elect Tories. The two northern seats, Athabasca and Cumberland, went to the NDP.

The NDP's success in the larger cities can be attributed to a number of things. The cities were experiencing high unemployment and a sluggish economy, without having the compensation of bail-outs from Ottawa. Organized labour, which had been disenchanted with the NDP in 1982, had concluded that the Tories were much worse. The lingering effect of the Devine government's purge of the civil service was also a factor, especially in Regina. The Tory sweep of rural Saskatchewan had much to do with Devine's record of giving assistance to agriculture and his ability, half-way through the campaign, to extract a deficiency payment out of Ottawa. The NDP had not renewed itself in rural Saskatchewan; the party had taken such a beating in 1982 that many people were still demoralized and believed the NDP could not win in 1986. Young farmers who might otherwise have stood as candidates decided to sit the election out, and many constituencies ran the same "old guard" candidates who had lost in 1982. This lent credibility to the Tory claim that the NDP had not significantly changed. Perhaps the most frank assessment of the election result came from Paul Meagher, the defeated PC candidate in Prince Albert: "We were successful in buying the farmers, unsuccessful in buying the cities."[36] In any event, Devine had a mandate to govern Saskatchewan for another term.

The 1986 election and privatization

As far as anyone could tell from Devine's election statements, the nature of the mandate was very general. He had talked vaguely about building Saskatchewan and diversifying the economy, goals in line with what every premier of Saskatchewan since 1905 had wanted to do. The Conservatives had received no specific mandate to embark on an ambitious program of privatization. Indeed, it could be argued that the Tories came out strongly against it. Twelve days before election day, Blakeney suggested that the government was planning to sell SaskTel to Bell Canada.[37] Gary Lane, the minister responsible for SaskTel, immediately denied the allegation, saying the government had no plans to sell the corporation or any portion of it. He called the rumours "totally false, totally unfounded...We have never looked at selling SaskTel nor will we."[38] Blakeney then released a copy of a leaked report, prepared by the investment firm of Pemberton, Houston and Willoughby at the request of the Saskatchewan government to examine "various issues relating to a possible divestiture by the Province of Saskatchewan of all or part of its equity interest in SaskTel."[39] The report was not the only evidence that the Tories were planning the privatization of SaskTel. In May of 1985, a group of influential Tories, including Dave Tkachuk, the premier's principal secretary, Terry Leier, the Crown Management Board's general counsel, and Spence Bozak of Dome Advertising, the government's advertising agency of record, had travelled to Britain to study how the Thatcher government had privatized the British phone company. Devine expressed open admiration for the sale and commented approvingly that at last the British people were "able to participate" in their own phone company.[40]

Despite all the evidence of an impending privatization of Sask-Tel, Devine insisted that Blakeney was "fishing." The Tory leader said that bonds might be sold, but there would definitely not be a disposal of assets.[41] To this, Blakeney replied that the Pemberton, Houston and Willoughby report did not mention bonds: "It talks about selling shares. Some people may be able to claim they don't know the difference between a plan to sell bonds and a plan to sell shares. Some people, but not a PhD in economics."[42] Blakeney warned that if the PCs were re-elected, they would "stoop to a bargain-bin sale of provincial assets for a quick fix of desperately-needed cash."[43]

Blakeney's predictions were not taken seriously. Gary Lane accused him of grasping at straws because he was losing the election. Nothing Devine said during the election led people to think that when he used the word "diversification," he really meant "privatization." After the election, it was evident that, in the minds of the Tories, the two words were closely connected. For the time being, though, everything was kept simple. Devine asked for a mandate to "Keep on building Saskatchewan" and that was what he received.

Notes for Chapter 6

1. *Western Producer*, 2 October 1986.

2. *Leader-Post*, 19 September 1986. 3. *Ibid.*, 20 September 1986. 4. *Ibid.*, 24 October 1986. 5. *Ibid.*, 11 October 1986. 6. *Ibid.* 7. *Ibid.*, 17 October 1986. 8. *Ibid.*, 12 September 1986. 9. Interview, Tom Brook, 27 May 1989. 10. *Leader-Post*, 22 September 1986. 11. *Star-Phoenix*, 7 October 1986. 12. *Leader-Post*, 26 September 1986. 13. *Ibid.*, 6 October 1986. 14. *Ibid.*, 20 September 1986. 15. *Ibid.* 16. *Star-Phoenix*, 27 September 1986. 17. *Ibid.* 18. *Leader-Post*, 15 October 1986.

19. *Ibid.*, 18 September 1986. 20. *Ibid.*, 23 September 1986. 21. *Ibid.*, 24 September 1986. 22. *Globe and Mail*, 24 September 1986. 23. *Ibid.*

24. *Leader-Post*, 1 October 1986. 25. *Globe and Mail*, 24 September 1986. 26. *Leader-Post*, 30 September 1986. 27. Susan Swedburg-Kohli, "Blakeney's Curious Resignation," *Western Report*, 1 December 1986. 28. *Leader-Post*, Eisler, 17 October 1986. 29. Interview, Garry Simons, 30 May 1989.

30. *Leader-Post*, 3 October 1986. 31. *Ibid.*, 6 October 1986. 32. *Ibid.* 33. *Ibid.* 34. *Ibid.*, 7 October 1986. 35. *Ibid.*, 17 October 1986. 36. *Ibid.*, Bruce Johnstone, 25 October 1986.

37. *Ibid.*, 9 October 1986. 38. *Ibid.*, 10 October 1986. 39. *Ibid.*, 16 October 1986. 40. *Ibid.*, 8 August 1985. 41. *Ibid.*, 16 October 1986. 42. *Ibid.*, 17 October 1986. 43. *Ibid.*, 11 October 1986.

7

CUTBACKS

◇ ──────────────────────── ◇

THE SUMMER
OF OUR
DISCONTENT

> It felt like I had been kicked in the stomach.
> – *fired dental worker* ELIZABETH HOOPER,
> *describing her reaction to the Devine government's
> decision to do away with the children's school-based
> dental plan. Star-Phoenix, June 1987.*

Central to the Devine government's 1986 election strategy was the need to conceal two things: the actual state of the province's finances, and the Tories' privatization plans. It seems unlikely that Devine's narrow margin of victory on voting day would have withstood either the bad news about the budget, or the truth about his party's privatization agenda. As it turned out, once the election was out of the way, Devine was able to use the bad state of the budget to win support for his plans to privatize Saskatchewan's large Crown corporation sector.

Although the March 1986 budget had projected a deficit of $389 million, Devine conceded during the campaign that this estimate was on the low side. The true figure, he said, was likely to be around $500 million. After the election, the Tories admitted that the deficit for 1986-1987 was $1.235 billion, much larger than any deficit previously recorded in Saskatchewan. Some very severe measures, Devine now said, would have to be taken to prevent the province's finances from spinning out of control.

Finance Minister Gary Lane hinted that the government's failure to disclose the size of the deficit was related to its privatization goals when he suggested that one method of dealing with the financial crunch would be to make government programs more cost-effective "perhaps through transfer to the private sector."[1] Allan Blakeney was also quick to see the connection. He warned the NDP provincial convention in June 1987 that Devine had followed a typical pattern of right-wing governments – run up a huge debt in the first term and then, in the second term, use the debt as an excuse to cut services and sell government assets. The debt provided the cover for the new right to carry out its program. Accordingly, in the period immediately after the election, the Devine government raised a great hue and cry about the debt, cut back drastically on government spending, and began to privatize aggressively.

The truth about the deficit

But first of all, the government had some explaining to do. How could the province's finances have slipped so far so quickly? During the election, upbeat PC television ads had given the impression that all was well in Saskatchewan. New industries were being established, plants were opening, the economy was diversifying. All that was needed was to "keep on building Saskatchewan." There was no sign that the government was short of money. Handouts of $1,500 were given to anyone who wanted to reshingle their house, replace their carpets, build a sundeck, or add a swimming pool. Who would have guessed that Saskatchewan faced a financial crisis?

The government needed some kind of explanation as to what had happened to bankrupt the province between October 1986 and March 1987. Part of the strategy adopted was to avoid calling the spring session of the legislature for as long as possible, thereby denying the opposition a forum to put the government on the spot. Furthermore, the longer the 1987 budget was delayed, the less conspicuous would be the contrast between election-time largesse and post-election austerity.

Traditionally in Saskatchewan, the budget is introduced before the last day of the fiscal year, March 31. Only one budget since 1905 was introduced later, that being the 1985 budget, which was brought down on 10 April. In 1987, the government shattered tradition by not calling the legislature into session until June. This enabled the Tories to put more time between the election and the bad-news budget, thereby defusing public anger. A June session meant that the budget debate would take place in the middle of the summer, when most people were on vacation and paying little attention to politics. Finally, a late budget allowed the finance minister to leak bits of it over an extended period of time. People could be gradually acclimatized to the idea of cutbacks so that when it was finally brought down, the 1987 budget would be less of a shock.

Despite all the manoeuvering, the glaring contrast between how the finances of the province had been presented during the election and the real numbers did not go unnoticed. Even Gary Lane came close to admitting that the public had been deceived. When asked why the size of the deficit had been so blatantly misrepresented during the election, he answered, "What do you expect? We're politicians."[2]

The opposition tried to get Devine to admit that he knew the deficit was far greater than his government had revealed. Why had he led people to believe that it would be $500 million rather than $1.2 billion? Eleven times during question period he was asked, and eleven times he referred the question to his finance minister. Finally, on the twelfth time, Devine asserted that $500 million was the best information available to him in October 1986 for the probable size of the deficit.[3] The answer strained credibility. Throughout 1986, the finance department received monthly expenditure reports and quarterly revenue reports. According to Art Wakabayashi, Deputy Minister of Finance, the information was available: "As a rule, once we get the second quarter, the picture starts to emerge."[4] Since the election took place during the third quarter of the fiscal year, Devine had a fairly accurate figure for the estimated size of the deficit.

The truth is that the budget presented in the legislature in March 1986 was never intended to be based on fact. As Blakeney remarked, it was "a strong candidate for the Governor General's award for fiction."[5] Revenue projections were consistently over-stated. For example, oil revenues for 1986-87, estimated at $511 million, came in at $213 million. The tobacco tax, expected to raise $92 million, raised only $78 million. Potash revenue was projected to double, but failed to do so.[6] Lane later attributed the deficit to the collapse in oil prices. This argument did not wash because when the budget was introduced, oil prices had already collapsed. Nor were Devine's vague allusions to falling agricultural prices, drought, and grasshoppers relevant. Blakeney pointed out that the government did not have any major economic information in March 1987 that it had not had a year earlier.

On the spending side, two major expenditures were not accounted for in the original budget. One was the home improvement program, sprung just before the election and announced even before it was approved by Treasury Board. The other was an advance to the Agricultural Credit Corporation to cover possible write-offs of farm production loans and livestock cash advances. The government obviously knew about these programs and could have revised its budget forecast accordingly. It wasn't that the government was not capable of producing an accurate budget; it had not wanted to. Winning the election took priority.

The axe falls

With the election out of the way, Devine and his ministers became fanatical believers in fiscal responsibility. It suddenly became very important for the government to show "how it could manage effectively in tough times." "Management" was the new buzzword, a euphemism for lopping $800 million from the expenditure side of the budget. Day after day during the spring of 1987 came a steady stream of announcements of services reduced, programs cancelled, and employees fired.

Transition houses caring for battered women and children were told that their budgets would be cut between 1.5 and 14.5 percent. Deanna Elias-Henry, chairperson of the Provincial Association of Transition Houses, angrily asked, "What kind of society are we sanctioning when we accept grants to paint our homes but we simply mourn and are able to do nothing when our social programming becomes eroded?"[7] The John Howard Society, which assists prisoners and their families, suffered a 25 percent budget reduction. This meant cancelling core funding that had been in place since 1958, prompting NDP justice critic Bob Mitchell to protest, "Is this supposed to be a cost-effective measure? Everyone knows it is cheaper to society to rehabilitate a criminal than to continue incarcerating him time and time again."[8]

Another victim of fiscal restraint was the Legal Aid Commission. Its funding was cut 8 percent, forcing staff lay-offs and curtailing services.[9] A minimum user fee of $60 was levied on all legal aid clients not receiving social assistance. Grant Schmidt, the minister responsible for the Legal Aid Commission, defended this cutback by reasoning, "Surely the prostitutes of Regina and the drug dealers who have capital to deal with drugs can come up with a little bit of money towards their defence."[10] This intemperate remark raised a furor. Members of a group called Lawyers for Equal Justice challenged Schmidt for stigmatizing all legal aid clients as prostitutes and drug dealers, when drug-related cases accounted for only 3 percent of the total legal aid case load.[11] Equally objectionable was Schmidt's insinuation that persons needing legal aid were guilty as charged. A minister of the Crown might have been expected to uphold the basic principle that one is innocent until proven guilty, critics said. But Schmidt only made matters worse, calling legal aid lawyers "scumbags working for scumbags."[12]

The cutbacks continued relentlessly: a 30 percent cut for the Mental Health Association; 37 percent for the Voice of the Handicapped; 16 percent for the Saskatchewan Human Rights Association; 10 percent for the Saskatoon Crisis Intervention Service; 100 percent for the Planned Parenthood Association and the Saskatchewan Pro-Life Association.[13] Some cutbacks involved the government's reneging on commitments made prior to the election. The students at the University of Regina had raised $2 million towards building a new students' centre after securing a government commitment for the remaining $3.4 million; Premier Devine himself came to the campus and announced the project with great fanfare at a special reception. After the election, the Tories said that there was no money for a student centre. The students would have to get by with the existing building, erected in 1969 as a facility meant to last only four years.[14]

Another broken promise involved St. Anthony's Home in Moose Jaw, a senior citizens home owned by the Sisters of Providence. Local citizens raised nearly $1.1 million for an expansion of the facility with the understanding that the provincial government would contribute $1.3 million. After the election, the province changed its mind. According to Gene Chura, the general campaign chairman, "We met all the criteria that were required, then – boom it's deferred." The director of the Moose Jaw Chamber of Commerce wondered aloud whether the city wasn't being punished for electing two NDP MLAs.[15]

A student summer employment program was cut in half. Grant Schmidt explained that "the need for high school students to have jobs was not as great as the government's need to save expenditures. Have you ever gone past a high school and saw how many high school students have cars?"[16] It became more difficult for university students to finance their education because the government tightened up the student aid program, putting more emphasis on loans and reducing bursaries. For the first time, the University of Saskatchewan imposed quotas on first-year arts and science students; 450 applicants who did not meet the cut-off average of 70 percent were turned away.[17] The technical institutes fared even worse, with 142 instructors fired from their jobs.[18]

Urban municipalities felt the pinch when the $16 million capital fund program was cancelled, an $8 million program to build sewer and water works was slashed to $4.2 million, and the funds from the revenue-sharing program were cut by 1 percent. The president of the Saskatchewan Urban Municipalities Association warned that vital construction projects might not proceed and municipal infrastructure could deteriorate.[19]

No one seemed immune from the cutbacks. Residents of nursing homes faced rent increases of $73 per month.[20] Finance Minister Lane announced that operating grants to schools, hospitals, municipalities, and universities would be frozen for two years, at a time when inflation was running at 4 percent. Wages for government workers were also frozen, even though wage increases on the average had not kept up with inflation since 1982.[21] The cost of living in Saskatoon and Regina had increased about 17 percent between October 1982 and October 1986, while public sector wages increased only 16 percent.

But in 1987 the burning issue for the public service was not wage and salary increases, but job security. A joke that went the rounds summed up the general mood. "What's the definition of an optimist? Answer: a civil servant who takes his lunch to work." In the spring of 1987 there were 16,544 government jobs (excluding Crown corporations) in Saskatchewan; of these, 2,868 were vacant. Devine wanted to cut 2,000 jobs from the civil service. However, this could not be done by simply eliminating the vacant positions – some of those jobs were essential and had to be filled. Calculations showed that at most 500 vacant positions could be abolished. The balance of the staff "downsizing" had to be achieved through other means. The government adopted the expedient of offering "voluntary" early retirements. Those with 30 years of service with the government or whose age and tenure added up to 75 years were presented with a retirement package.[22] Those who declined ran a high risk of dismissal. At the end of the exercise, 561 vacant jobs had been eliminated, 1,200 people had taken early retirement, and 407 people had been fired.[23]

The firm of Coopers and Lybrand had been hired by the government to plan the reduction and restructuring of the civil service. When asked how much the study would cost, Devine replied vaguely, "several thousands of dollars anyway." When pressed as to whether he thought it reasonable that in a period of severe restraint he did not know the cost of a contract that had been awarded without tender, Devine answered that he had a "pretty good idea" of the cost. He admitted it would be over $500,000, but did not say how much more.[24] He also confirmed that a consulting company headed by a recently defeated Conservative cabinet minister, Tim Embury, would work on a sub-contract for Coopers and Lybrand.[25] On the basis of the consultants' reports, decisions were made about who should go and who should stay in the public service.

The actual firing, however, was done by Stevenson, Kellogg, Ernst and Whinney, a firm of management consultants. The unionized workers' contracts required that they be given six weeks' notice. However, those who weren't covered by the union agreement were not so lucky. Senior-level civil servants were given the "red box" treatment, so called because of the red box in which they were asked to pack their personal belongings, and told to leave the building as soon as possible, sometimes under escort. This was in accordance with the recommendation of the Stevenson, Kellogg experts that a "surgical exit" was preferable. The firings were meticulously planned. Inquiries identified the employees who had illnesses that might flare up under stress, and steps were taken to ensure that a paramedic or staff nurse was available. Telephone numbers for in-house security and police were kept handy in case anyone reacted violently. The fired employees were offered counselling and psychological assessments to help them plan a new career.[26]

The efficiency of the process only added to its callousness. For those fired or forced to take early retirement, expulsion from their jobs was an ordeal. Many felt that their hard work and sense of professional commitment as career civil servants had been ill-rewarded. The government did itself no favour, getting rid of some of its best and most experienced people at the peak of their careers. Indeed, some had to be hired back on contract in order to keep departments running smoothly. The end result was that the morale of the public service, already battered by political purges and patronage hiring, sank even lower.

Health: The deepest cuts of all

A government that is firing people and slashing budgets is not likely to be a popular government. But of all the cutbacks, the ones most resented were those related to health. Medicare occupies a special place in Saskatchewan, and the record shows that the politician who tampers with it does so at his peril. The imposition of utilization or deterrent fees on visits to the doctor helped defeat Liberal Ross Thatcher's government in 1971. Then, in 1978, the NDP attacked with telling effect the alleged lack of PC commitment to medicare. During the campaign, Tory leader Dick Collver and Gary Lane had felt compelled to issue "certificates of guarantee" bearing their signatures and a solemn pledge not to take away health benefits. When Devine and Lane began to look for ways to economize on health spending, they knew the political risk they were taking.

Under the Prescription Drug Plan established by the Blakeney government in the 1970s, Saskatchewan residents received prescribed drugs at no cost except for a $3.95 processing fee paid to the pharmacist for each prescription. The changes to the plan in 1987 imposed a deductible of $125 per year for single people and families, $75 per year for families with one senior citizen, and $50 per year for single seniors. After the patient had paid the full cost of drugs up to the level of the deductible in a given year, he could apply to the government for reimbursement of 80 percent of the cost of any additional prescriptions. The government argued that the annual cost of the plan had skyrocketed from $100 million to $417 million over a ten-year period and that some restrictions were justified.[27]

The NDP responded that the restrictions worked undue hardship upon some people. Blakeney cited the case of a Regina family who had to pay out $1,700 a year for prescription drugs for their 3-year-old daughter who had an allergy problem. Even with the 80 percent rebates after the $125 deductible, the family still had to foot a bill of more than $400 annually. Moreover, some families simply did not have the cash to pay the full cost of prescriptions up front. The aforementioned family was on a tight budget, even though the father held down both a full-time and a part-time job and the mother earned extra money by babysitting. She went to Conservative MLA Gerald Muirhead to explain the problem created by the time lag between paying for her daughter's prescription and receiving the rebate, and was told to shop around for a druggist willing to supply credit. "Druggists are free-

enterprisers," Muirhead told her, "and, because they are competing for business, it would make sense that they would provide
credit to customers."[28]

These and other criticisms left Devine unmoved. He insisted
the changes were not a painful cutback, but a much-needed
reform. "Free prescription drugs and drug abuse go hand in hand,"
he said. "If it is a free good that has value someplace else, it's traded in the street and you have crime and abuse linked to it." The
NDP tried to call Devine's attention to those families who were
not drug abusers, addicts or criminals, but who were experiencing
hardship. Julie Shepherd, the mother of four children, appeared
at the legislature to say that she could not afford the up-front cost
of $132 to renew prescriptions needed by herself and her daugh-
ter. She said that she did not wish to malign Premier Devine, but
that "if he did his homework a little more, he would find out not
everyone who needs a prescription is a criminal...We're not
criminals, my husband and I."[29]

The government was eventually forced to retreat from its hard-
line stance. In the fall of 1988, just before the federal election, it
issued a plastic health card to all Saskatchewan residents. After a
patient had paid his deductible, the card enabled him to pay only
20 percent of the prescription costs up front. This eliminated
paper work and the long wait for rebates.

Another controversial decision was the elimination of the
school-based children's dental plan. Established by the Blakeney
government in 1974, the plan provided free dental health education, preventive services, and treatment to 144,000 Saskatchewan children aged 4 to 16 in 578 school dental clinics across 338
communities. The plan, which emphasized prevention rather
than treatment, employed dental therapists trained in a two-year
dental therapy program at Regina's Wascana Institute instead of
fully qualified dentists.

One of the advantages of locating the clinics in schools was
that virtually every child in the province could receive proper
dental care. No one was left out, not even those children whose
parents did not send them to the dentist for regular check-ups.
The plan made dental care for children convenient, accessible,
and comprehensive, and the emphasis on prevention meant that

cavities and dental irregularities were caught before they became serious problems. In 1976, an independent evaluation of the Saskatchewan Dental Plan was conducted by a three-member team headed by the dean of the faculty of dentistry at McGill University. They examined a randomly chosen sample of 410 children of all ages and from different regions of the province. The results showed that just over 30 percent of fillings on baby teeth done by dentists tended towards a rating of unsatisfactory, compared to 3 to 6 percent of those done by dental therapists. Conversely, about 15 percent of dentists' fillings were rated superior, compared with 45 to 50 percent of fillings by dental therapists.[30]

Despite the plan's evident success, the Devine government did away with it. Children between the ages of 5 and 13 could still receive free dental care, but only if their parents took them to a dentist. Older children were cut out of the plan completely. Cancelling the plan involved firing nearly 400 dental therapists, dental assistants, and support staff. They were herded into hotel rooms to receive the bad news:

> "It feels like a gas chamber," said the dental assistant as she was directed to her assigned meeting room in the luxury downtown hotel. She picked a chair at the back, blending in with the other dental assistants and therapists, all dressed the same in spotlessly clean pastel pink, green and blue uniforms. When the rows were full, the doors were locked. Reporters stared through the bars on the window. Some of the women cried, so the television crews stuck their cameras against the window, taking turns to get the best view of the scene.[31]

The televised spectacle of dental professionals, most of them women, sobbing and hugging each other for comfort, left many viewers shaking their heads.

The government's claim that as much as $5.5 million could be saved each year was immediately disputed. Some critics estimated the actual saving in providing care to 5 to 13-year-olds to be as low as $400,000 a year. Even if savings were actually $5.5 million a year, that amounted to merely .458 percent of government spending on health – hardly a huge dent in the budget.[32] The financial argument for cancelling the school-based children's dental program simply did not hold water.

Besides, the real cost of the cutback would not become apparent for some years. The great advantage of the plan was that it covered all children, and their dental problems were identified and treated early, so the dental health of the whole population gradually improved. The new plan was tailored to urban middle and upper-middle class children whose parents took them regularly to the dentist; it did not work well for native and poor children who did not get periodic check-ups. Minor dental problems left undetected and untreated eventually become major problems. Any money saved by eliminating the school-based plan would be more than lost in the long term.

Rural children were also losers under the new dental plan because dentists did not find it profitable to set up practices in small towns. Gravelbourg, a town of 1,305 located 187 kilometers southwest of Regina, lost its dentist. A Moose Jaw dentist had spent two days a week in the town, but when the government fired all the dental therapists, the dentist was now so busy that he had no time to travel to Gravelbourg. The town launched a nation-wide hunt for a dentist, but without success.[33]

Devine initially refused to admit that eliminating the school-based dental plan had been a mistake. As usual when cornered, he attacked. He insinuated that there had been something inadequate or substandard about the work done by the dental therapists and dental assistants. "Many parents let me know that they would rather have their children go to a dentist than they would have an assistant deal with their teeth in school," he claimed. These were the same therapists whose work had impressed the special committee led by the head of McGill's dentistry school. Without citing any evidence, other than what "many parents" had supposedly told him, Devine discredited an entire profession.

Devine's other attempts to defend the government's action were equally feeble. For instance, he justified the decision to drop adolescents from the plan by arguing that these funds were better spent on programs needed to fight alcoholism and drug abuse[34] – as if it was an either-or question, and that Saskatchewan did not have the will or the means to attack both problems.

After it became clear that the public was not accepting his reasons for abolishing the children's dental program, Devine began to modify his position. At the Tory convention in November 1987, he admitted that mistakes had been made, and that a new rural dental program for children and adults was on the way.[35] He promised to provide "drilling incentives" for small-town dentists, similar to the incentives given to the oil industry. Row upon row of dental chairs, cabinets, and other equipment, which had been removed from the school clinics, were lined up in warehouses and sold off at bargain prices to private dentists. Some equipment was unloaded for a fraction of the cost of new replacements, but even so, only $700,000 of the $2.2 million worth of dental equipment had been sold by June 1989. The rest was stored in a warehouse.[36]

But making dental equipment available to dentists at bargain prices was not enough to convince them to set up satellite offices in rural areas. One year after the elimination of the old plan, only 71 of the 338 rural communities that had formerly been covered had even a part-time dentist.[37] Abolishing the school-based children's dental plan was a disaster for everyone directly concerned – except, perhaps, the dentists, many of whom had considered the dental therapists' role in the clinics as a threat to their turf.

As an early experiment with privatization, it was something the government wanted to forget. It broke all the rules that are supposed to be followed to make privatization popular. People are not supposed to be fired, but hundreds were. Services are not supposed to be reduced, but they were slashed. Costs are to be reduced; that was doubtful. Privatization of the children's dental plan failed on all counts.

The changes to the dental plan and the prescription drug plan were but two of the more dramatic examples of health care cutbacks. Underfunding took its toll on virtually all health services. According to the head of the psychiatry departments at the University of Saskatchewan and University Hospital in Saskatoon, spending on care for the mentally ill fell precipitously. Dr. David Keegan charged that Saskatchewan, which had once led other provinces, now spent the least per capita on mental health.[38] Despite a 1986 election promise to spend an extra $100 million "to enrich hospital and special-care home services, including the provision of about 500 additional nursing positions," the funds did not materialize.[39] Instead, the University of Saskatchewan medical school was forced to eliminate 33 full-time teaching positions and 24 support-staff positions at its teaching facility in Regina. Operating grants to hospitals were frozen, and waiting lists for surgery lengthened. Dr. Tom MacLachlan, president of the Saskatoon and District Medical Society, revealed that in Saskatoon, with a waiting list of 11,000 in July 1987, the distinction between "urgent" and "elective" surgery was fading. "Because the system is so jammed with emergencies, 'urgent' is hardly even a category any more,"[40] MacLachlan said.

The health situation in the province during the 1987 season of cutbacks – "the summer of our discontent" – was summed up by Dr. Ron Ailsby at the annual meeting of the Saskatchewan Medical Association in April 1987. He described a patient who faced a nine-month wait for an operation on his hip. Hoping to help him in the meantime, his doctor outlined several options. Crutches? No good; the man's eyesight had deteriorated since his ophthalmologist left town. A walker? No such luck; there was a six-week waiting list if he wanted to get one under the Saskatchewan Aids to Independent Living Program. Still, the patient sat and grinned. Puzzled, the doctor asked the elderly man's wife why her husband wasn't upset. "He's a little hard of hearing," she said, "He's been waiting to get a hearing aid."[41]

The public reaction

The severity and extent of the cutbacks were an affront to many people, especially after an election campaign in which money flowed like water. The discontent mounted during the spring, as the government kept postponing the actual disclosure of the budget. The 1986-87 fiscal year ended 31 March. April went by, then May, and still there was no budget. The government financed its day-to-day expenditures by special warrants approved by cabinet. Opposition leader Blakeney protested that this was a misuse of special warrants, which were intended as emergency tools to meet unexpected spending needs when the legislature was not in session, not as an alternative budgeting process.[42]

The Legislative Counsel and Law Clerk, Merrilee Rasmussen, lent support to Blakeney's view when she submitted a nineteen-page legal opinion casting doubt on the legality of the government's use of special warrants.[43] Bob Andrew, the justice minister, accused Rasmussen of having given "questionable legal opinions in the past." Asked what opinions, Andrew said, "I forgot exactly what it was, it was something last year, I just can't recall." In the legislature he referred to her as "the lawyer for the Opposition," a remark for which he was forced by the speaker to apologize.[44]

When the government finally brought down a budget in June, it produced an explosion of angry protest. On top of all the cutbacks, there were substantial tax increases. The flat tax on net income was raised from 1 percent to 1.5 percent. The gasoline tax was re-introduced, despite the great hullabaloo about abolishing it during the 1982 election. Saskatchewan residents were allowed to save their gas receipts and submit them to the government at the year's end for a rebate. Individuals qualified for the rebate, but not corporate bodies like businesses, municipal governments, and school boards. Another 1982 Tory election promise falling by the wayside was the Public Utilities Review Commission. It had kept a lid on utility rate increases, in some instances even ordering rollbacks, but now the Devine government abolished it.

The toughness of the budget provoked a strong public outcry. More than 7,000 people, probably the largest demonstration in the history of the province, marched on the legislature. Walking through the streets of downtown Regina, they shouted in unison: "Hey, hey, ho, ho, Grant Devine has got to go," and "Grant Devine, you son of a bitch, you steal from the poor and give to the rich." Car drivers honked their horns in support, and bystanders waved and clapped. As thousands filled the streets, one demonstrator captured the mood of the moment when he said, "For a while at least it seems as if the people control the province again."

Devine tried to dismiss the event as being of no importance. The demonstrators, he said, were drawn by "free buses and free food and free games."[45] But the polls exposed the depth of dissatisfaction with the government: Tory support had fallen from 44.8

percent in October 1986 to 27.7 percent in June 1987.[46] The Tories had paid a heavy political price for the onerous regime of cutbacks.

Notes for Chapter 7

1. *Leader-Post*, 5 March 1987.

2. *Ibid.*, Eisler, 5 March 1987. **3.** *Ibid.*, 30 June 1987. **4.** *Ibid.*, 17 March 1989. **5.** *Debates and Proceedings, (Hansard)*, Legislative Assembly of Saskatchewan, 5 December 1986, p. 57. **6.** *Leader-Post*, 22 March 1989.

7. *Ibid.*, 4 April 1987. **8.** *Ibid.*, 10 April 1987. **9.** *Ibid.*, 2 July 1987. **10.** *Ibid.*, 25 July 1987. **11.** *Ibid.*, 6 August 1987. **12.** Murray Dobbin, "Tory Blitzkrieg in Saskatchewan," *Canadian Dimension*, September 1987. **13.** *Leader-Post*, 2 April, 29 April, 23 May, 26 June 1987; *Star-Phoenix*, 25 April 1987. **14.** *Leader-Post*, 3 April 1987. **15.** Moose Jaw *Times Herald*, 22 May 1987. **16.** *Leader-Post*, 4 July 1987. **17.** *Ibid.*, 10 September 1987, 12 July 1988. **18.** *Ibid.*, 9 September 1987. **19.** *Ibid.*, 28 March 1987. **20.** *Ibid.*, 27 May 1987. **21.** *Ibid.*, 13 March 1987. **22.** *Ibid.*, 20 March 1987. **23.** *Ibid.*, 12 December 1987. **24.** *Star-Phoenix*, 5 February 1987. **25.** *Leader-Post*, 31 January 1987. **26.** *Ibid.*, 12 December 1987.

27. *Ibid.*, 12 June 1987. **28.** *Ibid.*, 11 July 1987. **29.** *Ibid.*, 23 April 1988. **30.** Elizabeth Smillie, "Dental Plan Dropped," *Briarpatch*, December 1987/January 1988. **31.** *Leader-Post*, 12 June 1987. **32.** *Ibid.*, 13 June 1987. **33.** *Ibid.*, 25 March 1988. **34.** *Ibid.*, 27 June 1987. **35.** *Ibid.*, 17 November 1987. **36.** *Ibid.*, 13 June 1989. **37.** *Ibid.*, 11 June 1988. **38.** *Ibid.*, 1 May 1989. **39.** *Ibid.*, 4 April 1987. **40.** *Star-Phoenix*, 8 July 1987. **41.** *Leader-Post*, 13 April 1987.

42. *Ibid.*, 27 April 1987. **43.** *Ibid.*, 16 May 1987. **44.** *Ibid.*, 20 May 1987. **45.** *Ibid.*, 23 June 1987. **46.** *Ibid.*, 25 June 1987.

8

PRIVATIZATION

◇ ──────────────────────────────── ◇

MARGARET THATCHER COMES TO SASKATCHEWAN

> Saskatchewan is not Britain, where the many
> nationalized industries that were sold were
> uniformly disliked. In Saskatchewan, our
> Crowns are widely appreciated.
> – SASKATCHEWAN DEPARTMENT OF
> PUBLIC PARTICIPATION, *March 1989.*

The premier's reply to the Speech from the Throne is the occasion when he sets out in general terms his government's objectives for the coming session. When Devine addressed the Legislative Assembly on 12 December 1986 in the short session that followed the election, he gave no clue that privatization would be the centrepiece of the government's second term. The government, he said, had a mandate which it would take "very, very seriously,"[1] but when he talked about the nature of the mandate, he scarcely mentioned privatization. Instead, he interpreted the election result to mean that the people of Saskatchewan wanted him to build and diversify the economy while assuring protection for families from high interest rates.

Between December 1986 and November 1987, privatization moved to the top of the government's list of priorities. Part of the reason for this was the fact that the Tories were in deep trouble in the aftermath of the 1986 election. The economy was in bad shape with no relief in sight, and the only options that presented themselves were raising taxes, cutting programs, and wrestling with debt. Devine was fundamentally uninterested in the day-to-day business of government, tedious policy discussions, and the detailed refinement of programs. He much preferred to be on the road, stirring up audiences with his creative rhetoric. Whether it was "Open for Business," "Give 'er snoose," or free trade, he seemed to need a cause to champion or a gospel to preach. The trouble was that cutbacks and belt-tightening did not lend themselves to inspiring speeches. Privatization, on the other hand, would. It was new and exciting, and it seemed to be popular in Great Britain. Here was a chance for Saskatchewan to be "world class" (again), a "world leader," and here was a chance for Saskatchewan's premier to go everywhere spreading the wonderful news.

There were other reasons why the Devine government was attracted to privatization in 1987. It allowed the Tories to set the agenda for public debate. In the same way that the Mulroney government swept away discussion of its mistakes and scandals by focusing attention on the free trade issue, the Devine government polarized public opinion over privatization. If nothing else, it gave people something to talk about other than high taxes, high unemployment, government ineptitude, and waste of taxpayers' dollars. It also served the very important purpose of rallying the Tory caucus and the grassroots activists in the party behind the government. The terrible cutbacks and firings in the spring of 1987 had the potential to bring about disintegration of support among the Tory rank and file. Stories circulated that PC backbenchers were on the brink of resigning, and one, Ray Martineau, the MLA for Saskatoon Eastview, did quit. Privatization would rally discontented and restless Tory party members behind an ideological crusade.

Nor should the crass considerations of patronage be overlooked. The ability of the government to hand out jobs, contracts, and other benefits has traditionally been the glue of party loyalty for the party in power. Privatization, among other things, opened up entire new vistas of patronage. Valuable publicly owned assets could be put into the hands of well-connected private owners. Shares in Crown corporations could be put on the market for less than their real value and then resold for a profit. For those who had the money to participate on a large scale, privatization could be lucrative indeed.

Conservative party activists in Saskatchewan had always been more right-wing than the mass of PC voters. Evidence can be found in resolutions passed at Tory conventions which strongly endorsed privatization as early as 1984. In that same year, the Saskatchewan Chamber of Commerce, a key partner in the new right coalition, called on the government to "divest itself of all Crown corporations, except those providing essential public services."[2] Thus, when Devine embraced privatization, he was not breaking new ideological ground; he was merely doing what the new right in Saskatchewan had always wanted to do. Concerned about crumbling public support in 1987, his reaction was to consolidate the loyalty of the Tory rank and file. These were the people who served on constituency executives, attended conventions, and worked for the party at election time. Catering to them inevitably meant moving to the right. Privatization, therefore, was an expedient cause for Devine to adopt. It shored up the support of his most devoted followers because it harmonized with the cherished goals of the new right.

Another aspect of Devine's political problems in 1987 was that his economic development strategy was on the skids. Soon after being elected in 1982, he had declared the province "Open for Business," and waited for the inrush of entrepreneurs and capitalists. When they didn't come, other slogans were tried – "Partnership for Progress," "Keep on Building Saskatchewan," "Diversification" – but the economic miracle remained elusive. The economy was struggling, and people were leaving the province by the thousands. What was to be done? If a strong private sector could not be willed into existence, perhaps the answer was to build a private sector out of the public sector. If red-hot entrepreneurs were inexplicably not flocking to Saskatchewan to take advantage of the free enterprise environment, maybe they could be lured with public assets. Privatization was, in part, the economic development strategy of last resort.

Paradoxically, the Devine government was driven to a full disclosure of its ideology by pragmatism. In his first term, Devine had not seen fit to launch an all-out attack on the Crown corporations. He had limited their growth and chipped away at a few of them, but basically left them alone. Privatization was, at one and the same time, both perfectly consistent with neo-conservative principles and pragmatically expedient. It was a ready-made economic development strategy – or at least the appearance of one – for a government in desperate need of some fresh ideas.

Privatization: A British policy import

Saskatchewan Tories drew inspiration and borrowed expertise from their British counterparts. When Margaret Thatcher was first elected in 1979, privatization had not figured prominently in her stated plans either. The word "privatization" was barely mentioned in the Conservative party election manifesto of that year, and, in the first term, only a handful of profitable government-owned companies were sold. The avalanche came in Thatcher's second term, when companies like British Telecom, British Gas, and British Airways were privatized. By 1989, Britain had sold off assets worth $44 billion, the nation's largest transfer of power and property since the dissolution of the monasteries under King Henry VIII.

In carrying out these sales, British neo-conservatives developed a philosophy and a methodology of privatization. They filled essays and books with the arguments for privatization, and developed techniques to disarm the opposition and make privatization popular. To the Devine Tories, the privatization package must have seemed like a gift from above. There they were in the spring of 1987, hitting rock bottom in the polls and casting about for something to rally their supporters. Privatization was a ready-made program with a ready-made rhetoric. Not only was it philosophically in tune with the new right in Saskatchewan, it also appeared brand new because all the old arguments were presented in a novel way.

Articulate British spokesmen for privatization like Madsen Pirie, the head of the Adam Smith Institute in London, and Oliver Letwin, director of the International Privatization Unit for

N.M. Rothschild and Sons Ltd., began showing up in Saskatchewan. Both men had been employed as advisers to Margaret Thatcher, and both eventually ended up on the Devine government's payroll. In early 1987, dozens of photocopies of an essay by Pirie entitled "The Buying out of Socialism" circulated through the Saskatchewan civil service.[3] Tapes of Pirie's speeches made the rounds among members of the PC caucus, and there was a special screening of a three-hour British television documentary, *The Death of Socialism*, which celebrated the achievements of the Thatcher government.

In July 1987, the Fraser Institute, a right-wing think tank based in Vancouver, sponsored a conference on privatization. Saskatchewan sent the largest delegation of any government represented at the event. At this conference, the Saskatchewan delegates were brought up to date with the most recent thinking on privatization. That same fall, a right-wing lobby group called the National Citizens' Coalition brought Madsen Pirie to Regina, and 1,200 people came to hear him extol the virtues of privatization.[4] Meanwhile, outside the hall, a few dozen people gathered for a demonstration – the first sign of the political polarization that would soon develop. Although the dominant external influence on privatization in Saskatchewan was British, the American new right also had some input. Philip Fixler arrived from the Reason Foundation in Los Angeles to speak to the Regina Chamber of Commerce and the Saskatchewan Urban Municipalities Association. He told his audiences that everything should be privatized, including the police force and the fire department.[5]

Devine took the privatization plunge at the PC convention in November 1987, when he announced that all Crown corporations except the utilities were candidates for transfer to the private sector.[6] The government now had a clear ideological cause of the first order. It had come to this juncture as a result of a combination of circumstances: the need to rally a party that threatened to come apart; the need to divert public attention away from the government's poor record; the need to satisfy the ideological yearnings and patronage requirements of the Tory party rank and file; the availability of freshly minted privatization propaganda; and the hope that selling government assets would be as popular in Saskatchewan as it had apparently been in Britain.

The selling of privatization

An important step in implementing the privatization program was the establishment of a new government agency, the Department of Public Participation, whose job it was to supervise and coordinate all privatization activities. Chosen to head the department was Graham Taylor, who was known as a down-to-earth politician with "people skills." Devine thought he would be the ideal person to sell privatization.

The government was under no illusion that its new initiative would be instantly popular. Because of the province's social democratic past, Crown corporations were well-established and well-respected in Saskatchewan. Taylor knew he had to present privatization as non-threatening and non-revolutionary or there would be a backlash. He spoke reassuringly. "There's no need for everyone to get all excited and shook up about this," he said. "I don't want a fight. Let's talk about it as rational people. I'm not going to ram a whole bunch of things at the public."[7]

Taylor knew he needed to make people feel that privatization was of their own choosing. They had to be encouraged to think that they were participants and that privatization was being initiated at the grassroots. This was not all that easy, given that the grassroots were precisely where it was not being initiated – privatization was a classic example of a revolution engineered from the top. Nevertheless, it was absolutely crucial, from the public relations perspective, that privatization not be seen as the work of an elite from which only the elite would benefit. The public had to feel that it could participate – hence the choice of the name "Department of Public Participation" for the agency whose job it was to sell privatization. Taylor was candid about all this. "My role will be to talk to Saskatchewan people and I don't want any secrets. It's all going to be laid out," he reassured the public. "I don't want this to be a club for the elite, so to speak. These things will be offered in such a way that the ordinary person in Saskatchewan feels they have an opportunity to participate and see the value in doing it."[8]

The Department of Public Participation soon organized a series of public meetings in small towns across Saskatchewan to pitch privatization to voters. Graham Taylor described this well-orchestrated and costly exercise as "going right back to the roots of Athenian democracy."[9] He even proposed that the study of privatization be added to the school curriculum, an idea that was immediately attacked by NDP education critic Pat Atkinson. Education Minister Lorne Hepworth was forced to beat a hasty retreat on behalf of the government. "Schools under this PC government shall not be agents for dogma," he reassured parents.[10]

The Department of Public Participation had a private sector partner in its propaganda campaign. The Institute for Saskatchewan Enterprise, loosely modeled on the Fraser Institute and other right-wing "think tanks", was established by the province's business elite and given the job of coming up with the hard evidence to back up the government's claims for privatization.[11] The Institute billed itself as a non-partisan, non-ideological research organization. "It [privatization] is not ideology," asserted ISE president Roger Phillips, whose day job was head of Inter-Provincial Steel Company (Ipsco), "it's plain common sense."[12] Directing the Institute's research efforts was Morley Evans, once connected with the Reason Foundation in Los Angeles, a think tank devoted to privatization. No one was too surprised when the research reports emanating from the Institute uniformly endorsed privatization.

The new right's case for privatization

The arguments advanced for transferring government ownership and activity to the private sector are numerous and complex, but they can be briefly summarized under four headings. It was asserted that privatization (1) extended the benefits of share ownership to the people, (2) reduced government debt, (3) increased efficiency, and (4) stimulated an entrepreneurial culture. All these arguments were used by the proponents of privatization in Britain, and they also cropped up in Saskatchewan. However, not all the arguments worked equally well in both places. Some of Margaret Thatcher's pet justifications for privatization could not be used effectively by Grant Devine, and conversely, the Saskatchewan government developed variations on the standard arguments that weren't applicable to Britain. Saskatchewan made its own unique contribution to the privatization debate.

The 'shareholders' democracy' argument

This argument was based on the premise that government-owned companies were not truly owned by the people and that privatization would create a "shareholders' democracy" or a "people's capitalism." Ownership was "returned to the people," in the sense that a large number of individual citizens were given the opportunity to own shares. The social democratic concept of the people acquiring ownership through their government was thus turned on its head. The privatizers' message also contained a strong dose of populism. People were encouraged to think that they could have their own personal stake in the economy. Individual ownership was said to be much more concrete and meaningful than collective ownership.

Privatization experts like Madsen Pirie advised that government-owned enterprises should be sold so shares were distributed as broadly as possible; the worst possible scenario was the one in which the corporation was transferred to one buyer. The desirability of spreading ownership widely justified, at least in the minds of the privatizers, what would otherwise be considered dubious practices. For example, Pirie openly recommended selling public corporations at less than they were worth so that many people would be attracted to buying the shares: "You watch the big flotations in Britain and you see that several million new shareholders are attracted. There is invariably a premium. The price goes up on the first day, and everyone says the government sold it too cheaply. Yes, of course it did, because it's very important that the people who buy shares should perceive an immediate gain. That makes them support privatization."[13]

Contrary to what the privatizers claimed, the actual experience in Britain was that, in spite of heavy advertising and juicy incentives to buy shares, privatization did not lead to a "people's capitalism." In 1987, after four years of intensive privatization, only one in five British adults owned any shares. The shareholders who took advantage of the disposal of public assets tended to be, in the phrase of the *Times of London,* "the financially articulate middle class."[14] Because the government deliberately sold the shares at less than their real value, the price of the shares invariably went up as soon as they were traded on the open market. Many people were tempted to sell their shares to make a quick profit. And why not? If there were government giveaways lying around, one was a fool not to take advantage of them.

The result was that large volumes of shares were resold soon after the initial share issue, and the shares ended up concentrated in relatively few hands. In Britain, the number of shareholders in Cable and Wireless, a telecommunications company, fell from 150,000 to 26,000 within a year of its being privatized. The shareholders in British Aerospace declined in one year from 158,000 to 27,000. Despite the ballyhoo surrounding the transformation of British Telecom into a "shareholders' democracy," a third of the shares changed hands on the first day of trading. Within two years, the number of shareholders was down a third. The same pattern was observable among all the British privatized companies.

The Thatcher government sometimes attempted to legislate restrictions on share ownership, for example by limiting the number of shares in a company that one owner could hold, or by requiring that a fixed percentage of the shares be held by British citizens. This tactic worked poorly because market pressures built up to have the restrictions eliminated. Artificially limiting the number of people who could buy a certain share restricted the demand for the share and thereby lowered the price. The owners did not like to see the value of their shares depressed and constantly pressured the government to lift the restrictions. After all, the whole idea of privatization was that the market should prevail. In one instance, the Thatcher government tried to limit to 10 percent the shares owned by a single interest in Enterprise

Oil, formerly owned by the British government. Rio Tinto Zinc made a fool of the government by buying up 30 percent of the company.[15]

Critics also questioned the ethics of deliberately selling off public assets at less than their true worth. Was it fair for some people to receive a financial windfall at the expense of the rest of the population? A fortunate minority made a lot of money when the value of British Telecom shares rose by $2.3 billion (Canadian) on the first day they were traded on the stock exchange.[16] Generally speaking, privatization has been rewarding for the participants. A study by researchers at the London Business School showed that a purchaser of eleven privatization stocks between 1981 and 1987 would have earned a return of 166 percent on the investment, a performance two times better than that of the market as a whole. Those who held their shares for only a week after their issue made a quick killing of 32 percent, as compared with virtually no upward movement in the rest of the market in that same time span.[17]

Privatization was also a bonanza for advertising agencies, investment dealers, and stockbrokers. The advertising costs for the British Telecom sale alone were $67 million, and the underwriting fees another $185 million – a business deal that was virtually risk-free because the shares were underpriced.[18] When shares were purchased they were resold almost immediately, which meant that the broker collected two commissions. Little wonder that the investment services community "swarm[ed] around privatization as if it were a honey pot."[19]

All the evidence points to the conclusion that some gained a lot more from privatization than did others. Furthermore, the transformation of public corporations into private corporations did not turn them into democratic institutions; the individual with a few shares in a privatized company had virtually no say in how the company was run. The annual shareholders' meeting was a perfunctory affair, not exactly a vibrant example of grassroots democracy. And if it should happen that a single owner gained control of more than 50 percent of the shares, all pretence of democracy ended.

In Saskatchewan, the Conservative government tried to get

mileage out of the argument that privatization gave the residents of the province an opportunity to have a direct stake in the economy. Devine exploited this rhetoric when he claimed that his government was not "selling" the Crown corporations, but was "turning them back to the people."[20] Even the choice of the term "public participation" indicated the government's strategy of presenting privatization in a populist light.

A policy paper prepared by the Department of Public Participation took the line that the people did not really own the Crown corporations. Effective ownership was defined as the right to use the property at the owners' discretion, the right to alter the property, the right to exchange the property, and the right to sell, lend, give away, or bequeath the property.[21] The argument, basically, was that you don't own something unless you can sell it. By this definition, the residents of a province could not really "own" anything through their government, but only as individuals. The real owners of Crown corporations, according to this view, were senior politicians and bureaucrats. By contrast, the real owners of a private corporation were the shareholders who had the ability both to earn dividends and, if they chose, to sell their shares.

Interestingly, this line of argument came from the bureaucracy, not out of the mouths of politicians. One did not hear Tory cabinet ministers saying that the people of Saskatchewan did not own their Crown corporations. The argument itself hinged on whether or not one accepted the possibility of collective as opposed to individual ownership. Was it valid, for example, to say that the community "owned" a public park even though no member of the community had the right to sell the park? Similarly, did Saskatchewan people "own" the public power company, even though as individuals they did not have the ability to sell it?

Those who answered "yes" pointed out that the owners of a Crown corporation were citizens with votes. Through their elected representatives, they had a say in how the corporation was run, and politicians who wanted to be re-elected were well advised to heed what the shareholders had to say. Furthermore, the dividends earned by the corporation flowed to the public treasury, to the benefit of all the owners. From this point of view, it made little sense to say that privatizing a Crown corporation meant "turning it back to the people." At best, privatization meant turning it over to some of the people.

Even though Devine refrained from brashly asserting that the people of Saskatchewan did not own their Crown corporations, that idea was implicit in some of his public statements. For example, during the campaign to sell an issue of SaskPower bonds in 1988, he identified the true purpose of the exercise: "Our aim is not just to raise money for SaskPower, but to create participation from all walks of life in Saskatchewan. We're going to turn this province over to the people of Saskatchewan."[22] Devine obviously believed that the people of Saskatchewan did not already own and control SaskPower.

There was another dimension to the Tories' promotion of privatization as a movement to return ownership to the people. Public sector employees were encouraged to take over ownership of government enterprises or, alternatively, to do government work on a contractual basis. Devine suggested that employee ownership and contracting-out would appeal to hundreds of people who wanted something more fulfilling than a government job: "It's the excitement, it's the money, it's the satisfaction, the running your own show."[23] Privatization was not confined to Crown corporations. The Tory government envisaged a significant transfer of services from government departments to private companies which would be given government contracts. In the short term, some departments had more potential for privatization than others, but in the long term almost everything could be considered for removal to the private sector. This was the impression left by Public Participation Minister Graham Taylor. "There is quite a potential in the line departments – within highways, parks, and agriculture," was his assessment. "Where there is less opportunity, certainly in the beginning, are the soft side departments. I don't see it happening in health, or much of it in social services and not so much in education."[24]

The debt reduction argument

The second major rationale for privatization, one used heavily by Margaret Thatcher, was the need to reduce government debt to manageable proportions. The Tories in Britain inherited a huge debt when they came to power in 1979. Through privatization, the treasury received a massive infusion of cash. By 1987, the proceeds totalled 5 billion pounds a year, equal to 40 percent of the revenue the government was raising through the income tax. For those who wondered how long this could go on before the government ran out of things to sell, the answer appeared to be – quite a long time. Madsen Pirie projected that the British government could keep selling assets (water, electricity, the remainder of the auto industry, the steel industry, railways, the post office, coal mines, publicly owned land, etc.) at the same rate and not run out of things to sell for 40 years.

Selling assets seemed to have short-term rewards, but even that was deceptive. If the government sold an asset that was earning an income, the government did not improve its financial position unless it obtained a price that was larger than the debt that the income from the asset was carrying. Suppose that the asset earned $1 million a year and the money was applied to service a debt with an interest rate of 10 percent. That meant the $1 million in annual earnings was capable of carrying a $10 million debt. If the government sold the asset for less than $10 million, it would have made its financial position worse. If, for example, the asset were sold for $9 million, the government would have to find another source of revenue to cover the $1 million in debt that remained on the books.

The history of privatization in Britain has been the sale of profitable assets, not unprofitable ones. In some cases, where a part of a government-owned company was making money, that part was hived off and sold separately. The government was then stuck with the money-loser, while the money-maker joined the private sector. It was not surprising that profitable assets were easily sold. Who wants to buy an asset that is not capable of earning income?

The Saskatchewan government used the debt-relief argument selectively in its privatization campaign. When it came to debt, Devine had a public relations problem that Margaret Thatcher did not share. Whereas the British prime minister inherited a pile of debt when she assumed office, Devine took over a treasury with a modest surplus. Thatcher could blame the socialists for having plunged the country into debt and offer to clean up the mess, but what was Devine to say? He could hardly say that privatization was the solution to the problem his own government had created. Privatization had to be promoted as something good in itself, not just a handy solution for the government's self-created debt problem.

Although the Devine government avoided linking government debt to privatization, the argument was used with respect to specific Crown corporations. For example, SaskPower's debt was given as one of the main reasons for selling off the natural gas division. Since the Crowns were somewhat distanced from the government, it was easier to talk about their burden of debt without dealing with the awkward question, "What kind of management allowed this debt to accumulate in the first place?" Devine focused on the supposed need to exchange equity for debt. He argued, with more passion than logic, that "New York bankers" were the real owners of the heavily indebted Crown corporations and that the corporations had to be sold so that the people of Saskatchewan could own them. That was tantamount to saying that a homeowner with a mortgage should sell his house and then rent it as a means of acquiring ownership. Devine overlooked the fact that whereas debt can be paid off by the owners, the sale of equity means the loss of ownership.

The efficiency argument

A third argument for privatization was the assertion that the private sector was more efficient than the public sector – an article of faith among neo-conservatives, although it's proved hard to demonstrate. Government departments and corporations were said to be over-staffed with over-paid employees. Government enterprises were dismissed as inflexible, non-innovative, and chronic money-losers. The privatizers noted that when a privately-owned company failed to keep up with the competition, it lost money and ultimately faced bankruptcy. A government company, on the other hand, could anticipate a bail-out from the taxpayers.

The privatizers believed that only private ownership operating in a free market was capable of producing good corporate management, and that as soon as a state-owned enterprise was subjected to the discipline of the marketplace its performance would improve. This argument was weakened by the fact that some of the largest corporations considered candidates for privatization were monopolies, and neither a privately nor a publicly owned monopoly could ever be whipped into shape by the discipline of the marketplace. Moreover, other incentives, apart from market forces, existed to ensure that government-owned companies were well-run. Taxpayers did not like to see their money squandered and they were capable of registering a protest at the ballot box if public assets were mismanaged.

The biggest flaw in the neo-conservative argument that government corporations are necessarily inefficient is the contrary example provided by many successful Crown corporations. Studies have shown that Canada's well-established Crowns, generally those operating in railroad, air transport, telecommunications, and electrical generation industries, are as cost-efficient as their counterparts in the private sector.[25] In Saskatchewan it was not easy for the privatizers to say that the Crown corporations were flops, and Devine and his cabinet ministers pointedly avoided saying they were, even though they may have harboured the thought. This political fact of life was also appreciated in the Department of Public Participation. "Saskatchewan is not Britain, where the many nationalized industries that were sold were uniformly disliked," admitted a Department of Public Participation policy paper. "In Saskatchewan, our Crowns are widely appreciated."[26]

This did not mean that the Saskatchewan new right accepted the possibility that the public sector could function as efficiently as the private sector. Clearly, they did not. According to a briefing package circulated among the members of the provincial Tory caucus, privatization would result in substantial savings for the government.[27] Norman Baker, a Regina businessman, spoke for the hard-core privatizers when he advocated cutting back government to the basic role of keeping the peace. "Government can be involved in policing, in law and order," Baker declared. "But any place where private enterprise can do it, it should be done by private enterprise, because private enterprise does it better."[28]

The 'entrepreneurial culture' argument

The final major argument coming out of Britain was that privatization stimulated the emergence of an "entrepreneurial culture." It brought about, in the words of Madsen Pirie, "a complete social revolution."[29] A bracing free market environment inspired businessmen to compete aggressively rather than merely "get by." Privatization nourished the capitalist mentality. As people acquired their own economic stake, whether it was their own business or their own stock portfolio, they stopped thinking of themselves as workers or trade union members and started considering themselves part of the class of independent owners.

This was more than simply an economic change; it was a social and cultural transformation. According to the British privatizers, Britons had to be weaned off socialism if they were to be competitive in the global economy. Only then would the long British decline be arrested and national pride restored. So far the economic results of the neo-conservative program have been mixed. In 1989 Britain had an estimated 100,000 homeless people, and the poorest 4 million citizens had seen their living standards drop by an average 6 percent under Thatcher's administration.[30] Interest rates stood at 15 percent, inflation was up, and the pound was down.[31] The emphasis on market economics and individual acquisitiveness brought about the deterioration of public institutions and community services. The phrase "private affluence and public squalor" summed up the situation. The privatizers shrugged off such criticisms, saying that the true test of privatization was not so much the performance of the economy in a given time period, as the transformation in ideas and attitudes. They were heartened by what they saw as a movement away from a "dependency culture" to one that stood for rewarding individual effort.[32]

The privatization project in Saskatchewan aimed to do the same thing. The people in the forefront of the privatization drive believed they were not only restructuring the economy, but also bringing about a cultural revolution. This view was probably prevalent within the ranks of the Conservative party, but when front-line Tory politicians tried to convince the public, they did not engage in Crown-corporation bashing. Here was a distinct difference between the British and the Saskatchewan privatization campaigns. Just as there was no "socialist debt" in Saskatchewan to attack, there were no shoddily-run Crown corporations to rally public opinion against. Otherwise, the distaste many privatizers felt for the public sector would have been expressed much more openly. "If I had said in 1982 we'd have tens of thousands of people investing in Crown corporations, you would have asked what's that boy been smoking," Premier Devine told a PC fundraising dinner in April 1989. "In seven years, we have made changes beyond my expectations, which are fairly high." These changes were but a prelude. "We've got a tiger by the tail on a downhill drive and we're going for it."[33] The social democratic vision of Crown corporations taking a leading role in the economic development of the province would be erased. This was the death of socialism and Devine was the dragon-slayer.

Other cabinet ministers voiced similar thoughts less dramatically. Economic Development Minister Bob Andrew spoke professorially about a fundamental transformation of the "economic sociology" of the province. In his opinion, government enterprise was not capable of meeting the challenge of an intensely competitive global environment. A class of robust entrepreneurs in the private sector was needed. Andrew felt that without such a class of high-flying risk-takers, Saskatchewan would fall behind in the race for new products, markets and jobs.[34] Finance Minister Gary Lane agreed that the goal of the PC government was to awaken the entrepreneurial spirit of the people, a spirit that he accused the NDP of trying to smother.[35] At the heart of the privatization, added Graham Taylor, was the need "to change the thinking of Saskatchewan people."[36]

This theme of fundamental cultural change was picked up by some people outside the government. Herb Pinder, Jr., a Saskatoon businessman appointed to the board of directors of Saskoil, wrote: "We are experiencing our own mini-cultural revolution – Saskatchewan style."[37] Business columnist Paul Martin dubbed Grant Devine "the new Tommy Douglas."[38] Martin suggested that just as Douglas had steered the province in an entirely new direction in 1944 by implementing an economic development strategy based upon Crown corporations, Devine's privatization program represented a fundamental shift of equal historical significance.

The curious aspect of the government's bold declaration of fundamental change was that it was accompanied by assurances that privatization was in keeping with how things had always been done. The government wanted to have it both ways. It wanted to have a revolution, but remain true to Saskatchewan tradition. It wanted to privatize almost all the Crown corporations Tommy Douglas had established, but at the same time insist that Douglas would have wanted them privatized. This was what was unique about privatization in Saskatchewan. One cannot conceive of Margaret Thatcher claiming to be the spiritual descendent of Clement Atlee in the way that Grant Devine tried to appropriate the legacy of Tommy Douglas. Mrs. Thatcher kept it simple. She said that privatization spelled the end of the socialist era and signalled a clean break with the past. Devine muddied the issue. He announced that, yes, a new era was dawning, but, no, it would not be that different from the old era.

An example of this tactic was Devine's attempt to compare privatization with the co-operative movement. Historically, producer and consumer co-operatives were major forces in the development of Saskatchewan's economy. Rather than being dependent on business institutions headquartered in central Canada or elsewhere, local people got together to establish enterprises. They created the Saskatchewan Wheat Pool, the credit unions, the Co-operative oil refinery, the Co-operative insurance company, and other co-operatives that thrive to this day. Devine attempted to graft his privatization initiative onto this movement. "We are going to take what we've been blessed with, and we're going to get Saskatchewan people involved and roll up their sleeves as deep as they want to go," he declared. "It will go back to the co-op movement, it will go back to my grandparents that homesteaded here, it'll go back to anybody that ever believed in building – building, diversifying, growing, manufacturing, and providing opportunities for people all over this province."[39] Just as in a co-operative where every member has a share, Devine promised that privatization would extend share ownership to anyone who had the money to participate. "I want my share, my share, my share, my share. I want a crack at this; I want to vote on it. Very popular in Saskatchewan."[40] However, in his enthusiasm, Devine overlooked the fact that co-operatives, unlike private corporations, operate on the principle of one member, one vote. Furthermore, whereas co-operatives are locally controlled, there is no assurance whatsoever that a private corporation's shares which are traded on the Toronto or New York Stock Exchange would remain in Saskatchewan hands. Despite these important differences, Devine wanted to promote privatization as something compatible with the well-established and popular co-operative movement.

The other technique Devine used to play down the revolutionary nature of privatization was to link it with diversification. Throughout the years, diversification had been a long-standing goal of all Saskatchewan governments. The reason is rooted in the very nature of the economy. Saskatchewan has always made its livelihood exporting a small number of products – chiefly wheat, potash, uranium, oil, and a few others. The commodity markets are notoriously fickle; prices swing up and down, and boom alternates with recession. Governments, whether CCF, Liberal, NDP, or Conservative, have all tried to encourage manufacturing and diversify the economy beyond the resource base. In short, there was nothing more typically Saskatchewan than the desire to diversify. When Devine tried to tell people that privatization and diversification were intimately connected, this was another way of suggesting that privatization did not represent radical change.

It was understandable that the Devine government would want to blend continuity with discontinuity, revolution with evolution, in packaging privatization. In Britain, the old regime had been discredited, and Thatcher had no trouble blaming her political opponents for all of the country's economic woes. Even if the Labour party was not responsible for the loss of the empire and the decline of Britain, a scapegoat had to be found. The desire for fundamental change prepared the ground for Mrs. Thatcher's revolution. The situation in Saskatchewan was quite different. Like Britain, Saskatchewan had a large number of government-owned corporations and a left-of-centre party in power (though the Saskatchewan NDP was not nearly as left-wing as the British Labour party). The key difference was that when Devine launched his privatization revolution, the old regime had not been discredited. The NDP had presided over a strong economy, brought in eleven consecutive balanced budgets, and left the Tories a healthy surplus in the treasury. Faced with making a revolution when there was no pressing demand for one, Devine had to try to suggest that the revolution had a lot of non-revolutionary content.

The Devine government's adaptation of privatization to the Saskatchewan setting was not just a matter of style or rhetorical presentation. The Saskatchewan version of privatization was also less ideologically pure than the model held up by Madsen Pirie and the other philosophers of privatization. Privatization was supposed to mean the triumph of the free market and the end of government intervention in the economy, but that was not what it meant in Saskatchewan. The province's hinterland economy forced the Devine government to intervene extensively in the economy in support of private enterprise, completely contradicting the essential purpose of privatization. The arguments for privatization were either flawed, inapplicable to Saskatchewan, or both.

Notes for Chapter 8

1. *Debates and Proceedings (Hansard)*, Legislative Assembly of Saskatchewan, 12 December 1986, p. 204. 2. *Leader-Post*, 3 May 1984.

3. Interview, Peter Holle, 12 May 1989. 4. *Leader-Post*, 30 October 1987. 5. *Ibid.*, 2 February 1988. 6. *Ibid.*, Eisler, 14 November 1987.

7. *Globe and Mail*, 19 March 1988. 8. *Ibid.*, 20 March 1989. 9. *Ibid.* 10. *Leader-Post*, Eisler, 11 April 1989. 11. *Ibid.*, Eisler, 3 September 1988. 12. *Ibid.*, 29 October 1988.

13. Madsen Pirie, "Principles of Privatization," *Privatization: Tactics and Techniques* (Vancouver: Fraser Institute, 1988). 14. Herschel Hardin, *The Privatization Putsch* (Halifax: The Institute for Research on Public Policy, 1989). 15. *Ibid.*, p. 50. 16. *Ibid.*, p. 51. 17. *Globe and Mail*, 9 May 1989. 18. Hardin, pp. 64, 72. 19. *Ibid.*, p. 71. 20. *Leader-Post*, 16 January 1988. 21. *Public Participation: Some New Directions in Saskatchewan's Public Policy Agenda*,

Department of Public Participation, March 1989. **22.** *Leader-Post*, 9 July 1988. **23.** *Ibid.*, 16 January 1988. **24.** *Ibid.*, 25 January 1988. **25.** Tupper and Doern, "Canadian Public Enterprises and Privatization," in *Privatization, Public Policy and Public Corporations in Canada*, p. 23. **26.** *Public Participation: Some New Directions in Saskatchewan's Public Policy Agenda*, March 1989. **27.** Progressive Conservative Caucus briefing package, 5 May 1988. **28.** Adriane Paavo, "Privatization Man," *Briarpatch*, March 1988. **29.** Pirie, p. 5. **30.** *Globe and Mail*, 3 May 1989. **31.** *Leader-Post*, Richard Gwyn, 27 October 1989. **32.** *Globe and Mail*, 4 May 1989. **33.** *Leader-Post*, 22 April 1989. **34.** *Ibid.*, 21 March 1989. **35.** *Ibid.*, 20 April 1989. **36.** *Globe and Mail*, 20 March 1989. **37.** *Star-Phoenix*, 10 May 1989. **38.** *Ibid.*, 15 April 1989. **39.** *Debates and Proceedings (Hansard)*, Legislative Assembly of Saskatchewan, 20 March 1989, p. 259. **40.** *Ibid.*

9
PRIVATIZATION

◇ ——————————————— ◇

SASKATCHEWAN
FOR SALE

> We're going to make it very difficult for you
> people [the NDP] to take it over again, when
> you get back into power, if that ever happens.
> – *Deputy Premier* ERIC BERNTSON, *reflecting on
> what he hoped would be the permanence of
> privatization in Saskatchewan. Globe and Mail,
> 20 March 1989.*

The Devine government announced late in 1987 that it was going ahead with privatization in a big way. Almost all Crown corporations were up for sale, and a broad range of government services were being considered for transfer to the private sector. The Department of Public Participation was set up to ensure that privatizations were carried out in an orderly way and that potentially hostile interest groups were pacified. Although some of the early privatizations were executed rather ineptly, the process gradually became smoother. Through 1988, privatization rolled along without encountering too much in the way of open, public resistance.

The Crown corporations up for sale included SaskMinerals, the Saskatchewan Mining Development Corporation (SMDC), the general insurance side of Saskatchewan Government Insurance, the Saskatchewan Computer Utility Corporation, parts of SaskTel, the natural gas division of SaskPower, the Potash Corporation of Saskatchewan, Saskatchewan Government Printing, and Saskatchewan Forest Products. These enterprises varied widely in size and significance. The Printing Company, for example, sold for $1.5 million, while the assets of SMDC were valued at close to $1 billion. Large or small, big profit-makers or modest profit-makers, they were all slated for privatization.

The prelude to privatization: SaskPower bonds

The first stage of the privatization campaign was the marketing of SaskPower bonds. The bond issues served a dual purpose, raising capital for the power utility and at the same time getting people used to the idea of investing in Crown corporations. The personal savings of Saskatchewan residents formed a large pool of capital, estimated at $6 billion, which could be channelled into privatized companies. For this to happen, people would have to be made comfortable with the idea of risking their money through the purchase of shares. They had to be coddled and coaxed – trained to be risk-taking investors. The purchase of bonds was the first step; from there, they could be eased into the stock market.

This strategy explained the hoopla that surrounded the promotion of the SaskPower bonds. One would have thought that by the time the fifth series of the bonds went on sale in June 1988 most people would have been familiar with the product. Nonetheless, SaskPower spared no expense for television, radio, newspaper and billboard advertising. The exact cost was never disclosed by the government. Mail-outs went to every household in the province, and 27 public meetings were held to inform investors of the terms of the issue.

A bond purchaser had the option of paying a quarter of the purchase price as a down payment and borrowing the balance from SaskPower at an interest rate of 10.25 percent, with the loan repayable in three months. Once the bonds went on sale, the publicity machine moved into high gear. SaskPower announced that the first application came from Terry and Carolynn Meadows of Pense who bought $300 worth of bonds in their son's name. Daily news releases whipped up excitement, urging people to "buy your bonds, before they sell out."

At the close of the campaign, it was announced that applications to purchase $343 million worth of bonds had come from 41,748 Saskatchewan residents.[1] To ensure a wide distribution, the bonds were marketed in multiples of $100, with the maximum allowable purchase fixed at $100,000. They had a government-guaranteed interest rate of 9.25 percent, a rate that could be adjusted upward, but not downward.[2] But the most interesting feature was that the bonds could be either redeemed for cash or converted to Saskoil shares. By this means, bond buyers were being encouraged to become shareholders and participants in privatization.

SaskMinerals: How not to privatize

One of the ironies of these elaborate measures to promote "public participation" was that one of the first Crown corporations to be privatized went to two out-of-province buyers. The sodium sulfate division of SaskMinerals was sold to Kam Kotia Mines of Toronto for $12.1 million, and the peat moss division to Premier Sask of Riviere-du-Loup, Quebec for $3.4 million.[3] It was difficult to see how this transaction did anything to "turn the province back to the people" – a company that had been entirely Saskatchewan-owned was now entirely Ontario- and Quebec-owned.

SaskMinerals had been a case study of successful entrepreneurship in the public sector. Established by the T.C. Douglas government in 1946 to develop the province's deposits of sodium sulfate, a product used in the manufacture of pharmaceuticals, glass, detergent, and textiles, the company turned a profit in every year but one, that being 1972, when it lost $243,000. Accumulated net earnings over 40 years were $47,565,674. Far from being a burden on the taxpayers, SaskMinerals had paid the same royalties to provincial coffers as had private producers and, in addition, had paid substantial dividends. Its success was based on a commitment to research, innovation, and the development of new markets – a classic model of public sector enterprise.

Many aspects of the privatization were questionable. The price the province got was $5.5 million less than the company's book value as stated in the SaskMinerals annual report for 1988. It was also less than the profit the corporation had earned in its three best years. The government maintained the deal was a good one, but refused to make public the professional appraisal of the company's assets. The government also tried to argue that Sask-Minerals had to be sold because some of its equipment was worn out and needed to be replaced. For 40 years, the Crown corporation had been able to purchase new equipment and acquire new technology, but suddenly this was deemed to be impossible. Moreover, if the capital expenditures were profitable ones for a private company to make, why wouldn't they also be profitable for a public company?

The manner in which the sale was conducted also left much to be desired. The employees were not given a chance to purchase shares, and received only a vague promise of a profit-sharing plan from one of the new owners. There was no guarantee that the employees would even be able to keep their jobs. As privatization minister Graham Taylor bluntly informed the workers, "You cannot write in and bind companies' hands for years to come."[4] To make matters worse, the employees were given almost no advance information about what was going on. A few days before the deal became public knowledge, Taylor drove out to Chaplin, the site of one of the mines. He gave the employees a lecture about how they shouldn't fear change and that there was nothing to worry about, but refused to provide them with any details.[5]

The SaskMinerals privatization was a disaster from beginning to end. A profitable Saskatchewan company was sold to Ontario and Quebec corporations for a paltry sum. The employees were treated inconsiderately, and Saskatchewan people lost ownership and control of a valuable enterprise with an impressive track record.

SMDC: *Resource wealth and social responsibility*

Although the Saskatchewan Mining Development Corporation (SMDC) was sometimes confused with SaskMinerals, the two Crowns were very different operations. Whereas SaskMinerals produced modest amounts of sodium sulfate and was sold for only $15 million, SMDC owned rich, low-cost uranium mines and made a profit of over $60 million in 1987. The Devine government's plans to privatize SMDC were complicated by the Mulroney government's desire to unload the federal Crown corporation Eldorado Nuclear, so a scheme was developed to merge the two Crowns and then privatize them as a combined unit. The plan was more beneficial to Eldorado than to SMDC, given the very different histories of the two companies.

SMDC was a strong corporation with excellent prospects. It had assets in 1987 valued at $914 million, with revenues of $194 million for a return on equity of 20.2 percent. The corporation did not carry an excessive debt load, with the ratio of debt to equity being an eminently manageable 1.4:1. Over the years, SMDC had astutely acquired desirable properties, thereby positioning the company well to earn large future profits.[6]

Eldorado Nuclear had a less promising future. The federal Crown dated back to World War II when the Canadian government considered it important to have a secure supply of uranium for the production of nuclear weapons for the Western Allies. The corporation had done well financially until the mid-1960s when a glut in the world uranium market developed. In the mid-1970s, markets began to improve, and Eldorado undertook a major expansion at Beaverlodge mine in northern Saskatchewan and built major processing facilities at Blind River and Port Hope, Ontario. The Beaverlodge mine was not cost-competitive and had to be shut down in 1982. The processing facilities were also less profitable than expected, partly because the Canadian government stopped enforcing the policy that had required uranium concentrates to be upgraded prior to export. Owing to these two factors, Eldorado had a bleak balance sheet.[7]

Despite the mismatch, the federal and provincial Tory governments ordered the merger. The new company, called the Canadian Mining and Energy Corporation (Cameco), came into existence in October 1988. With assets of $1.6 billion, it was owned 61.5 percent by the government of Saskatchewan and 38.5 percent owned by the government of Canada, a split based on appraisals of the worth of the unmerged companies carried out by independent consultants. The plan was to privatize Cameco in stages, 30 percent within two years, 60 percent within four years, and 100 percent within seven years. Individual Canadian investors were limited to 25 percent of the shares and individual non-Canadians to 5 percent. In addition, non-Canadians were allowed a maximum of 20 percent of the votes cast at shareholders' meetings, and the government of Saskatchewan reserved the right to keep the head office in the province. Even before any shares were put on the market, the cries went up from the financial community that the restrictions on share ownership were too limiting. The writing was on the wall – market pressures were such that the people of Saskatchewan would in all probability eventually lose ownership and control of Cameco.

Equally unfortunate was the fact that ownership was being lost at a time when uranium was at the bottom of its price cycle. Some industry analysts forecast a significant upturn in prices in the early 1990s, when 130 nuclear reactors in various stages of construction around the world were scheduled to go into production. One expert predicted that the uranium industry would have to open a new mine of 3.56 million pounds capacity every year for the next ten years.[8] Judging from their investment plans, some private mining companies took these predictions seriously. Denison Mines, which accounted for about 5 percent of total global uranium production, sold off its oil and gas assets in 1989 in order to concentrate on uranium mining. It planned to develop two uranium sites, one in northern Saskatchewan and the other in Australia. Rio Algom also declared itself bullish on uranium and bought properties in Wyoming and New Mexico.[9] The government of Saskatchewan was hurrying to dispose of its mines at the very time when private companies were anticipating a uranium boom.

Privatization was not only ill-timed, it would do nothing to improve the efficiency of SMDC. The Crown corporation had been well-managed, a fact acknowledged by the man brought in from the private sector to take over the company. "Like many people, I probably had a misinformed judgment that Crown corporations were lax, did not have a purpose, probably were careless with money," said Bill Gatenby, who had been hired away from his former job as president of Texaco Canada Resources to head up Cameco. "I say honestly that through this merger process I found out I was 100 percent wrong."[10]

Deputy Premier Eric Berntson solemnly assured the workers at SMDC and Eldorado that the merger would not result in job losses. "You can rest assured the people who work at SMDC today will be working there at the new merged company as well," he said.[11] Five months later, Cameco announced the permanent lay-off of 170 employees, 100 of whom worked at the Rabbit Lake mine in northern Saskatchewan.[12] The reason given for the lay-off was not the merger as such, but rather the depressed uranium markets.

In addition to the usual considerations surrounding a privatization – the impact on employees, efficiency, revenues, and ownership – the sale of SMDC had some distinctive features. As a Crown, the corporation had given the government a "window" on the industry, making it easier to set appropriate taxes and devise suitable regulations. The Blakeney government had moved vigourously to capture maximum revenue for the province. This had been accomplished in an atmosphere of harmonious government-industry relations attributable in large part to the government's inside knowledge of how the industry operated. Crown ownership and effective taxation and regulation of the private sector went hand in hand.

A unique aspect of SMDC related to the nature of the uranium industry itself. It posed special threats to the health and safety of the workers and to the environment. Unlike a private company, which is narrowly focused on profit, a Crown corporation can have social, as well as economic, goals, and SMDC was able to set high standards for employee safety and environmental protection. While opponents of Crown ownership maintained that the government was in a conflict-of-interest position when it tried to regulate itself, the fact remained that the government ultimately had to take responsibility and be accountable for its decisions to the electorate. If a government places a high priority on the welfare of workers and preservation of the environment, a public corporation can be an instrument of that policy. By contrast, private corporations operating on market principles have the primary goal of making money for their shareholders.

Another dimension of SMDC's social policy role related to the location of the uranium industry in one of the most economically disadvantaged regions of Canada. Through policies designed to ensure that northerners received training and jobs as well as business opportunities spun off by the mining activity, the Blakeney government had tried to extend the benefits of mineral resource development to the native people of the area. Of course, this all cost money, and inherently conflicted with the desire of shareholders in private companies to maximize profits. The Devine government made it clear that in the conflict between profit-seeking shareholders and northern Saskatchewan's economy, the shareholders took precedence. In 1985 the Tories admitted that only 35 percent of the work force at Key Lake consisted of northern natives, in spite of the fact that the 1980 lease agreement between the government and the mine (half owned by SMDC) called for a 60 percent native work force.[13] A committee established to ensure compliance with the lease agreement had not even met since 1982.

SGI: 'A very well-run company'

Whereas SMDC had a short history dating back to the 1970s, the roots of Saskatchewan Government Insurance (SGI) went back to 1946. The insurance corporation had a solid reputation and was a fixture of the provincial scene, guaranteeing that its privatization would generate more controversy than the sale of SMDC. Stories of an impending sell-off began to drift into the media early in 1987. The rumours were fueled by a trip to England made by Joan Duncan, the minister responsible for SGI, to confer with Margaret Thatcher's privatization advisers. When the NDP called upon the government to hold public hearings, however, Deputy Premier Eric Berntson assured the public that the government had made no decision to sell SGI, and accused the NDP of jumping the gun.[14] That was in September. In October, Duncan announced that a proposal to privatize the general insurance side of SGI would soon be presented to Cabinet, but guaranteed that automobile insurance would continue as a Crown utility;[15] apparently, government auto insurance was still considered untouchable.

The government's case for privatizing SGI was not based on a belief in the superior efficiency of the private sector. Duncan emphasized that the Crown corporation was already operating efficiently: "SGI is a very well-run company with great growth potential."[16] Nor did the government argue that private capital had to be injected to ease a debt problem, because there was no debt problem. SGI made $19.8 million in 1988, the largest profit in its 40-year history. Even more impressive, it made an underwriting profit, which meant that income from insurance premiums exceeded claims and operating expenses, exclusive of investment income – a feat achieved by just ten of about 200 general insurance companies in Canada in 1987.[17]

The main argument advanced in favour of privatization was that it would allow the company to expand. Alex Wilde, the SGI president and an advocate of privatization, observed that the corporation already handled 40 percent of the general insurance sold in Saskatchewan; no further growth was possible unless it could reach beyond the borders of the province for new markets.[18] Grant Devine took up this theme. "Why confine ourselves to a Regina market, a Moose Jaw market, when we could have an international corporation?" he reasoned. "They [the NDP] can cry all they want, but they will find that when it happens, it will be very, very popular."[19]

Insurance industry officials wondered whether SGI would have such an easy time expanding beyond its borders. Jack Hamilton, general manager of the Insurance Brokers Association of British Columbia, pointed out that the B.C. market was already saturated, and to obtain a toe-hold there SGI would either have to undercut going rates or offer unique packages. In the highly competitive Canadian general insurance market, Hamilton reported, rates had already been cut to the bone and money was being lost. Walter Krochak, president of the Insurance Brokers Association of Alberta, echoed these remarks and pointed out that jumping borders was a two-way street – if SGI wanted to compete outside Saskatchewan, it could expect other private companies to move aggressively into its own home market.[20]

If the Devine government was convinced that there was an untapped insurance market in Alberta, Manitoba or elsewhere, it had the option of encouraging the private insurance companies based in Saskatchewan to go after those markets. The Saskatchewan Mutual Insurance Company, for example, was privately owned and headquartered in Saskatchewan and was presumably capable of expansion. There was no necessary link between a policy of expansion and a policy of privatization.

Furthermore, SGI's status as a Crown corporation gave it some unique advantages. Private insurance companies were obliged to pay federal corporate income tax, and to deposit reserves with the federal superintendent of insurance to protect policy holders in the event of bankruptcy. But as a Crown corporation backed by a provincial government, SGI was required to do neither, to the advantage of its bottom line. The existence of a publicly owned insurance company had the further advantage of giving consumers an alternative to the private and co-operative companies, thereby enhancing the competitive market place. Indeed, the competition offered by SGI exerted downward pressure on the rates charged by the private insurance sellers. When all the practical benefits of having a Crown corporation in the insurance business were considered, it was clear that the government's drive to privatize was based primarily on ideology, and hardly at all on pragmatic considerations – unless the pragmatic consideration was one of letting the private insurers raise their rates.

SaskTel: Piecemeal privatization

Although the Devine government promised during the 1986 election campaign not to sell SaskTel or any part of it, this was not a commitment it took very seriously. The telephone utility was carved up into units, some of which were sold. The computer division, for example, was transferred to Westbridge, a private computer services company. SaskTel International, a wholly-owned subsidiary that marketed SaskTel's technology and skills worldwide, was another candidate for privatization. In September 1987, Gary Lane, the minister responsible for the corporation, talked publicly about a share offering, but action was delayed.[21] Speculation also centered on Diginex, a division of SaskTel set up to serve the communication needs of businesses. Although a spokesman for SaskTel promised that Diginex would not be privatized and would continue as part of the Crown corporation, this assurance was greeted with skepticism. Assurances of this type had been given before, only to be broken later on.

Another component of SaskTel slated for privatization was the telephone directory division. A deal was consummated in 1989 whereby this highly profitable division was sold to a private company called DirectWest Publishers Ltd., which was owned 46 percent by the DirectWest employees, 44 percent by Brigdens, a privately owned publishing company, and 10 percent by SaskTel. The government did everything in its power to persuade employees to leave SaskTel and join the privatized company, including inviting them to a wine and cheese party featuring a slide presentation set to upbeat music, at the conclusion of which each employee was given a videotape of the sales pitch for home viewing.[22] Even more tempting were the financial incentives. Each worker buying shares in DirectWest qualified for federal and Saskatchewan tax credits totalling 40 percent of the amount invested to a maximum of $1,400. The government also offered interest-free loans for the share purchase. With terms like these, it was not surprising that 53 of the 81 permanent staff in the directories division opted to join the new company, and 80 percent of those bought shares.[23]

The employees were further reassured by the fact that DirectWest had a seven-year agreement to publish SaskTel directories. The new company would also be able to compete for other business, such as trade and data-base directories. If the company's gross revenues were below $23.5 million annually by April 1993, DirectWest could force a renegotiation of the contract or a sale of DirectWest's directory assets back to SaskTel on favorable terms. In other words, the employees were being given an escape hatch in case the venture did not work out.[24] It was also a good deal for Brigdens, which picked up 44 percent of the company for a mere $220,000. In the past, Brigdens had received printing contracts from both the Conservative government and the Conservative party, prompting NDP MLA Dwain Lingenfelter to refer to it as "the Tory printing company."[25] Patronage tarnished this privatization, and SaskTel lost a valuable source of revenue which had been used to subsidize other parts of the operation.

Westbridge: A government-assisted computer company

The privatizations of the computer division of SaskTel and the Saskatchewan Computer Utility Corporation (SaskComp) occurred at the same time. SaskComp had been established in 1973 to provide computer services to the Government of Saskatchewan. While it also offered its services to the private sector, 90 percent of its business was with the public sector. It made money during every year of its existence, and in both 1982 and 1984, annual net income was greater than the total equity in the company. In February 1988, SaskComp, the computer division of SaskTel, and two private companies (LeaseCorp and the Mercury Group) were brought together to form a new company – the Westbridge Computer Corporation. The merger of these diverse entities created an integrated computer company capable of supplying a wide range of computer services.

The new company was aggressive and expansion-minded. Leonard McCurdy, its president and chief executive officer, a 42-year-old former IBM employee, set his sights on making Westbridge "Canada's leading corporate computer solutions supplier to medium and large corporations."[26]

The growth strategy included the purchase of Management Services Ltd. (MSL), a Regina-based computer software company with 100 employees and $7.5 million in annual revenues. MSL had extensive contracts in the United States and gave Westbridge an entry into the American market.[27] In 1989 Westbridge bought all the outstanding shares of Superior Business Machines Ltd., a company that sold and serviced IBM office products and personal computers across the country. Superior, with headquarters in Montreal and with branches in many Canadian cities, employed 200 people.[28] Westbridge's rapid expansion made it the fastest growing company in the province, jumping from 43rd largest in 1988 to eighth place in 1989.[29] In the fiscal year ending 31 March 1989, it posted a net income of $5.5 million (after taxes) on revenue of $127.7 million.[30] McCurdy projected even greater things for the future. "This is our shot in Western

Canada – Saskatchewan – to build a multi-million-dollar company," he said. "This privatization is working gangbusters."[31]

Although the Devine government presented Westbridge as an example of the economic benefits created by privatization, the company was not entirely cut loose from the purse strings of the public sector. Westbridge was still 58.8 percent owned by the government of Saskatchewan, and received all the government's big computer services contracts. The company was not exactly freewheeling in the market on its own. It had a SaskPower contract worth $60 million, a SaskTel contract worth $100 million, as well as service agreements with a variety of government departments including finance, health, social services, highways, and agriculture. The steady cash flow from the public sector gave the company a valuable competitive edge. Help came in small, as well as large, ways. For example, when SaskPower instituted a personal computer purchase program for its employees, the only computer company allowed to make direct written proposals to the employees was Westbridge. Only Westbridge had permission to set up personal computer displays at SaskPower offices around the province.[32]

McCurdy as much as admitted that the Tory government still had a hand on the wheel of the company. "The government wants to make sure this is being done properly," he said. "Obviously, if it weren't, it would represent high risk in terms of all privatizations."[33] This also explained why all the government computer business went to Westbridge – their privatization flagship could not be allowed to sink.

Saskoil: Shareholders' interest versus Saskatchewan's interest

Saskoil was privatized before the 1986 election, but significant developments also occurred in the government's second term. A second share offering, which took place in July 1987, raised $50 million and reduced the government's stake in the company from 58 percent to 47 percent. The day after the shares were issued, they traded on the stock exchange for $8.50, nearly a dollar more than the offering price. In addition, Saskatchewan purchasers received a tax break of $2.25 a share. With incentives like these, it was little wonder the issue sold out. As opposition leader Allan Blakeney pointed out, "Obviously we can get everybody to invest if they are all going to get a major bonus from the Saskatchewan treasury."[34] Further share issues reduced the government's stake to 25 percent.[35]

In the fall of 1987, Bill Douglas, who had been president and chief executive officer of Saskoil for five years, was replaced by Ted Renner. The reason for the change, according to Herb Pinder, Jr., Saskoil's chairman of the board, was that Douglas was not "tough enough." Pinder believed that, as a private company, Saskoil needed a hard-driving entrepreneur at the top.[36] Renner, the former president of Mark Resources in Calgary, declared that his objective was to make Saskoil "a world class company, one that would be among the top 30 oil and gas producers on the Toronto Stock Exchange."[37]

One of his first steps was to "innovate the cost-control side" – in other words, cut costs. Soon after his arrival, about a dozen senior employees, including two vice-presidents, were fired.[38] Renner aimed to transform Saskoil into an aggressive, dynamic, profit-driven company: "I'm hoping to get our finance guys challenged. We want our people to stretch. We have reservoirs, technology and research. Why can't we be industry leaders?"[39] The new president's approach was symbolized in a major remodelling of the company's corporate offices. The quiet, understated earth tones were abandoned in favour of up-scale blue-grey glass and chrome.[40] Shortly afterwards, the decision was made to construct a new building in Regina for the company's head office.

Renner set his sights on expansion and diversification. For $325 million, Saskoil bought additional reserves of 787 billion cubic feet of natural gas and 495,000 undeveloped exploration acres from SaskPower.[41] The timing of the purchase was excellent for Saskoil, but terrible for SaskPower, because natural gas prices were depressed. SaskPower had regarded these assets as an insurance policy, to be called upon during some energy crisis in the future. It had developed the reserves sufficiently to make them self-supporting, but no real effort had been made to maximize profitability. With these acquisitions, Saskoil could now increase production from 55 million cubic feet per day to 160 million cubic feet per day just by developing existing reserves, and exploration on the 495,000 undeveloped acres would add additional volume. This open-ended volume potential set the SaskPower purchase apart from normal sales transactions of this kind. According to the *Financial Post's Investor's Digest*, "On any basis of comparison, it is obvious Saskoil acquired the SPC assets at a very low price...We cannot overemphasize the opportunities presented by the acquisition."[42]

The development of the properties purchased from SaskPower was expected to result in a rapid expansion in Saskoil's natural gas sales and profit growth. Deregulation of natural gas, instituted by the Devine government, provided opportunities for natural gas producers to market increasing volumes directly to local distribution companies. In 1987, before purchase of the SaskPower properties, Saskoil's natural gas sales averaged 11.5 million cubic feet per day (mmcf/d). In 1988, sales increased to about 58 mmcf/d, and were forecast to rise to between 190 and 210 mmcf/d by 1990.[43]

Saskoil's expansion program continued with the purchase of oil and gas assets from the Inter-City Gas Corporation of Winnipeg for $111 million. This enabled Saskoil to balance its oil and gas reserves, with natural gas making up 55 percent of the total. It also reduced the company's dependency on heavy oil to the point where 75 percent of total oil production now came from light and medium crudes. Another acquisition was Metro Gas Marketing Inc., which gave the corporation increased capacity to market natural gas and the control of related pipeline space.[44]

Saskoil's assets increased from $300 million at the time it was privatized to about $1 billion in 1989. This was partly the result of the sale of the natural gas reserves of SaskPower for a low price. The beneficiaries of the transaction were the shareholders of Saskoil, and the losers were the owners of SaskPower, the residents of Saskatchewan. They suffered a loss in another sense, too. Saskoil's accumulated tax benefits, made up of all the tax write-offs it did not require as a Crown corporation, were inherited by the privatized version of the company. This meant that Saskoil would not have to pay corporate taxes for years. The benefits of

Crown status, which had once been shared equally by all Saskatchewan residents, were essentially transferred to the private shareholders, most of whom did not live in Saskatchewan. By January 1988, 75 percent of the Saskoil shares available on the open market were owned by non-residents.[45] Notwithstanding the government's promises, the benefits of owning Saskoil were leaving the province.

Employee buy-outs: The preferred method of privatization

Not every privatization initiative of the Devine government was a bad move. The sale of the Saskatchewan Government Printing Company is an example of the most socially desirable type of privatization – the employee buy-out. This Crown had fallen on hard times after 1982 because the Devine government gave increasing amounts of its printing work to private firms, and the private companies had mounted a campaign to have the government-owned printing company completely dismantled. The workers at Saskatchewan Government Printing saw employee-ownership as a means of saving their jobs.[46] Although 22 employees became shareholders in the operation, 51 percent of the shares were held by one person. The government was anxious to see the privatization succeed and went to great lengths to ensure that all the employees participated. When eleven of them showed no interest, each employee was given $2,000 to purchase shares.[47] The terms of the sale were also generous, with the $1.5 million purchase being financed through a venture capital corporation set up for the purpose by printshop workers, thus giving the new employee-owners a 40 percent tax break. In addition, the venture company received a government loan covering 30 percent of its financing needs at an annual rate of 10 percent, as well as an interest payment holiday for the first year of the five-year deal.[48]

The privatization was cushioned in yet another way. At the time of the sale, government business accounted for $1.7 million, or about 85 percent, of the work done by the printing company. The government guaranteed a certain amount of work for the next five years, to allow the company to adjust to life in the private sector. The amount of guaranteed work was to gradually decline over the five-year period until the company stood completely on its own.[49]

Another privatization which featured an employee buy-out involved some of the holdings of the Saskatchewan Forest Products Corporation. In June 1988, more than 3,000 people gathered at a park near Meadow Lake, 156 kilometers north of North Battleford, for a barbecue and a celebration. The occasion was the announcement that two sawmills, one at Meadow Lake and the other at Green Lake, had been privatized. The new company, called NorSask Forest Products, was owned equally by two partners: the Meadow Lake Tribal Council, made up of ten local Indian bands, and the employees of the mills. Of the 157 employees, 90 percent were shareholders. The employees retained their pre-privatization wage levels and benefits, and the old management, which now held 58 percent of the shares, stayed in place. NorSask paid $6 million for the mills: $1 million up front and the remaining $5 million over the next five years. The government absorbed the debt carried by the two sawmills so that the new owners began with a clean balance sheet. The size of the debt was not revealed, but one official estimated it to be more than $10 million.[50]

This was a textbook privatization. Rather than being fired or losing benefits, workers became co-owners, which would presumably give them an added incentive to be productive. The large native population in the area also gained because of the equity participation of the Tribal Council and because the largely native communities were given the first right to timber harvesting, transportation and reforestation contracts in the region. Of all the privatizations carried out by the government, this was one of the most progressive and well-executed.

Contracting out: The privatization of government services

Although the sale of Crown corporations attracted most of the attention, the privatization campaign also included the contracting out of government services. This began tentatively in the first term when then-Highways Minister Jim Garner gave 394 employees what he called "the opportunity to transfer to the private sector."[51] The privatization generated a great deal of adverse publicity, especially when it was learned that $40 million worth of highway equipment had been auctioned off for $6 million.[52] The move to eliminate the government presence in highway construction and repair work also opened the door to allegations of patronage, cost-cutting, and bid-rigging.

The government's argument was that private contractors could do the work more cheaply. Matt Campbell, the president of the Saskatchewan Road Builders and Heavy Construction Association, cited statistics showing that in 1984, 45,900 tonnes of paving were put to tender at an average price of $11.20 a tonne; just three years later, in 1987, 84,700 tonnes were put out to tender at a cost of just $8.84 a tonne.[53] However, he failed to point out that the fall in the price of oil had made asphalt less expensive, and, because of government cutbacks to highway construction and maintenance, the road-building industry was working at only 65 to 70 percent capacity, a circumstance that tended to keep prices down.[54] There seemed to be agreement that bids for road construction work in remote areas had risen on account of privatization because private contractors in those areas knew they did not have to compete with low government bids for the work.

Any savings that were realized from privatization appeared to be at the expense of the workers. Government highway workers were unionized, but the employees of private contractors were not. In 1988, unionized operators of light trucks, land packers and oilers made between $10.54 and $11.27 an hour, while employees of private roadbuilders were getting $9.95 an hour, and worked a longer week which gave them fewer opportunities for overtime.[55]

Apart from highways and a few minor services like court reporting, the Tories steered away from contracting-out until after the 1986 election. With the renewal of their mandate, however, they again tried to present privatization in a positive light. Public Participation Minister Graham Taylor invited government employees to half-day seminars to hear about the advantages of quitting their jobs and doing the same work on a contractual basis. A privatization "hot line" was set up to handle inquiries.[56] The message was that privatization was not something for civil servants to fear, but rather an opportunity to be seized.

The argument found few takers among those whose jobs would be privatized. An exception was the audio-visual tape duplication and film/video loan operation of the Department of Education. Bruce Solilo, a technician in the media services branch of the department, organized a company to do the job on contract. Sixteen employees were affected by the change, eight of whom joined Solilo's company. The others were protected from lay-off by the union contract and had the right to bid for other government jobs.[57]

A more significant privatization in education was the expansion of private vocational schools. In 1989, there were 5,000 students in 55 such schools, compared to 1,600 students in 16 schools in 1982. Government supervision was inadequate, resulting in complaints from students and staff of shoddy courses, lax admission requirements, late paycheques and high dropout rates. The better-run private schools urged more stringent regulations to preserve the reputation of their institutions. The irony of this venture in the privatization of schooling was that it was funded through the public purse – few students could afford the $2,000-$6,000 tuition fees without government student loans.

One of the government departments most affected by privatization was Parks and Recreation. In May 1987, 10 condominiums and 25 cabins at Duck Mountain Provincial Park were leased to businessmen Darryl and Vaughn Binkley and their partner John Dutchyshyn. In return for taking over these facilities built entirely with public money, the Binkleys were required to pay the provincial treasury 7.5 percent of gross sales. In addition, the leaseholders received a $375,000 government grant to help build a new $1.3-$1.4 million lodge. As a result of the privatization, fifteen permanent seasonal jobs at Saskatchewan Government Employees Union rates were lost. "There would never be a profit [with union wages]," explained Vaughn Binkley. Critics of privatization say the Duck Mountain deal has cost the provincial treasury revenues; the actual amounts of money involved are in dispute. Although the businessmen denied that political connections helped them to obtain the leases, one of the partners had been an executive assistant to provincial Tory cabinet minister Neal Hardy and was active enough in the party to contest a federal riding nomination.[58]

Deals of this kind were made in other provincial parks where rental accommodation, golf courses and ski lifts were turned over to private businessmen. As many as 31 campgrounds, ranging from mere campsites to small beach-front parks, fell into private hands. The Moose Jaw Wild Animal Park was leased to entrepreneurs who then turned to the government for grants and loans.

The Saskatchewan Government Employees Union opposed the privatizations on the grounds that well-paying, secure jobs were being exchanged for minimum-wage, short-term jobs with private operators,[59] and that the profit motive conflicted with the goal of avoiding excessive commercialization of the parks. In Cypress Hills Park, for example, no environmental impact study was done prior to the construction of a hotel, new road, and parking lot. Several thousand lodgepole pine, a tree that grows naturally in Saskatchewan only in the Cypress Hills, were cut down to make room for the development. Privatization and user-pay also resulted in steep increases in fees for certain services such as golf course green fees and ski lift tickets. Because the revenues from profitable services now flowed to private entrepreneurs, the parks could no longer use profits to subsidize low-enrollment programs such as swimming lessons and guided nature hikes. The government defended privatization by saying that private investors were building new facilities, but failed to acknowledge that the profit motive distorted public policy, harmed the natural quality of the parks, and denied reasonable access to all citizens regardless of income.

A similar issue involving a conflict between profit-making and the public good arose when the government tried to privatize liquor vending outlets. Graham Taylor stated that buying into liquor board stores "could be just the kind of thing that employees could feel good about."[60] The employees did not see it that way. Their union cited studies linking private sales to increased consumption of liquor, especially among young people. Research also indicated that the public purse received more revenue from alcohol sales when profits were not shared with private operators.[61] To combat the privatization, the union took out a series of strongly-worded radio and newspaper ads featuring a liquor board employee and the caption, "I am not saying that all special vendors will sell to minors, but I am sure a lot of them will, to make that extra profit."[62] The Regina Chamber of Commerce and other business organizations considered the ads an attack on the morals of businessmen, and the SGEU was forced to apologize, but the hardball tactics seemed to work, because the government backed off from its plans to privatize the sale of liquor.

Privatization rampant

Throughout 1988 and early 1989, while announcement followed announcement of Crown corporations put up for sale or public services contracted-out, there were few signs of strong public opposition to the Devine government's privatization campaign. People seemed to have adopted a "wait-and-see" attitude. At a Progressive Conservative fund-raising dinner in April 1988, Oliver Letwin, a British privatization guru hired by the Devine government, praised the Saskatchewan privatization program as one of the best-planned schemes he had seen. He warned, however, that the government should expect some resistance. "It's not going to be a smooth ride and you shouldn't expect it to be," he cautioned. Then, gesturing to Devine, who was sitting next to him, Letwin continued, "But if ever I've seen a leader capable, he is right here."[63]

If the Tories were going to have a rough ride, this was not obvious in June 1988, when the government released a poll suggesting that 53 percent of those surveyed said they supported privatization if it led to economic growth and job creation. The poll seemed to show that privatization was not opposed on ideological grounds; people apparently did not mind public assets being transferred to the private sector as long as there were tangible economic benefits.[64] Letwin was sufficiently encouraged to declare that the pace of privatization was "about right." He said that there were two mistakes that could be made in the "privatization game." One was to go too fast; the other was to suppose that, because things were going slowly, progress was not being made. He was sure that gradually the privatization concept was being accepted. "I think what is important is to develop – slowly and effectively – momentum."[65]

Letwin may have been right. In 1988, opposition was centred in the NDP and the unions, but there was no evidence of a widespread public rejection of privatization. For the time being, privatization was rampant. Only later did it become clear that many people were beginning to wonder whether the government was going too far. Given the right kind of issue and the right opportunity, the latent opposition to privatization could explode, and in April 1989, it did.

Notes for Chapter 9

1. *Leader-Post*, 9 July 1988. 2. *Ibid.*, 7 June 1988.
3. *Globe and Mail*, 29 March 1988. 4. *Ibid.* 5. *Leader-Post*, Johnstone, 26 March 1988.
6. *Ibid.*, 14 April 1988. 7. Doug McArthur, "An Analysis of the Merger of SMDC and Eldorado and their Subsequent Privatization," in *Minutes of Proceedings and Evidence of the Legislative Committee on Bill 121*, House of Commons, Issue 4, 19 May 1988. 8. *Globe and Mail*, 30 May 1989. 9. *Ibid.* 10. *Leader-Post*, 8 July 1988. 11. *Ibid.*, 24 June 1988. 12. *Globe and Mail*, 29 March 1989. 13. *Leader-Post*, 24 May 1985.
14. *Ibid.*, 19 September 1987. 15. *Ibid.*, 14 October 1987. 16. Moose Jaw *Times Herald*, 8 June 1987. 17. *Leader-Post*, 6 June 1989. 18. *Ibid.*, 23 July 1988. 19. *Ibid.*, 30 September 1987. 20. *Leader-Post*, 23 July 1988.
21. *Ibid.*, 24 September 1987. 22. Interview, Jeff Smith, 27 June 1989. 23. *Leader-Post*, 22 July 1989. 24. *Ibid.* 25. *Leader-Post*, 8 March 1989.
26. *Ibid.*, 13 March 1989. 27. *Ibid.* 28. *Ibid.*, 8 July 1989. 29. *Star-Phoenix*, 10 May 1989. 30. Westbridge Computer Corporation, Annual Report, 1989. 31. *Star-Phoenix*, 4 May 1989. 32. *Leader-Post*, Eisler, 8 July 1989. 33. *Financial Times*, 20 March 1989.
34. *Leader-Post*, 7 August 1987. 35. *Star-Phoenix*, 30 March 1989. 36. *Leader-Post*, 10 December 1987. 37. *Ibid.* 38. *Leader-Post*, 26 February 1988. 39. Paul Martin, "Change the Only Constant," *Saskatchewan Business*, June 1988. 40. *Leader-Post*, 4 April 1988. 41. *Investor's Digest*, 7 March 1989. 42. *Ibid.*, 5 July 1988. 43. *Ibid.*, 7 March 1989. 44. *Leader-Post*, 4 April 1989. 45. *Globe and Mail*, 22 January 1988.
46. *Leader-Post*, 23 September 1989. 47. *Debates and Proceedings (Hansard)*, Legislative Assembly of Saskatchewan, 20 March 1989, p. 255. 48. *Leader-*

Post, 11 March 1989. **49**. *Star-Phoenix*, 7 December 1988. **50**. *Leader-Post*, 17 June 1988.

51. *Commonwealth*, March 1989. **52**. *Ibid.* **53**. *Saskatchewan Business*, January/February 1988. **54**. *Leader-Post*, 26 January 1988. **55**. *Ibid.* **56**. *Leader-Post*, 13 October 1988. **57**. *Star-Phoenix*, 14 October 1988. **58**. Adriane Paavo, "Big Great Country," *Briarpatch*, July/August 1989. **59**. *A Brief to the Government and People of Saskatchewan by the Provincial Parks Workers Committee of the SGEU*, April 1988. **60**. *Leader-Post*, 7 June 1988. **61**. *A Brief on Behalf of Saskatchewan Liquor Board Employees Members of SGEU*, May 1988. **62**. *Leader-Post*, Johnstone, 10 December 1988.

63. *Ibid.*, 23 April 1988. **64**. *Leader-Post*, Eisler, 14 June 1988. **65**. *Ibid.*, 8 July 1988.

10

THE MOMENTUM SHIFTS

Only government-owned utilities will be exempt
from a major policy of privatization that will
unfold in the coming months.
– GRANT DEVINE, *Leader-Post*,
14 November 1987.

At the opening of the legislature in March 1989, Grant Devine declared that the main business of the session would be the privatization of three of the province's largest and most prominent Crown corporations: Saskatchewan Government Insurance, the Potash Corporation of Saskatchewan, and the natural gas division of SaskPower. Exuding confidence and determination, Devine predicted that the privatizations would be extremely popular. He said it was the end of the line for the New Democratic Party – their "Alamo," their "Waterloo." Brandishing a copy of *Newsweek* with a cover story entitled "The Decline of the Left," he bashed the NDP as a "radical, left-wing organization" which was out of step with the times: "The whole world is opening up. If Mikhail Gorbachev was the premier of Saskatchewan, he'd be way out ahead of me."

According to Devine, people around the world were excited about privatization in Saskatchewan. In Europe they talked about little else: "It's all over Europe that we have opportunities in Saskatchewan. The French are phoning, the Germans are phoning, companies are phoning."[1] Here at home, the people couldn't get enough of privatization: "They've got the bit in their teeth now and they're saying, 'I like this.'" Devine was riding a triumphant wave of his own creation. The key was momentum; if enough people began to think privatization was unstoppable, it would be.

The Potash Corporation of Saskatchewan

The Potash Corporation of Saskatchewan (PCS) had been the pride of the Blakeney government, a powerful symbol of the NDP philosophy of natural resource development through public enterprise, and the Tories seemed to take particular delight in undoing what their opponents considered a major accomplishment. Although the *Globe and Mail* wondered whether the privatization might be described as "the revenge of the nerds," the Devine government saw itself as striking a blow for private enterprise. It was oblivious to the fact that in this case private enterprise meant out-of-province and foreign ownership of a major resource industry.

The preliminary moves

The first steps leading to the privatization of PCS can be traced back to the days immediately following the 1986 election, when Gary Lane was appointed minister responsible for the corporation and Paul Schoenhals, who had lost his seat in the election, became the chairman of PCS's board of directors. In March 1987 most of PCS's senior executives were fired and replaced with a new management team.

The new president was Chuck Childers, an American and the former vice-president of the International Minerals and Chemical Corporation (IMC), the Potash Corporation's chief competitor. Childers was a friend of Schoenhals, the two having met on several occasions when Schoenhals was Minister of Energy and Mines. Shortly after the 1986 election, Childers invited Schoenhals and his wife to Chicago for a few days' holiday, where the two friends played some golf and took in a Blackhawks hockey game as well as some professional basketball.[2] When Schoenhals was casting about for a PCS president to prepare the corporation for sale, he immediately thought of Childers. Childers accepted, bringing with him another top IMC executive, William Doyle, who became the president of the PCS sales division. The new management moved quickly to cut staff, firing 115 non-union and 55 union workers in 1987.[3] This was followed, in 1988, by the shutdown of the Cory mine, throwing 200 miners out of work. The next step to get the corporation ready for privatization was the transfer of $662 million of PCS debt to the Crown Management Board, the holding company for the Crowns. This made the Potash Corporation much more attractive to a buyer, who would be able to assume the assets without the liabilities.

At this point, the owners of two nearly depleted New Mexico potash mines inadvertently threw a wrench into the Saskatchewan government's plans when they accused Saskatchewan producers of dumping their product in the United States market at less than the cost of production. The Americans enlisted the support of New Mexico Senator Peter Domenici and mounted a powerful lobby which resulted in a ruling from the United States Department of Commerce in August 1987 which found the Canadian producers guilty of dumping, and imposed heavy retaliatory duties. This meant that an extra levy was added to the purchase price of any potash from Canada sold in the United States. The level of duty on Saskatchewan potash averaged 43 percent, but there were variations from company to company. Central Canada Potash, for example, was hit with a levy of 85.2 percent, while IMC got off fairly lightly at 9.1 percent. PCS was in the middle range at 51.9 percent.

The American government's trade action threatened the viability of the Saskatchewan industry, which supplied 70 percent of the potash consumed in the United States. Devine had up to this time urged a policy of friendly co-operation, even suggesting at one point that the best way to resolve disagreements with the Americans was "to go down there and give them a big hug." Now he adopted a bombastic "get tough" stance: "We're the OPEC of potash...The government of Saskatchewan and the people of Saskatchewan are going to be deciding the future of our resources – not another country, not the U.S. Congress, not anybody else."[4] At the height of the dispute he even threatened to cut off all potash exports to the United States.[5]

Devine was understandably embarrassed by the American ruling. The United States, whose political and economic system he greatly admired, had delivered Saskatchewan's potash industry a serious blow. Why had the U.S. put its own economic interests ahead of those of Saskatchewan? For Devine, the real villain was, of course, the NDP. "The NDP, the black-armed people from the socialist side, nationalize an industry, burn the American flag and will not even stand with their allies in the free world and defend . . . this part of the world when it comes to NATO," the premier raved, "and the Americans are looking up here and saying, 'What kind of people are these?'"[6]

In fact, what was happening was that New Mexico producers were trying to keep their inefficient mines operating in the face of inexpensive potash coming into the United States from Canada. Their first concern was not to register a protest against the opposition party in Saskatchewan; nor was the PCS likely their primary target, since many of the privately-owned potash companies had higher duties slapped on them than did the public corporation.

The potash crisis led to the introduction in the Saskatchewan legislature of the Potash Resources Act, which gave cabinet the power to control the volume of potash produced in Saskatchewan in any given period, and provided for the appointment of a board to allocate production levels among the companies. Restricting the supply of potash would cause the price to go up, answering the New Mexico producers' complaint that low prices were driving them out of business. With half the productive capacity of the Saskatchewan industry, and with Saskatchewan supplying about 40 percent of the world's potash, PCS had considerable market leverage, and in September 1987 it announced a price increase from $58 to $93 U.S. per tonne. The other companies operating in Saskatchewan followed suit, as did producers in Israel, Jordan, and Europe.[7] The price rose to $101 U.S. per tonne before stabilizing, and the New Mexico producers, satisfied with the higher prices, voluntarily dropped their anti-dumping suit for a five-year period.[8]

The crisis had been resolved through the Potash Resources Act and through PCS. When PCS cut back production, no private producer moved to increase production because of the threat of legislated controls. But at the same time, PCS bore the brunt of the cutbacks – while the private companies in Saskatchewan operated at 80 to 85 percent capacity, PCS operated at only 55 percent. At the same time that PCS closed one of its mines, two nearly played-out mines in New Mexico re-opened.[9] PCS president Chuck Childers as much as admitted that his corporation was the industry scapegoat. While in Japan on a trade mission, Childers had discussions with Koichi Kamashita, the general manager of the Mitsui and Company fertilizer division. Kamashita related what Childers had said about the way PCS was being treated compared with the other producers: "It is PCS that is adjusting its product amount so prices can go up. It is being done on the sacrifice of PCS, Mr. Childers said."[10]

By the middle of 1988, a mood of quiet optimism began to overtake the potash industry. Prices were up and markets seemed to be improving. John Douglas, an industry consultant and former manager of the U.S. Fertilizer Development Center, forecast that world demand for potash would increase by 1 million tonnes annually for the next three to five years, and PCS was well positioned to take advantage of the upswing in the market.[11] Once the initial capital investment in a mine had been made, there were relatively few additional capital costs. PCS, operating at only 55 percent capacity, made a profit of $106 million in 1988; if demand for potash increased, the corporation would likely capture most of the increased market, and the bulk of the additional revenues would be pure profit.

As PCS began to look like a more attractive investment, it became easier to sell. During his trip to the Far East in early 1989, Premier Devine openly hawked the corporation, which he seemed embarrassingly eager to unload. Hardly a day went by when there was not an announcement of a substantial percentage of PCS being offered to the governments of China, India, South

Korea, and Japan. In fact, by the end of the trip the premier had, according to press reports, offered for sale more than 100 percent of the corporation. Clearly Devine saw nothing wrong with selling more than 50 percent of the corporation to foreign interests,[12] and he did not seem to be afraid that if PCS were sold to the governments that purchased potash from Saskatchewan, the new owners would have an interest in keeping the price low. Nor did he deal with the contradiction inherent in selling a 25 percent interest in PCS to the government of China, while maintaining that the government of Saskatchewan should have no equity.

As Devine began to feel the political heat generated by his statements, he revised his position. In a press release issued from Korea, where he was trying to sell part of PCS to the Namhae Chemical Corporation, he promised that a majority of the company would stay in Canadian, though not necessarily Saskatchewan, hands.[13] He denied a story that had appeared in a potash industry publication claiming that he had offered a ten-year payment holiday to the government of India if it purchased shares in PCS. The confusion created by Devine was not dispelled when PCS minister Gary Lane announced that the cabinet had not yet discussed what portion of the corporation would be sold to foreigners.

Privatizing PCS: Pros and cons

Despite this shaky start, in April 1989 the government introduced the bill to privatize PCS. Bill 20 stipulated that a maximum of 45 percent would be sold to foreign investors, and that foreigners would not be allowed to cast more than 25 percent of the votes at annual meetings. Individual shareholders, with the exception of the government of Saskatchewan, were limited to 5 percent of the total shares, and the corporation's head office would remain in the province. A majority of the board of directors would be Canadian citizens, with a minimum of three being Saskatchewan residents.[14]

The Tory government called PCS an "albatross" around the neck of the province.[15] Devine endorsed the opinion offered by business reporter Bruce Johnstone, who described the corporation as "essentially worthless."[16] If this were true, the government was going to have a hard time finding buyers. The long-term economic prospects of the company were, in fact, very good.

Saskatchewan has the largest potash deposits in the world. Estimates place them as high as 40 percent of the world's total, with only the reserves of the Soviet Union approaching similar proportions. The grade mined in Saskatchewan averages between 21 and 27 percent K2O (the index used to measure the richness of the ore), which compares with grades of 15 percent or less that were mined in many parts of Europe, the United States, and the Soviet Union. The reserves are of such size and quality that Saskatchewan could supply the entire world's potash needs for hundreds and even thousands of years. Nor is the market for potash likely to disappear: potash contains potassium, one of the vital nutrients needed for plant growth, and therefore an essential requirement of agriculture.

Under the NDP, PCS had been a successful business. Between 1976 and 1982 it made profits of $414 million and paid the provincial treasury more than $270 million in taxes and royalties and $100 million in dividends. The original equity investment of the province in PCS was $418 million; by the time the NDP left office the value of the assets had increased to $1 billion, and total debt was only $221 million. The performance of the corporation under the PC government was less satisfactory. From 1982 to 1988, PCS lost a total of $78 million, and long-term debt increased from $221 million to over $660 million.[17] While PCS was partly a victim of a recession in the industry, it also suffered from mismanagement. The Devine government's decision to force PCS to remain in Canpotex damaged the corporation's ability to market its product, and Saskatchewan became the supplier of last resort.

Prior to the formation of the Potash Corporation in 1976, the ten mines in the province were owned by a dozen companies, eight of which were American, one South African, one French/German, and two Canadian. There were no head offices in Saskatchewan and no industry research was carried on in the province. With the creation of PCS, all this changed. Saskatchewan people were hired in executive positions, the corporation's requirements, from engineering contracts to legal services, went to Saskatchewan businesses, and research and development were done in the province. If Saskatchewan lost ownership, it would give up these benefits as well as the profits.

Another justification for privatization centred on the corporation's debt. Devine even made the extraordinary statement that the Potash Corporation was foreign-owned because it owed money to non-Canadian banks. "PCS is now owned by banks in New York, which are foreign," he said. "All we own is a debt. We don't own the equity in that corporation."[18] This was, of course, incorrect. How could the government privatize something it did not own? And while Devine objected to paying interest on foreign debt, he was all for paying dividends to foreign shareholders. He further suggested, "The money we pay in interest [on the PCS debt] is money I can't spend on health and education."[19] In reality, no money was being transferred from general revenues to pay interest charges on the PCS debt; PCS carried its own debt from the money it earned selling potash. Far from taking funds away from health and education, PCS dividends helped pay for these programs. Finally, the debt argument broke down completely because $662 million of long-term debt had been transferred to the Crown Management Board – the new owners would get the corporation minus the debt. Furthermore, the government gave no assurance that the proceeds from the sale would be applied against the debt. In the words of Finance Minister Gary Lane, "There's no guarantee that the money will go for debt reduction. It will depend on what the public's views are on this process."[20]

The final defence of privatization rested on the well-worn diversification theme. Despite all the evidence to the contrary – for example, the successful records of such government-owned fertilizer companies as Norsk Hydro of Norway, Kemira Oy of Finland, and Dead Sea Works of Israel – the Tories insisted that Crown corporations could not diversify or develop new products. During the entire history of the potash industry in Saskatchewan, only one new product was developed with potash as an ingredient – potassium sulfate fertilizer, developed by the only locally owned potash company, which also happened to be the only publicly owned one. There was no reason to assume that only private companies could diversify.

The Devine government failed to appreciate PCS's value as an instrument of public policy. The government could use the Crown corporation to influence world supply and price. By adjusting supply in such a way as to maintain price at a fairly high level, but not so high as to make it profitable for countries with inferior reserves to start production, Saskatchewan could maximize its own advantage. As the demand for fertilizer increased around the world, the province had the potential to capture the new markets.

A second public policy role for PCS arose from the conflict between the federal and provincial governments over control of natural resources. During the 1970s the battle raged, resulting in a constitutional amendment in 1982 which gave the provinces the right to levy indirect taxes on resources, something the federal government had previously maintained it alone had the right to do. However, the amendment has never been tested in the courts. The federal government retains authority over natural resource exports and still has the power to levy indirect as well as direct taxes on resources and resource production. The possibility exists for the federal government to tax away the profits of the potash industry, thereby depriving the province of wealth. Public ownership is the only secure way to keep potash revenue in the province, because a Crown corporation cannot be taxed.

These public policy considerations had no weight with the Devine government. For them, 1989 was the season for privatization and PCS was at the top of the list. Furthermore, their political judgment was that there would be very little public outcry if the corporation were sold. Public opinion seemed to be receptive to the idea of privatization, and the government seemed to have momentum on its side.

SaskEnergy

The decision that finally turned public opinion against the Devine government's privatization campaign was the attempt to sell SaskEnergy, the natural gas division of SaskPower. When Devine initially announced his privatization program, he had specifically exempted public utilities. Despite this clear and unequivocal commitment, Eric Berntson, the minister responsible for SaskPower, informed the legislature in May 1988 that Sask-Power was being split into two parts, an electric utility and a natural gas utility, the latter renamed SaskEnergy. When asked whether this separation was preliminary to the privatization of the gas division, Berntson answered that it had "absolutely nothing to do with the sell-off of anything."[21]

Despite this assurance, George Hill, the president of Sask-Power, stated in January 1989 that the only thing holding back the privatization of SaskEnergy was cabinet approval.[22] Hill, a lawyer from Estevan, was a former provincial PC party president and had helped arrange for Grant Devine to be parachuted into the Estevan constituency. He was both a power to be reckoned with in the Tory party and a strong supporter of privatization; when British privatization expert Oliver Letwin came to Regina, he worked out of an office down the hall from Hill's office in the SaskPower building.[23] Given Hill's political influence, his public statements hinting at the sale of SaskEnergy had to be taken seriously.

Deputy Premier Berntson began to go through various verbal contortions to explain away the fact that the government intended to privatize a utility. When asked what Devine had meant when he said "basic utilities" would not be touched, Berntson replied that the natural gas distribution system was not a utility. Pressed to define what he meant by a "utility," he irritably advised the reporter, "Look, if you're looking for a definition, ask Webster."[24] Webster's dictionary defines a utility as "something useful to the public, especially the service of electric power, gas, water, telephone, etc." George Hill did not bother with these linguistic gymnastics: "The opposition will attempt to say he [Devine] changed his mind. I say, so what? It happens every day of the week in everybody's life."[25]

Privatizing SaskEnergy: Pros and cons

One of the main reasons Hill gave for the privatization was the need to reduce SaskPower's $2.2 billion debt, which consumed 40 cents of every dollar paid by Saskatchewan consumers to meet interest charges. According to Roy Billington, an engineering professor at the University of Saskatchewan and former member of the Public Utilities Review Commission, the debt had swollen so large because from 1975 to 1985, the government had skimmed off about $100 million in SaskPower profits and added them to general revenue. If the corporation had been allowed to keep those profits as retained earnings, its borrowing requirements would have been reduced. Billington also suggested that power rates had been kept artificially low, reducing revenue and forcing SaskPower to borrow more.[26]

George Hill attempted to pin the blame for the debt on the NDP. He charged that the NDP had demanded dividends from a company that could ill afford huge payouts, and had lacked the political guts to raise electricity rates, preferring instead to borrow huge sums in New York. He also alleged that the NDP had spent money wastefully, eventually amassing a SaskPower payroll of 3,610 employees, 801 of whom had been eliminated by the PC government.[27] In all his railing against the SaskPower debt, Hill failed to mention that it soared from about $1.4 billion in 1982 to $2.1 billion in 1987. Since he had been either chairman of the board or president of the corporation during most of that period, he had obviously been slow in coming to the conclusion that the size of the debt was insupportable.

But now that the debt had been identified as a problem, the Devine government proposed the sale of the natural gas side of SaskPower, which had assets of $879 million, as the solution. The cash raised would be used to retire a portion of the debt, thereby reducing SaskPower's interest charges and enabling it to keep electricity rates down. The Tories promised that in the three years following the privatization of SaskEnergy, electrical rate increases would be kept below 3 percent per year, and that they would be kept below the rate of inflation for ten years. To sweeten the pot even more, the government promised to cut electricity rates for all skating and curling rinks in Saskatchewan by 50 percent, a policy that was sure to win votes in the province's many small towns where the ice rink served as the main community centre. In addition, all Saskatchewan residential and farm customers would be provided with a 5 percent discount on their electricity bills up to $100. This could be taken either as a cash saving or in the form of free shares in SaskEnergy. And, in the event that all of these inducements were not enough, the government pledged to put some of the money raised from the privatization into a fund to support economic diversification. The fund would make available to new industries $10 million per year for a minimum of four years.

The natural gas side of SaskPower was far more profitable than the electrical side. Over the preceding ten years, the gas division had made $407 million while the electrical division lost $25 million,[28] and the gas side accounted for 27 percent of the corporation's assets and 82 percent of the retained earnings, but only 13 percent of the long-term debt.[29] Privatization opponents pointed out that the sale of an asset would not, in the long term, improve the corporation's financial position; if an asset was capable of generating a profit in the private sector, there was no reason why it should not be capable of generating a profit in the public sector.

It seems odd that for decades SaskPower had been able to manage in both good and bad economic times, including the Great Depression, without having to resort to selling income-earning assets, but in 1989, apparently, this was no longer possible. Debt had its cost in the form of interest charges, but so did equity investment, because investors expect a return on their investment in the form of dividends or capital gains. The money that would be going to the shareholders in SaskEnergy was money that would not be going to the owners of the Crown corporation – that is, the citizens of Saskatchewan. According to the terms of the privatization of SaskEnergy, shareholders would receive a guaranteed annual dividend of "approximately 10 percent" and a five-year guarantee of the principal. That was a share that bore a suspicious resemblance to a bond.

The various lures attached to the privatization proposal – the 50 percent reduction in electricity charges for hockey rinks and curling rinks, the $100 worth of free shares to all SaskPower customers, the diversification fund – were essentially window dressing; even such a devoted privatization booster as business columnist Bruce Johnstone admitted that these inducements "reeked of political opportunism."[30]

Another concern raised by the privatization centered on gas

rates. With SaskEnergy as a private sector monopoly, what assurance was there that service would not deteriorate, or that consumers would not be charged excessive rates? The government proposed to appoint a commissioner with a ten-year term empowered to review SaskEnergy's rates every three years, but the absence of an annual review and the refusal to allow the commissioner to hire any staff beyond a secretary ensured that the rate regulation would be ineffective.[31] The proposed method of regulating TransGas, the SaskEnergy subsidiary in the business of transporting natural gas long distances and for large industrial users, was similarly toothless: the regulatory board was allowed to review TransGas rates on a "complaint basis" only, and for no longer than twelve-month periods.

Another major criticism of the privatization focused on the question of who would control SaskEnergy after the sale. The government attempted to put these concerns to rest by legislating restrictions on the private company. The head office was to remain permanently in Saskatchewan; two thirds of the board of directors were to be Saskatchewan residents; the initial share offering was to be made to Saskatchewan residents only, and no foreign ownership was to be allowed; and no shareholder, apart from SaskPower, could hold more than 8 percent of the total shares. However, there was nothing to stop Saskatchewan shareholders from subsequently selling their holdings to out-of-province buyers. Given the typical pattern of privatizations, the shares would probably be underpriced, providing a strong inducement to immediately flip the shares for quick profit. They would then be snapped up by investors in central Canada, where much of the country's money is concentrated. As soon as a large volume of SaskEnergy shares was made available on the stock exchange, continued local ownership of the corporation would be very much in doubt.

The government, significantly, didn't offer any promises about share offerings subsequent to the first one, which probably meant that they would not be restricted to Saskatchewan residents. Shareholders do not appreciate it when the government says certain people are not allowed to buy their shares, because that reduces the demand for the shares and, inevitably, their value.

Governments consequently have a difficult time upholding regulations about share ownership. A case in point was the loosening of restrictions on the ownership of SaskPower bonds, where restrictions designed to keep the securities in Saskatchewan hands were initially placed on the sale. At first, out-of-province residents were not allowed to buy the bonds, and no one person was permitted to purchase more than $100,000 worth. In May 1989, both these restrictions were lifted. Since the market for the bonds, which had a feature whereby they could be exchanged for Saskoil shares, was now much larger, the value of both the bonds and the shares went up. It seemed clear that when there was a conflict between local ownership and profit-making, profit-making won out.

What had been true of SaskPower bonds would be no less true of SaskEnergy shares. There was no real guarantee that a majority of them would continue to be owned by Saskatchewan residents, and the legislated guarantee that SaskEnergy's head office would remain in Saskatchewan did not amount to much, because while the government could pass a law determining the location of the head office, it could not effectively legislate what was done in that office.

Roy Romanow, who succeeded Allan Blakeney as NDP leader in November 1987, argued that local ownership had been a key reason for establishing the Crown corporations in the first place. Through the Crowns, the people of the province were able to defy market forces and gain some control over their own economy. Profits were invested in the province, and policies were instituted to direct spin-off activities to local businesses. SaskPower, for example, purchased $400 million in goods and services from Saskatchewan companies in 1988. "Can we be assured that buying from Saskatchewan businesses would be the first priority of a privately owned utility owned by out-of-province investors?" Romanow asked.[32] Another benefit was that a Crown corporation did not have to pay federal tax. Had the gas utility been a private corporation from 1978 to 1988, it would have paid $113 million of its $407 million profit to Ottawa.[33] Privatization would likely divert money from Saskatchewan to federal coffers.

The government had one final argument in support of its case.

Pointing to the example of Nova, which began modestly as the Alberta Gas Trunk Line Company and developed into a $7 billion corporation, George Hill predicted that privatizing SaskEnergy would lead to economic diversification: "There will be very much of an expansionist philosophy. The things that SaskEnergy could get into are limited only by one's imagination."[34] Hill did not explain why it was necessary to sell the utility that delivered natural gas to people's homes in order to have economic diversification. If, for example, opportunities existed in the petrochemical industry, those projects could be undertaken whether the gas utility was publicly or privately owned.

The bells ring

Up to the time when Devine announced the imminent sale of part of SaskPower, the NDP had appeared to be losing the battle over privatization. Devine had boasted that he would use the issue to bury the socialists. Just as Mulroney won the 1988 election by polarizing the electorate over free trade and in so doing had managed to cover up the government's mistakes and scandals, Devine was in a position to do the same thing with privatization. Privately, NDP strategists worried that the Tory premier might be able to pull this off and sweep into power for another term.

The tide began to turn against privatization on 21 April 1989, when the bill to privatize SaskEnergy was introduced in the legislature. When the bells rang to summon the members for the vote, the NDP MLAs walked out in protest. Saskatchewan was one of two provinces, the other being Ontario, where the government was not able to force a vote with the opposition absent, so the bells kept ringing, and the legislative proceedings ground to a halt. It was a calculated gamble for the NDP to dramatize its opposition in this way, because there was a chance that the public might see their boycott as irresponsible and undemocratic. The Tories certainly hoped for this response, declaring angrily that they had been duly elected to govern and that the NDP had no right to arbitrarily shut down the legislature. If the New Democrats were so sure of their case, they should not be afraid to debate the details of the government proposal in the proper forum.

Complicating things for the NDP was the fact that since the budget had not yet been approved, government departments were dependent on interim supply bills for operating funds. There was enough money to last into the middle of May, but after that pressure would mount for the NDP to return to the legislature so that money could be allocated to maintain government services. By stopping the business of the house, the NDP MLAs took a major risk. If the voters were indifferent to the privatization of SaskEnergy, they would have to creep back, humiliated, to the legislature.

As it turned out, the NDP's bold stroke succeeded beyond even their expectations. The protest against the sale of SaskEnergy touched a nerve. The latent public antipathy to Devine's privatization crusade welled to the surface and was channelled into a fierce campaign to save SaskPower. Within a matter of weeks 100,000 people had signed a petition demanding that the government back off from the sale. Romanow addressed huge, emotional rallies in Prince Albert, Yorkton, Saskatoon, and Regina. The anger in the crowds was palpable, and Romanow was interrupted by ovation after ovation and shouts of "Ring those bells," and "Let's fight back."

Six days into the walk-out, Devine called a press conference to urge the NDP to come back to the legislature. "We knew they would go crazy," he said. "All I am saying is the legislature is the place to debate it. Let's debate it." Devine denied that natural gas was a utility and thus that he had gone back on his word, and also rejected the idea of calling an election. "Why would I call an election when I haven't built Rafferty and they're holding it up? When I haven't provided shares for natural gas and I haven't allowed people to invest in potash?"[35] A few days later, an Angus Reid poll showed how out of touch with public opinion the premier was. Sixty-seven percent of those polled said they were opposed to the privatization of SaskEnergy by means of a public share offering, 22 percent approved, and 10 percent had no opinion. Not only that, 58 percent said they were generally opposed to the Devine government's privatization initiatives.[36] This was a major reversal for the government. Before the furor broke out over SaskEnergy, the government's privatization campaign had not encountered any major opposition, but all that now changed.

At first, Devine shrugged off the poll, declaring, "I'm not going to be intimidated by somebody running around and asking the wrong questions."[37] People did not understand the issue, he added, and once they had been properly informed they would come to see that the government was right. Subsequently, television ads paid for by the taxpayer lauded public participation as "the Saskatchewan way," and SaskEnergy president Oscar Hanson sent 400,000 letters to gas consumers in the province explaining why the privatization of his company was an opportunity not to be missed. A SaskEnergy road show, complete with slides, music, glossy pamphlets and speakers, was dispatched to 80 communities across Saskatchewan.

Meanwhile, the NDP boycott of the legislature stretched to seventeen calendar days, eclipsing the fourteen-day walk-out by the federal Conservatives in 1983 against one of the Trudeau government's energy bills, and setting a new parliamentary record in Canada for this kind of protest.[38] As government funds began to run out, the NDP came under increasing pressure to return to the legislature; if the NDP stayed out too long, it risked a reversal of public opinion, as the focus shifted from the government's duplicity over privatizing the gas utility to the opposition's abuse of the legislature.

Finally, the NDP returned to the legislature with the understanding that the bill would die on the order paper. The government appointed a three-member panel chaired by Lloyd Barber, president of the University of Regina and a member of the board of the pro-privatization Institute for Saskatchewan Enterprise, to examine the impact of a SaskEnergy share offering. For the time being, the plans to privatize the natural gas utility were put on hold.

Privatizing PCS through closure

Having experienced a major setback with SaskEnergy, the Devine government was desperate to salvage something from the 1989 session of the legislature and decided to proceed with the sale of PCS. Public opinion was less resistant to this privatization because PCS, unlike SaskEnergy, was neither a monopoly nor a utility, nor did it have a long history as a Crown-owned enterprise. Even so, the Tory privatization campaign had lost its aura of euphoria. The government proceeded with grim determination to push through the privatization of PCS with as little fuss as possible.

This was evident from the taciturnity of the Tory MLAs during the debate on the PCS privatization bill. The long, impassioned speeches of NDP MLAs failed to evoke more than a perfunctory response from the silent, stony-faced members opposite. In an effort to wear out the NDP speakers, the government refused to present any other legislation and increased the legislature's sitting hours to eleven per day. The opposition talked on; the Tories said little. On 4 August 1989, the government moved to cut off debate, the first time in the history of the province closure had been used. It was invoked after 80 hours of discussion during which only nine of 38 Conservative MLAs had bothered to speak.[39] Privatization minister Graham Taylor gave a short speech just before closure was introduced, and Gary Lane made a few remarks when he moved second reading of the bill. Neither Devine nor most of his front-bench ministers entered the debate prior to closure.[40] Linda Haverstock, the provincial Liberal leader, scornfully concluded: "It [the imposition of closure] proves to me that we have a government unwilling to govern. We have a government that is unwilling to debate or obviously thinks it lacks the talent to do so."[41]

The Tories' reluctance to debate reflected the coolness of public opinion toward the idea of privatization. Had there been strong support, the government would have prolonged the discussion to keep the NDP dangling in the wind. Nonetheless, when all was said and done, the Tory majority got its way. After closure had been applied and the bill to privatize the Potash Corporation passed, the Tory MLAs rose and cheered. A major symbol of the NDP years in power had been demolished.

The share offering was loaded with financial inducements to enhance its popularity. Saskatchewan residents were offered potash bonds at 10.75 percent interest annually for three years (compared with 10.5 percent for one year on Canada Savings Bonds). The bonds, issued by the government rather than by PCS, carried virtually no risk. The real kicker was that after one year they were convertible to PCS shares at the original share issue price.

At the beginning of November, about 13 million PCS shares went on the market. The $18 share price meant that the government placed a market value of $630 million on PCS, which was about half the book value and one quarter of the replacement value of the corporation. The share price was further depressed by the weakness of the potash market at the time of the issue. However, the low initial share price worked to the advantage of the bondholders. If, after a year, share prices rose, they could exchange their bonds for shares at $18, resell them and take the profit. PCS employees were even better off; they could buy 50 shares at $1 each and an additional $10,000 worth at 90 percent of the share issue price through payroll deduction, or with money loaned by PCS at 5 percent. No expense was spared for a lavish promotion campaign which included full-page newspaper ads, brochures, posters, public meetings, a toll-free information line, and mailings to every household in the province.

The potash bonds were snapped up because they had a high, guaranteed rate of return plus the possibility of a capital gain. The normal rules of the market are that risk should be rewarded by the possibility of gain, but in their determination to make the PCS privatization a success, the Devine government took the risk out of equity investment, at the expense of the taxpayers of Saskatchewan. The $100 potash bonds issued in November 1989 had a market value of $106 in February 1990. The shares did not do so well, however. Issued at $18, their market value reflected a slump in the potash industry and fell in three months to $13.75. If the government had not taken the risk out of the investment, it would have had some irate Saskatchewan investors on its hands.

Devine recognized that his government had lost popularity because of its privatization campaign. The potash privatization lacked the spirit of populism and excitement that had surrounded some of the early privatizations in Britain. In Saskatchewan, there was a distinct lack of popular enthusiasm for the whole exercise.

Hanging over the government was the SaskEnergy debacle. The Devine government crossed a line that it had said it would not cross when it threatened to privatize a public utility. The New Democrats were able to rally public opinion and set the government back on its heels. It could no longer be claimed that the people were clamouring for privatization. If they were clamouring for anything, it was for a halt to the privatization onslaught.

Devine moved to repair his bridges by shuffling his cabinet and promising to run a "more sensitive and open government." "I've been back to the kitchen tables, talking to people," he said. "That's how I got here, quite frankly."[42] Everything was up for review and reconsideration, including the privatization of SGI and SaskEnergy. Even when the Barber Commission reported that the sale of the gas utility made "good business sense," the government vowed privatization would not proceed until the people were ready for it.

Devine's strategy of offering apologies and promising to listen was almost identical to his performance in the months leading up to the 1986 election. Then, too, he had played down ideology until another mandate had been secured. Devine did not say he had been wrong, only that he had been "too far ahead" of the people. The Tories had not abandoned their new right program; they had gone into tactical retreat.

Notes for Chapter 10

1. *Globe and Mail*, 9 March 1989.

2. *Leader-Post*, Eisler, 14 March 1987. 3. *Ibid.*, 11 March, 18 March 1987. 4. *Ibid.*, 28 August 1987; Johnstone, *Leader-Post*, 5 September 1987. 5. Johnstone, *Leader-Post*, 29 August 1987. 6. *Ibid.*, 12 September 1987. 7. Eisler, *Leader-Post*, 9 January 1988. 8. *Globe and Mail*, 8 January 1988. 9. Eisler, *Leader-Post*, 9 June 1988. 10. *Ibid.* 11. *Globe and Mail*, 15 March 1989. 12. *Star-Phoenix*, 9 February 1989. 13. *Ibid.*, 17 February 1989.

14. *Leader-Post*, 18 April 1989. 15. *Ibid.*, 19 April 1989. 16. *Ibid.*, 5 August 1989. 17. Allan Blakeney, Notes for an address, 19 July 1989. 18. *Star-Phoenix*, 9 February 1989. 19. *Ibid.* 20. *Globe and Mail*, 12 August 1989.

21. *Leader-Post*, 10 May 1988. 22. *Ibid.*, 10 January 1989. 23. Eisler, *Leader-Post*, 25 April 1989. 24. *Ibid.* 25. *Globe and Mail*, 11 April 1989.

26. *Ibid.* 27. Petrie, *Leader-Post*, 27 July 1989. 28. *Ibid.*, 27 April 1989. 29. *Ibid.* 30. Johnstone, *Leader-Post*, 13 May 1989. 31. *Ibid.*, 21 September, 23

September 1989. **32.** *Ibid.*, 2 May 1989. **33.** *Ibid.*, 27 April 1989. **34.** *Globe and Mail,* 11 April 1989.

   35. *Leader-Post*, 27 April 1989. **36.** *Ibid.*, 3 May 1989. **37.** *Ibid.*, 4 May 1989. **38.** *Ibid.*, 9 May 1989.

   39. *Leader-Post*, 4 August 1989. **40.** Eisler, *Leader-Post*, 5 August 1989. **41.** *Ibid.*, 8 August 1989. **42.** Eisler, *Leader-Post*, 4 October 1989.

11

THE NEW RIGHT
AND THE WELFARE STATE

◊ ──────────────── ◊

THE BREAKDOWN
OF PUBLIC WELFARE

There is no poverty in Saskatchewan.
— *Social Services Minister* GRANT SCHMIDT,
Leader-Post, 8 *June* 1989.

Neo-conservatives believe in private enterprise, the free market, the autonomy of the individual, and reducing the size of government. As a result, they have unleashed an unprecedented attack on social services based on both economic and moral arguments. The program of the new right is based on the theory of incentives. They argue that because the rich are getting too few incentives, they are not investing their money and creating jobs. On the other hand, the poor are getting too many incentives and, therefore, are not working. Thus, the rich need more incentives in the form of tax cuts, and the poor need fewer incentives by way of declining benefit levels. This policy must be followed, according to George Gilder in his Reaganite Bible, *Wealth and Poverty*, because " . . . the effort to take income from the rich, thus diminishing their investment, and to give it to the poor, thus reducing their work incentive, is sure to cut American productivity, limit job opportunities, and perpetuate poverty."[1] This theory gives a semblance of intellectual credibility to a program that could otherwise be perceived as a cynical grab for a greater share of the wealth by the rich.

This theory of incentives leads naturally to an acceptance, indeed an endorsement, of greater social inequality. The market mechanism is said to be the only effective method of resource allocation, and, in order for the market to work as efficiently as possible, the rich must be permitted to retain most of their money. Ironically, the best way to address poverty, according to neo-conservative orthodoxy, is to dismantle welfare provisions which burden the economy and only benefit meddlesome bureaucrats and welfare spongers. The only possible hope for the poor comes from encouraging economic growth through a reduction of redistributive taxation measures which penalize effort, reduce incentives, and slow down economic growth. Once the welfare burden is lifted, energy, thrift, and invention will flourish, untrammeled by the heavy load of the welfare state.

The modern idea of social welfare was enshrined in the Canada Assistance Act of 1966. It states that those who are without means of support through no fault of their own have the fundamental right to have their basic needs met, meaning an adequate allowance for food, shelter, clothing, fuel, utilities, household supplies, and personal requirements. The Act further states that "no person shall be denied assistance because he refuses or has refused to take part in a work activity project."[2] This guaranteed that any person who was eligible for assistance did not have to perform a work test in order to prove that he was truly deserving of help. Under the Act, the federal government pays one-half of the cost of social assistance, the other half being paid by the province.

The basic principle underlying the Canada Assistance Act conflicts with the philosophy of neo-conservatism. The idea that society has a collective responsibility for its members is incompatible with the idea that individuals are responsible for themselves in a competitive market. Neo-conservatives, unlike traditional conservatives who perceived society as an organism made up of interdependent parts or a community based upon mutual obligation, reject collectivist values. They see society merely as an aggregation of individuals. The role of government is not so much to serve the common good as to referee the competition among private interests. For the new right, the concept of social welfare is at best residual. They believe that social services should be provided by families, friends, volunteers, and profit-making organizations, with the government reluctantly doing the rest.

Welfare 'reform': The first phase

The Devine government's embrace of neo-conservative principles resulted in policy and program revisions euphemistically called "welfare reform." The first phase began in March 1984, when Social Services Minister Gordon Dirks introduced a package of changes whose stated purposes were to provide productive training and job opportunities for employable welfare recipients; to provide greater equity in benefits through reductions for some groups and increases for others; and to make social assistance programs administratively more efficient. The Tories knew they had an increasingly severe unemployment problem on their hands, and wanted to deal with it along neo-conservative lines. As Dirks noted, "The average people out there agree that government should assist people, but don't go overboard, don't provide too much because they know what human nature is like. That too much government help can be a disincentive for initiative." This echoed George Gilder, who expressed the view that "in order to succeed, the poor need the spur of their poverty." With these "reforms," the Tories returned to the nineteenth century idea of distinguishing between the "deserving" and the "undeserving" poor. In the former category were women, children, the handicapped, and the elderly; in the latter category, bearing the brunt of the attack, were single "employable" people. By zeroing in on this group, the government was able to market its reforms as a way to get chiselers and bums working again. Social welfare would become the last resort for the truly destitute, the deserving poor.

The "undeserving" poor were subject to the newly created Saskatchewan Employment Development Program (SEDP), which was an attempt to brand the poor as fraudulent spongers whose poverty resulted from laziness. Under this program, fully employable social assistance recipients who had been on welfare for three months had to register with the Assessment Placement Unit (APU) of the Department of Social Services. The APU then referred them to jobs, sponsored by SEDP, providing "meaningful work experiences" and lasting between 20 and 26 weeks. That would be just enough to qualify someone for unemployment insurance benefits, which were 90 percent paid by Ottawa, and get them off welfare, which was 50 per cent paid by Ottawa. Saskatchewan's poor might still be out of work, but at least they would be less of a burden on Devine's provincial budgets.

The program had two goals. It was used as a method of social control, in that once a person had been categorized as fully employable he was so deemed until he could prove otherwise, a reversal of the old presumption of being innocent until proven guilty. The other goal was to help create low-wage jobs in the private sector. At least 50 percent of SEDP money was directed towards job creation for private businesses, with the remainder divided between local governments and non-profit organizations. Welfare rates were slashed in order to provide the money to set up SEDP. Thus, the government was engaging in job creation at the expense of people on social assistance.[3]

In an effort to give single employable people the "necessary spur" to get off welfare, their household and clothing allowances were eliminated, which represented a 41 percent cut in benefits covering basic needs. They had a further $100 cut from their accommodation allowance. But single employables were not the only ones targeted for reductions. Although families and seniors received modest increases, amendments to the Saskatchewan Assistance Plan rendered these increases meaningless. For instance, Saskatchewan became the only province where family allowances were deducted from social assistance cheques; the income tax exemption for the renter's property tax credit and property improvement grants were eliminated; and the amount of money a social assistance recipient was allowed to have in the bank was reduced. These changes created a situation in which the burden of unemployment was increasingly borne by the individual rather than by society at large. The principle that society has an obligation to help those in difficult situations not of their own making, was severely diluted.

The changes lessened the ability of many families to meet their basic needs. In 1985, one year after the introduction of welfare reform, the Regina Welfare Rights Centre reported that almost all of the 964 people who sought its help did so because of insufficient funding. While social assistance rates in Saskatchewan had for many years been below the poverty line as established by Statistics Canada, the gap was widening. Whereas social assistance rates were 10 percent below the poverty line in 1978, after the welfare reforms of 1984, they dropped to 50 percent below the poverty line for single people and 30 percent for a single parent with one child.

Another indicator of the inadequacy of benefit levels was the startling increase in the use of food banks in the province. Social Services Minister Gordon Dirks endorsed this trend, calling for a "joining together of public and private charity to meet the need of the people."[4] Privately-run food banks became an essential supplement to a deficient public welfare system. They also reinforced the principle of "less eligibility," a doctrine dating back to the early nineteenth century English Poor Law which stated that no one on relief should receive more than the lowest wage-earner. As Graham Riches, author of *Food Banks and the Welfare Crisis*, points out, "if those at work are concerned about losing their jobs and going on unemployment insurance or social assistance, their fears must be more than doubled at the thought of having to ask for food when their cash benefits run out. In this way the visibility of food banks preserves the notion of blaming the victim and assists in keeping the lid on wage demands."[5]

In retrospect, the welfare reforms of 1984, though introduced in the name of restoring the work ethic and self-reliance, did not improve the welfare system of the province. Instead, they caused hardships for the most defenceless, making people on social assistance feel unworthy and persecuted.

Grant Schmidt: Welfare 'reformer'

The first wave of welfare reform paled beside what happened in the second term. The driving force behind this second phase was Grant Schmidt, whose name became synonymous with Tory toughness in social services. Schmidt's early years were spent on a grain farm near Melville. Following Grade 12 he pounded spikes and shovelled gravel for the railway, earning enough money to enroll at the University of Saskatchewan. As a student, he lived frugally, an experience that later enabled him to lecture welfare recipients on how to budget. Graduating with a law degree, Schmidt articled and became a partner with a Melville law firm. Like his father and grandfather who had supported the CCF, Schmidt became active in the local NDP, only joining the Tories later.

He offered a variety of explanations for his conversion to conservatism. He had been a victim of "university disease," he said, which caused "idealism rather than realism."[6] On another occasion, Schmidt, a strong Lutheran, likened himself to Martin Luther 450 years ago: "I had my doubts." Finally, he had recourse to the standard Tory complaint that the NDP was dominated by labour unions.

Schmidt was elected MLA for Melville in 1982, but was not appointed to the cabinet until December 1985 when he became Minister of Labour. His major promotion came after the 1986 election, when he was put in charge of Social Services, Labour, the Employment Development Agency, the Women's Secretariat, and the Native Affairs Secretariat. Many of these functions were later rolled into one super-ministry called Human Resources. Schmidt emerged as one of the most controversial figures in the Devine government, evoking strong feelings of either approval or disapproval. He had a habit of speaking his mind, however inappropriate the comment might be. Addressing the National Council of Women, he began his speech with, "I'm about to give a braless speech . . . It has a point here, a point there and is shaky in the middle."[7] Schmidt often put his foot in his mouth, but always managed to retain a serene confidence in his own virtue.

Schmidt shared the convictions of the new Christian right and saw social problems in terms of personal morality. The new right did not acknowledge that the social and economic environment drastically reduces opportunities for some people. According to the neo-conservative world view, all achievements are individual achievements, and all problems are individual problems. This was based on the fundamental premise that society is not so much a community as an aggregation of individuals. If the community does not exist, it cannot have problems or weaknesses. All problems and weaknesses therefore must be the fault of individuals.

Grant Schmidt frequently expressed the view that poverty resulted from personal moral failure. He assumed that those who apply for social assistance are likely to be lazy cheaters. Challenged in the legislature by Ned Shillington, the NDP MLA for Regina Centre, who wanted to know what Schmidt planned to do about the high level of unemployment, the minister retorted, "There are jobs out there if people want to take them and they're not all minimum wage jobs. . . They're not all desk jobs either I can tell you, but people have to be prepared to do an honest day's work for their dollar and that is not common in Regina Centre."[8] In other words, the problem was not the scarcity of jobs, but the moral inadequacy of the unemployed.

A report from the National Council on Welfare stated that, in 1988, 19.8 percent of the population of Saskatchewan was living below the poverty line. The only province to have a higher rate of poverty was Newfoundland.[9] This gloomy fact did not faze Schmidt, who simply denied that there was any poverty in Saskatchewan. He further claimed that if any people were homeless, they were homeless by choice.[10] Welfare mothers in cities did not have the fortitude of the farm families in his Melville constituency: "When my constituents live on less money than your constituents and my constituents can still feed their children, then I say you've got to go to the character of the people and what they can do with their dollar."[11] Single mothers on welfare – many of them visibly upset – confronted Schmidt outside the legislature, but he refused to apologize or withdraw the remark.

Schmidt's habit of reducing socio-economic issues to issues of personal morality led him to judge social assistance recipients according to his own personal, moral standard. He seemed to think that if he could do something, then everybody on welfare should be able to do it, too. Thus, he defended low welfare rates by saying, "My wife insists she could feed our family on what I pay on welfare. . .I haven't put her to the test yet but she insists she could do it."[12] He said he liked to eat macaroni, hamburger, and the produce from his wife's garden. The message to those on welfare, apartment-dwellers included, was "grow a garden." Of interest, too, was Schmidt's use of the phrase "what I pay on welfare," as though welfare recipients were being paid out of his personal bank account.

Schmidt again used himself as the standard against which to measure the poor when the Department of Social Services placed a cap on the amount of money given to social assistance recipients to pay for utilities. Prior to 1987, the full cost had been covered, but the policy was changed in order to encourage those on welfare to conserve on their heating bills. Schmidt claimed that the cost of heating his 1,800-square-foot home in Melville was less than what would be allowed for a family living on welfare in the same community. He did not mention that he had the luxury of living in a modern, energy-efficient home, while welfare recipients were more likely to be renting old, drafty houses without proper insulation.[13] Schmidt resorted to a similar analogy when the government forced social assistance clients to do menial work like picking stones and clearing brush: "I cut my grass the other day and I didn't consider it demeaning," he observed.[14]

Schmidt's position, in essence, was that able-bodied people have no business being on welfare. He was uncomfortable with the concept of a social safety net, which he regarded more as a hammock than a net. Those who had the misfortune to rely on social assistance became candidates for moral instruction from the minister. He assumed he had the right to tell them how to live, as in this conversation between Schmidt and a welfare mother: "I said to her, 'You're dressed as well as my wife. Your daughter goes to play school with my son. I know I don't pay you a lot on welfare, but how do you get by?' She said, 'It is not easy, but I get by.' I said, 'You don't drink, smoke or any of those things.' She said, 'No.' I said, 'Good, because I don't pay you for any of those things. I don't give you any extra for that kind of activity.'"[15] Welfare was a kind of purgatory. After the recipient suffered for a while, he or she earned the right to rejoin society.

In Saskatchewan, in 1986, one in six families lived in poverty, not including Indians living on reserves, where poverty remained acute. The situation for single-parent families headed by women was especially alarming. Nearly 70 percent of them were living below the poverty line, compared with the national average of 56 percent. In 1988, the poverty line for a single parent and two children was $19,343 per year, but in Saskatchewan such a family was entitled to just $11,640 in social assistance. If the single parent happened to be employed and earning minimum wage, his or her annual earnings would be $9,331. By comparison, the poverty line for a single person was $10,984 a year, and his social assistance entitlement a meagre $4,500.

It was abundantly clear that all the poverty in Saskatchewan could not be attributed to the moral failings of individuals. Between 1981 and 1988 the number of unemployed increased from 21,000 to 37,000. The increased need for social assistance came not from a sudden deterioration in personal morality but from a lack of jobs. From 1971 to 1981, an average of 9,100 new jobs were created in Saskatchewan each year. In the period 1981 to 1988, the figure was only 3,714. Most appalling of all, the age group 15-24 suffered an absolute loss of 20,000 jobs from 1981 to 1988.

The opportunity to work was a key factor in determining a person's standard of living, as was the rate of pay. In 1988, average weekly wages were $411 – the second lowest among all the provinces. Not only that, Saskatchewan's weekly wage as a percentage of the national average declined. In October 1986 it had been 94 percent of the national average; two years later, it was 88 percent. Saskatchewan's minimum wage fell from being the highest in Canada to being one of the lowest. From 1982 to 1989 it increased by only 25 cents. Meanwhile, from August 1985 to February 1989, the cost of groceries went up 13 percent; shelter, 18 percent; and clothing, 15 percent. The tax burden increased, too. The ordinary Saskatchewan family paid $1,500 per year more in provincial taxes and charges in 1989 than it did in 1982.[16]

Given this picture of high unemployment, low wages, rising cost of living, and increasing taxes, it was bizarre for Schmidt to blame poverty on defects in moral character. Undeterred by criticism, he embarked on what he termed welfare reform, the main consequence of which was to make life even harder for those on welfare.

Grant Schmidt was not a maverick in the Tory party holding

eccentric views. On the subject of social welfare, he expressed the sentiments of the rank and file. At the Saskatchewan PC convention in 1987, the chairperson of the panel on social services put forward the view that anyone in good shape who couldn't find a job should be inducted into the military. Other delegates blamed the education system as one of the underlying causes of welfare abuse. "Socialistic" teachers were accused of ingraining in students the belief that "somebody owes them a living."[17] The guests at the premier's annual fund-raising dinner in 1989 reserved their longest and loudest applause for "Schmidtie," who was introduced by Devine as "the fellow who says what other people think."[18] Although Schmidt spearheaded the attack on social assistance, he was by no means acting alone.

Welfare 'reform': The second phase

Stripped of all the self-serving verbiage, the second phase of welfare reform amounted to the further curtailment of benefits to welfare recipients. Taking inflation into account, the real value of benefits paid to single employables declined 64 percent between 1981 and 1988. For welfare families with dependent children, the decline was 28 percent.[19] As a result of the cutbacks, basic needs were not being met. The inadequacy of the allowance was evident when the cost of a nutritious food basket, as determined by Agriculture Canada, was compared with the amount of money available from the Saskatchewan Assistance Plan after rent and utilities were paid. It was only half what Agriculture Canada said was necessary. Furthermore, if all the money left over after payment for rent and utilities were spent on food, the welfare recipient would have nothing for clothing, personal items, household goods, or travel.[20]

One particularly painful cut was the elimination in 1987 of the $27 per month transportation allowance. Schmidt explained that people on welfare "should be able to walk within the city... From what I know of the city of Regina, food is always available within walking distance."[21] As for the need for transportation to get to job interviews, he dismissed the problem: "If one of my relatives had a job interview in Saskatoon and was on welfare, I would make sure that that relative got there, and I wouldn't ask the government for any money."[22] Social Service Department regulations provided that welfare recipients who were attending sheltered workshops, receiving medical care, or were enrolled in a secondary school that did not have bus service, were still entitled to the transportation allowance.[23] Despite this regulation, many people needing medical care had their allowance cut off. Doctors and nurses at the Westside Community Clinic in Saskatoon reported that a large number of welfare recipients were delaying their visits to doctors, missing operations, and failing to keep appointments with specialists for tests and treatment. Fewer children were getting immunization shots and many women were unable to get prenatal check-ups. A survey of 80 patients on welfare found that 23 people with serious physical disabilities, including arthritis and respiratory ailments, had lost their travel allowance.[24]

Besides losing benefits, welfare recipients were humiliated and stigmatized for their failure and dependency. Welfare cheques were not mailed to people unless they were physically disabled; they were required to come to a government office in person to collect their allowance. If they failed to do so by the end of the month, the benefit was cancelled.[25] People suffering from mental illness who were too disorganized to pick up their cheques suddenly found themselves cut off social assistance benefits. In another crackdown measure, the government issued a separate cheque for the portion of the welfare payment intended to cover rent. Since the cheque had to be co-signed by the landlord, this procedure broke the Department of Social Service's regulation requiring that "every unit [of the department] shall administer assistance so as to protect the recipient's right of confidentiality."

The tightening of restrictions on welfare recipients was accompanied by a stronger anti-fraud campaign conducted by the newly formed Entitlement Control Unit. With the erosion of benefits and a new regulation that placed stricter limits on the amount of personal earnings a recipient was allowed to keep, some clients were suspected of concealing sources of income. The eighteen-man special investigative unit made up of former RCMP officers was instructed to place under surveillance selected social assistance recipients. In one instance, a Regina woman who approached a welfare investigator who had staked out her home was told, "It's a free country." The man pulled away in his car, only to reappear in the back alley a few minutes later. Neighbours were encouraged to provide information about the personal lives and spending habits of people on welfare. According to Harvey Stalwick, former director of the School of Social Work at the University of Regina, individuals suspected of fraud were not the only ones investigated; those who spoke out against government policy were also "targeted for surveillance."[26]

Although Schmidt estimated welfare fraud at $20 million or about 10 percent of the $200 million social assistance budget, the actual figure for inappropriate payments in 1988-89 was $1.3 million. Not all of the payments were the result of people trying to cheat the system. In several cases, administrative errors had been made or recipients had misunderstood the rules. Ray Barnard, an assistant deputy minister of Social Services, emphasized that welfare overpayments should not be confused with abuse: "If a welfare recipient makes a mistake, they make a mistake."[27]

In its zeal to come down hard on social assistance applicants, the Tory government landed itself in legal trouble. In 1984 Murray Chambers, a "single employable" person on welfare receiving a basic monthly allowance of $123 for food, clothing, and household expenses, filed a complaint with the Saskatchewan Human Rights Commission. He maintained that, in view of the fact that a childless married couple received a basic allowance of $356 ($178 per person), he was being discriminated against on account of his single status. In June 1988, the Court of Appeal ruled in Chambers's favour and ordered the government to repay him $55 per month (the difference between $178 and $123) for every month he had been on welfare. All the other welfare recipients who had been underpaid were similarly entitled to compensation. Schmidt did not receive the court judgments with good grace. Initially, he said he would settle accounts with Chambers, but the others would get nothing: "I don't believe in retroactive welfare payments... It may be that couples were paid too much."[28] Later, the government agreed to make the back payments, but the onus was on those who had been discriminated against to apply for them. Then the government vindictively cut the basic allowance for childless couples on welfare. This ended the discrimination by applying the same low rate to everyone.

From welfare to 'workfare'

A central feature of welfare reform was "workfare." When Grant Schmidt took over the Department of Social Services in 1986, he discovered that there were more people on welfare than when the Tory government had taken office. Displeased, he made it a priority to reduce the welfare rolls, and in 1987 he launched Saskatchewan Works, a program paying minimum-wage level subsidies to anyone who would hire a welfare recipient for 18 to 20 weeks. Most of the jobs were community-based: maintenance of skating and curling rinks, snow removal for senior citizens, building golf courses, road construction in northern Saskatchewan, and so on. In some cases, private employers were the beneficiaries of cheap labour. An example was the company building the $2.1 million Manitou Springs Mineral Spa near Watrous. The entire workforce was supplied by the Saskatchewan Works program, with their wages coming from the Department of Social Services. One of the principal investors in the project was a prominent local Tory.[29]

Saskatchewan Works was a no-frills program that made no pretence of offering training allowances, wage raises, or career-planning courses. These had been the hallmarks of the earlier Tory ventures in workfare. Welfare recipients who refused to participate were sent a threatening letter: "If you do not take advantage of this job opportunity, your eligibility for Saskatchewan Assistance Plan benefits will be reviewed immediately."[30] With this policy, the Saskatchewan government came close to breaking the law. Under the terms of the Canada Assistance Plan, which paid half the cost of social assistance, welfare recipients could not be forced to perform work in exchange for benefits. Because of the coercive features of the Saskatchewan program, Havi Echenberg, the Executive Director of the National Anti-Poverty Organization, denounced it as the worst in Canada. In April 1988, federal Health and Welfare Minister Perrin Beatty announced, "My officials are monitoring the situation. I know Saskatchewan is aware of the fact that we are watching it very closely as well."[31] Schmidt, however, was sure he was in the right: "Since when is work illegal?"[32] Devine concurred: "You've got to get a hold of them [welfare recipients] and jolt them a little bit, to help them out."[33]

Between 1985 and 1988, the Saskatchewan government spent $25 million creating 4,893 job placements for people on social assistance. This represented an average of only 16 percent of recipients who were fully employable in those years. The majority of jobs subsidized under workfare were short-term, lasting 20 to 23 weeks, just long enough for the individual to qualify for unemployment insurance benefits.

Did workfare succeed in getting people off welfare and into the work force? The government pointed to the fact that the number of social assistance cases decreased by 1,678 between 1985 and 1988. Nonetheless, the total caseload in 1988 was still 21 percent higher than when the Devine government took office in 1982. The decline in the number of social assistance cases after the introduction of workfare could be explained by other factors. Applicants were possibly deterred from seeking social assistance by stricter eligibility tests; others may have decided to leave the province. The latter possibility was quite likely, given the fact that between 1987 and 1988 Saskatchewan was the only province in Canada to have a decline in the size of its labour force and in the number of people employed.

The 1930s revisited

The Devine government brought back the old distinction between the "deserving" and the "undeserving" poor. Work tests, which had been discredited and abolished after the Great Depression of the 1930s, were re-imposed. Social assistance benefits were cut back so severely that recipients had to seek charitable aid. Between 1983 and 1988, food bank usage increased by 70 percent in Regina, 165 percent in Saskatoon, and 89 percent in

Prince Albert.[34] One study reported that one out of five social assistance recipients in Regina required groceries from the food bank, with the majority of users being children.[35] Food banks also appeared in some parts of rural Saskatchewan. For example, four churches in Lashburn (population 750) got together to establish one that fed 243 people in eight months, 53 percent of them children.[36] In the cities, voluntary organizations like "Chili for Children" and "Food for Learning" sprang up to feed school children. Schmidt adamantly refused to consider a school lunch program: "I would look at a lunch program that might be in the area of a school so that they could walk, have lunch and go back to school, but I'm certainly not going to look at a state-run lunch program."[37] He said that parents, not the government, should feed children.

This was in keeping with the new right's approach to the welfare state. Responsibility for dealing with poverty was shifted from the community to the individual, from the public sector to the private sector. In accordance with the neo-conservative strategy of giving the poor the necessary incentive to get off welfare, social assistance benefits were slashed and welfare was replaced by workfare. The result for Saskatchewan was the breakdown of the welfare system and ever-worsening poverty.

Notes for Chapter 11

1. George Gilder, *Wealth and Poverty* (New York: Basic Books, 1981), p. 73.
2. Canada, Parliament, *Statutes of Canada, Canada Assistance Plan* (Bill C-1), 1966.
3. Bonnie Jeffery, "Living Without Power," *Briarpatch*, June 1986. 4. Joe Ralko, "Non-Governmental Welfare: How Big is the Role of Charity in Helping the Needy?" *Saskatchewan Business*, March/April 1985. 5. Graham Riches, "Feeding Canada's Poor," *Briarpatch*, February 1985.
6. *The Font*, July/August 1988. 7. *Western Report*, 29 June 1987. 8. *Leader-Post*, 15 September 1987. 9. *Ibid.*, 4 May 1988. 10. *Ibid.*, 11 February 1988. 11. *Ibid.*, 8 June 1989. 12. *Ibid.*, 28 February 1987. 13. *Ibid.*, 11 December 1987. 14. *Ibid.*, 15 April 1987. 15. *Ibid.*, 28 February 1987. 16. *Saskatchewan Family Facts*, Saskatchewan NDP caucus, Regina, July 1989. 17. *Star-Phoenix*, 9 March 1987. 18. *Leader-Post*, 6 July 1989.
19. Graham Riches and Lorelee Manning, *Welfare Reform and the Canada Assistance Plan: The Breakdown of Public Welfare in Saskatchewan, 1981-89*

(Regina: Social Administration Research Unit, 1989), p. 5. **20.** Riches and Manning, p. 16. **21.** *Leader-Post*, 23 December 1987. **22.** Mark Stobbe, "Less is More: Schmidtspeak," *Briarpatch*, December 1987/January 1988. **23.** *Leader-Post*, 22 August 1987. **24.** *Globe and Mail*, 24 May 1988. **25.** *Leader-Post*, 19 April 1989. **26.** *Ibid.*, 28 June 1989. **27.** *Ibid.*, 29 June 1989. **28.** *Ibid.*, 15 July 1988.

29. Patricia Elliott, "Wage Slaves," *Saturday Night*, October 1989, p. 56. **30.** *Leader-Post*, 28 June 1989. **31.** Elliott, p. 59. **32.** *Leader-Post*, 18 April 1988. **33.** *Globe and Mail*, 16 April 1988.

34. Riches and Manning. **35.** Graham Riches, *On the Breadline: Hunger in Regina* (Regina: Social Administration Research Unit, 1986), pp. vi, vii. **36.** *Star-Phoenix*, 28 March 1989. **37.** *Ibid.*, 30 January 1988.

12

THE NEW RIGHT
AND THE WELFARE STATE

◊ ──────────────────────────── ◊

THE FAMILY
AND
HUMAN RIGHTS

The PC party is based on positive characteristics
of respect, honesty, and decency that keep
families together. The Conservatives are the
only party willing to take on crime,
prostitution and disease.
— GRANT DEVINE, *speaking at a Regina PC*
nomination meeting, 29 March 1988.

The new right's attack on the welfare state included a
moral component contributed by the new Christian
right, which claims to find sanction for private enterprise economics in the Bible. A good example of this approach comes from
Michael Novak of the American Enterprise Institute: "I advise
intelligent, ambitious, and morally serious young Christians and
Jews to awaken to the growing dangers of statism. They will better
save their souls and serve the cause of the Kingdom of God all
around the world by restoring the liberty and power of the private
sector than by working for the state."[1] The private sector would
not only make you rich, it would save your soul.

Believing as it does that the Bible endorses individual self-reliance, the new right asserts that the solution to society's problems
– whether economic or social – is fundamentally moral. Poverty,
unemployment, family breakdown, crime and drug addiction are
attributed to the immorality of individuals. This approach has the
appeal of simplicity – it is easier to blame everything on beer and

bingo than to come to terms with the complex causes of poverty. As an alternative to the welfare state, the new right proposes an enhanced and strengthened role for the family. By providing those services that in the neo-conservative utopia the government will no longer provide, the family will repair the shredding moral fabric of the nation. It is regarded as the key social institution to develop the ethic of competitive individualism needed to keep people off welfare. No one expressed this idea better than Margaret Thatcher: "The sense of being self-reliant, of playing a role within the family, of owning one's own property, of paying one's own way, are all part of the spiritual ballast which maintains responsible citizenship, and provides a solid foundation from which people look around to see what more they can do for others and for themselves."[2] When the state provides social services, families feel justified in abandoning their responsibilities. Therefore, the new right makes the strengthening of the family one of its major goals.

Rhetorical championing of the family justifies cutting government social expenditures. It also supplies a handy rationale for the redomestication of women, who are encouraged to return to their traditional caring and nurturing roles. The new right's view of the family also implies a dismissal of the services provided by social workers and other professional caregivers as an unnecessary state encroachment on the natural functions of the family.

The new right offers volunteerism as the other major alternative to a publicly funded welfare system. This offers a way for governments, intent on budget-cutting, to transfer responsibility for social problems to volunteer agencies. Volunteerism is justified by what it does for the givers and what it does for the recipients. Because it is essentially charity, it provides the givers with a sense of altruism and the satisfying feeling that comes from doing good. They also have a keener appreciation of their own good fortune in having a job and economic security. At the same time, the recipients are made to feel a little ashamed of having to accept charity, which gives them an incentive to get a job and become self-reliant.

Gay Caswell: Enemy of the welfare state

The Devine government engaged in a great deal of tough talk about welfare spongers, interfering social service bureaucrats, the need to strengthen the family, and the softness of the judicial system on criminals. One of the leading disseminators of the anti-welfare state, pro-family message was Gay Caswell, the Tory MLA who represented the predominantly working-class riding of Saskatoon Westmount from 1982 to 1986. Caswell, the sixth child in a family of nine, was raised on a grain farm 85 kilometres south of Saskatoon. She attended a three-room school where the teachers emphasized the "three Rs," an emphasis that she later cited as a decisive influence in her life, shaping her ideas regarding educational reform. As a young student at the University of Saskatchewan in the early 1970s she studied education, but most of her time was devoted to student politics. Surprisingly, her politics at that time were radical and included support for the pro-choice and anti-war movements.

Caswell's conversion to neo-conservatism began when she left university and began teaching school on an Indian reserve in northern Saskatchewan. She came to believe that the curriculum, which aimed at teaching students to be "caring" and "creative," was an unmitigated disaster. Instead, she returned to traditional methods: "Sit in your desk, be quiet, and do your work." This experience in northern Saskatchewan also led to outspoken scorn for modern social policy. She was convinced that social workers were doing damage to Indian family life. Returning to the city, Caswell was ready to take up a new faith. In 1979, now the mother of six children, she read one of Grant Devine's speeches and felt that he was saying the right things. His talk of God first, family second and politics third was instantly appealing to the recently born-again Caswell. After consulting her conscience and her family, she joined the Progressive Conservative party. Her campaign literature in 1982 highlighted her commitment to fight for the rights of the family in three crucial areas: social services, health, and education. The calling card she left on every doorstep read: "Stop bureaucracy, restore democracy."

When the Tories took office, they used the outspoken Caswell as a trial balloon to test politically volatile social issues with an electorate that was not nearly as attuned to new right thinking as the Tories would have liked. An indication of her influence in social policy was her appointment to the chair of the caucus committee on health and social services. While the direct influence of the committee was difficult to gauge, the fact that the government refused to distance itself from Caswell, and more often supported her, showed a high level of agreement with what she was saying.

And Caswell had a good deal to say. She was the champion of nearly every neo-conservative issue imaginable, and everything she undertook had one passionate aim – to strengthen the family. Thus, the vociferous Tory MLA advocated stricter divorce laws, defiantly opposing no-fault divorce which she believed would fragment the family. She opposed day-care, declaring it just another example of state interference with family responsibilities. She denounced abortion as a criminal assault on the unborn, and attacked Planned Parenthood as an agency whose sole purpose was to corrupt the morals of children.

Caswell's sworn enemies were feminism and socialism, which she regarded as being synonymous. She cringed whenever she heard the terms "women's rights" and "women's liberation" because of their links to socialist ideology. As she put it, whenever socialists "advance one of their causes supposedly for women it has the potential or actuality of doing great harm to women, to the institution of women, the family, to the free enterprise market-place and to democratic traditions."[3] Caswell was equally wary of those who believed that government had a role to play in detecting and punishing wife-beating and child abuse. She opposed giving social workers "massive discretion" for fear that families would be monitored and threatened with the loss of their children. Too broad a definition of "child care," she warned, "would mean more families would suffer loss of autonomy and cohesiveness from state intervention."[4] Above all, Caswell was concerned that the state not interfere with the efforts of parents to raise their children.

The new right and 'real' families

Most Tories joined Caswell on this pro-family bandwagon, but of course they supported only one type of family: the nuclear family with its sexual division of labour between male providers and female homemakers. According to the extremists of the new right, the ideal family was based upon the subordination of women and children to the husband/father. Exemplifying this attitude was a remark made by the president of the Indian Head-Wolseley PCs at an election rally for candidate Graham Taylor: "My good wife's here. She's at the back working, as I guess most of our men like to keep their wives."[5] A woman's natural role was that of homemaker, helpmate, and mother.

This view of the family led to policies aimed at the redomestication of women. The Devine government axed the Women's Division of the Department of Labour, which had been responsible for improving opportunities for women in the workplace. The division had, for example, encouraged and monitored affirmative action programs in the private sector. Under the NDP, preliminary steps had been taken to implement pay equity. Such initiatives were resented by the new right as government intrusions on the free operations of the market and unwarranted attempts to assist women to take jobs outside the home. In the name of the family, the Tories tightened child-care subsidies, limited access to abortions, and began a review of the Matrimonial Property Act.[6]

The Devine government continued in its second term to promote the family as the key feature of its social policy. In July 1989, it hosted a national symposium in Regina on the family, the cost being shared by all the provinces. Elected officials showed up from only three other provinces, and the organizers had to make desperate last-minute phone calls to drum up delegates. Nor was the content of the conference all that the Devine government would have wished. Since it was not footing the entire bill, it lost control of the speakers' list, allowing Roy Bonisteel and others to address both the government-sponsored conference and the protest counter-conference organized by the Saskatchewan Coalition for Social Justice. There, the Devine government was accused of hypocrisy for making a great show of sympathy for the family while allowing a situation where one out of every six families and one out of every four children lived below the poverty line. The conference also challenged the new right stereotype of the "normal" family where father goes to work and mother stays at home to look after the children. Of the 6,325,315 families in Canada in 1984, counter-conference delegates were told, only 24 percent were of this type; nearly 70 percent of Saskatchewan families living in poverty were single-parent families, and a majority of native households in Saskatchewan, most of them poor, were headed by women.

But of course the Coalition for Social Justice's counter-conference failed to convince the Devine government to re-examine some of its assumptions about the family. Instead, Devine created a new cabinet portfolio for family issues, and appointed Beattie Martin the minister responsible for families. The creation of the new portfolio served two purposes: to help Martin, whose seat was in danger, survive the next election, and to re-affirm the Devine government's symbolic commitment to families. However, meaningful policies to support families remained mired in new right ideology.

The privatization of child care

One area of family policy where there was a major, unfilled need was child care. According to the 1986 census, 58 percent of women in the province with preschool children were in the paid labour force, most of them working full time. As of 1989, Saskatchewan had only 5,400 licensed day care spaces. This meant there were spaces for only 7 percent of children whose parents were in the paid labour force, the second-lowest percentage in Canada. Unlicensed child care was the only option for many families, and even this was almost non-existent in rural and northern communities. Low-income families were hit the hardest, first because of the shortage of subsidized day care spaces, secondly because the maximum subsidy was only $235 per month. The subsidy had not been increased for six years and fell well short of the actual cost, which averaged $350 per month in urban centres.[7]

The Devine government did not consider day care to be a necessary public service. Many Tories shared Chantal Devine's view. "Outside of God's love, a woman's love is the most powerful force in our life," said the premier's wife. "Providing day care spaces encourages mothers to go back to work. Wouldn't it be better to look to the future and encourage mothers to stay at home with their children?"[8]

It was a surprise, therefore, when Social Services Minister Grant Schmidt announced in 1988 that the province would be spending $70 million over the next seven years to double the number of licensed and subsidized day care spaces in the province. Unfortunately, the commitment hinged on a major federal initiative promised by the Mulroney government during the November 1988 federal election,[9] and when the victorious federal Tories decided after the election that they had no money for day care after all, their Saskatchewan counterparts immediately abandoned their stated goal of doubling the number of spaces by 1995.[10]

Schmidt called upon private investors to pick up the slack. Legislation was introduced in 1989 to permit the establishment of profit-making day care centres. Until this time, Saskatchewan had been the only province requiring such centres to be nonprofit and controlled by parents. Schmidt defended market-oriented child care on the grounds that it gave parents more options, and ensured that the state did not control the raising of children. NDP MLA Peter Prebble predicted that day care for profit would inevitably lead to the lowering of standards: "Once profit operators and day-care chains are operating in Saskatchewan, there will be a consistent lobby group in place against improved day-care regulations."[11] To support his point, he cited a letter from the Ontario Association of Day-Care Operators to their government in which they opposed new regulations calling for lower children-to-supervisor ratios. The operators did not want to incur higher costs which would lead to lower profit margins.

The Saskatchewan Child Care Association also lobbied against for-profit day care. It quoted studies done in the United States and Canada showing that wages and per-child expenditures were about 30 percent lower at profit-making day cares. Profit centres often cut costs by not hiring enough staff. The resulting heavy workload and long hours led to low morale and a high turnover, with the result that children were constantly having to adjust to new staff.[12]

Governments in other provinces, for example Ontario, where private day care centres had dominated child care for years, were giving more money to non-profit groups all the time, while cutting back on funds for private operations. In Saskatchewan, the trend was the other way. The twenty-year-old Regina Day Care Co-operative closed its doors in September 1989 because of the government's refusal to give an interest-free $20,000 emergency loan.[13] As an alternative to profit-oriented day care, the NDP recommended increasing public funding for non-profit centres above the existing level of $12 million per year, and urged that more emphasis be placed on assisting parents who stayed at home to raise their children. However, the privatization mentality of the government skewed its thinking toward a market solution to the shortage of child care spaces.

Family violence

Neo-conservative thinking also impeded the government's ability to provide adequate child protection services. As early as February 1984, the problems had been clearly identified. A minister's advisory council chaired by Dr. Peter Matthews (later elected provincial president of the Conservative party) submitted a report calling for an overhaul of the Family Services Act. The main thrust of the report was to strengthen the rights of the child. The council proposed that a family guardian be appointed to mediate between the parents and the Department of Social Services in finding an acceptable plan for the care of an abused child. This guardian would have the authority to designate a lawyer to act as the child's advocate. By January 1985, the Department of Social

Services had prepared a set of amendments to the Family Services Act based on the Matthews report.

Social Services Minister Gordon Dirks had promised to introduce the amendments during the spring session of the legislature, but did not do so because an intense debate had broken out over them within the PC caucus. MLA Gay Caswell led the opposition to the amendments, claiming they undermined the autonomy of the family and encroached on the natural rights of parents. Caswell won Devine's support, and the amendments never reached the floor of the legislature.[14]

The issue lay dormant until January 1987, when Saskatchewan Ombudsman David Tickell released a shocking 36-page report on the crisis in the child protection system. The ombudsman, who acts as a watchdog on the government, had received a flood of complaints about the way child abuse cases were being handled, and based his report on 70 investigations conducted over a four-year period. Tickell concluded that many of the problems could be traced to the government's failure to make child protection a priority: "This is a system stretched to its realistic limits and frankly, incapable of guaranteeing safety to children in care."[15] Social workers had too many clients to look after, and some children had been placed in inappropriate foster homes. There were not enough foster homes, and support services were inadequate, Tickell said.[16]

He recounted the history of one family. Even though the stepfather had admitted to sexually abusing the eldest girl, the Department of Social Services twice took her out of foster homes where she had been placed for her own protection and sent her back home to live with her stepfather. The first time, she was returned home after a two-month stay in a foster home. Two weeks later, her stepfather had intercourse with her. She was placed in a different foster home, but in two months the girl was back with her parents. The department did not refer the matter to police for investigation until three years after the girl first alleged she had been sexually assaulted. When the police were finally called in, they found the stepfather had begun sexually abusing the girl's 14-year-old sister. A teenage son who twice attempted suicide told police his stepfather beat him with a belt. Sexual assault charges were eventually laid, and the stepfather was sent to jail for three years. Two of the children needed prolonged psychiatric treatment, while a third child exhibited "a lot of very violent behavior."[17]

Tickell made a number of recommendations, including the appointment of a children's ombudsman or guardian to investigate children's complaints and act as a legal representative for children in court. The guardian would act independently of the Department of Social Services. Tickell also recommended that the provincial government should consider banning the use of corporal punishment in foster homes, something that had already been done in five other provinces. Since foster children frequently come from a background in which they had been abused, there was a danger that corporal punishment would do more harm than good.

Grant Schmidt, who succeeded Gordon Dirks as Social Services Minister, responded to Tickell's report by speculating as to whether the office of the provincial ombudsman should be abolished. "Wouldn't I be better off putting that money into better foster parents than having him [Tickell] spend hundreds of dollars telling us there's a problem?"[18] Devine also called the future of the ombudsman's office into question by refusing to guarantee that the agency would survive the spring budget. It was a classic instance of shooting the messenger rather than listening to the message. As to the substance of Tickell's report, Schmidt had very little to say, except to focus on the recommendation against corporal punishment. He said he saw nothing wrong with corporal punishment, and declared that he spanked his own children on the driveway of his home, a practice he commended to other parents.[19] The recommendation to appoint a guardian to protect the rights of children under foster care was summarily dismissed, even though Alberta had such an official and the Manitoba ombudsman provided similar services. Despite Schmidt's rejection of the report, Tickell was vindicated when, two years later, his successor as ombudsman produced a second report which made some of the same recommendations.

The Department of Social Services gradually came around to

the view that some changes were necessary. In April 1987, Schmidt released a report listing 146 recommendations on discipline of children, procedures for investigating child abuse, training of foster parents, and many other issues.[20] Since roughly 68 percent of Saskatchewan children aged 12 to 17 living in foster homes, group homes, or with relatives were of Indian and native ancestry, the Social Services department hired an official to recruit more native foster parents. Reform and improvements in child care were, at last, slowly introduced.

The reluctance of the new right to allow the state to interfere with the autonomy of the family also contributed to the weak government response to the problem of wife battering. In Saskatchewan, 2,798 women and children found refuge at transition houses in the one-year period ending March 1989, and a further 771 were turned away because of lack of space. These figures did not include the hundreds of women who turned to temporary shelters, family, friends, or crisis centres for help. The shortage of shelters and counselling services was especially acute in rural Saskatchewan. Of thirteen applications to the government for operating funds for new shelter spaces, only one, a six-space transition house in Swift Current, was approved. There was also an urgent need for counsellors to help children deal with the trauma of family violence. More than half of all children admitted to transition houses had witnessed a serious attack against their mother, and more than a third had themselves been victims of violence. Funding to provide counselling services specifically for children was non-existent.[21] In this, as in other respects, the government failed to respond effectively to the needs of families.

Privatization of adoption

The privatization philosophy of the Devine government extended into the area of family services. Previously, all adoptions in the province had been arranged through the Department of Social Services and handled by professional social workers. The Tories brought in new legislation giving the social services minister discretion to approve any non-profit group to provide adoption services. A group in Saskatoon called Christian Counselling Services was given $100,000 a year to assign children to adoptive parents. This allowed natural parents to choose between three or four potential couples when giving up their children, enabling natural parents to make sure their son or daughter was adopted by someone of the same religious faith. [22]

Aside from the questionable wisdom of making adoption a private transaction, privatization could also lead to discrimination. There was a long waiting list in Saskatchewan for the adoption of healthy babies less than 6 months old. In 1986 there were about 1,000 couples on the list, but only 52 received babies. If adoption were placed under the control of privately run "born again" Christian agencies, non-Christian parents or Christian parents who belonged to other denominations would have more difficulty adopting children. As with most privatizations, a particular group benefited at the expense of the interests of society as a whole.

The new right and human rights

The new right supports the family unit as the custodian of basic human values. In a similar way, they support the market as the guarantor of individual freedoms. So great is their faith in the market and their distrust of the state that they oppose all government agencies set up to protect human rights. This explains their hostility to such institutions as the Office of the Ombudsman, the Human Rights Commission, the Legal Aid Commission, and the native courtworker program.

The Office of the Ombudsman was never popular with the Tories, and Premier Devine hinted more than once that it should be abolished. Although he did not carry out this threat, he ignored proper procedure when it came time to choose a successor to David Tickell. It had been customary to make the appointment in consultation with an all-party legislative committee. The government disregarded precedent and, at the last minute, unilaterally selected Gerald McLellan, a former law partner of high-profile Tory George Hill. The NDP charged that the process the Tories followed in choosing Tickell's successor showed a lack of understanding and respect for the role of the ombudsman as someone independent of the government and responsible to the legislature.

The government further undermined the office by underfunding it. As a result, two out of 15.4 staff positions had to be eliminated in 1987. Although McLellan warned in 1988 that any more cuts "would seriously limit our ability to provide this service to the public," another $8,700 was taken from the budget.[23] McLellan then asked to receive his funding from an all-party committee of the legislature rather than from Treasury Board: "I feel it is invidious for the government to be directly involved in reviewing the financial and staffing needs of this office. The conflict is obvious, the remedy simple."[24] The request was denied.

Budget cuts also hampered the effectiveness of the Human Rights Commission. Saskatchewan, the first province in Canada to legislate a Human Rights Code, had been known as a leader in this area. This reputation changed with the election of the Tories. Justice Minister Bob Andrew said seven commissioners were more than was necessary, and when commissioners' terms expired the vacant positions were frequently left unfilled. Lack of funding forced the closure of the Prince Albert office, and employees in Regina and Saskatoon had to take a 10 percent pay cut. In 1987, a year in which the commission's budget was reduced by 15.7 percent, its caseload increased by 43 percent. Of 521 complaints of human rights infractions under investigation, 282 cases represented the backlog from previous years.

Education programs and supervision of affirmative action plans were also curtailed, and the government's own affirmative action plan was a complete shambles. Provincial officials admitted that in the seventeen-month period ending 31 August 1987, the number of women employed by government in non-traditional, non-management positions dropped from 16.2 percent to 7.3 percent. In the same period, the number of natives and physically disabled people employed in such positions also declined. Saskatchewan was going backward rather than forward in providing job opportunities for disadvantaged groups.[25]

The Legal Aid Commission also experienced hard times. Set up in 1974, it was based on the principle that all were equal before the law and justice should not be determined according to the amount of money in one's pocket. Legal aid proved to be an easy target for the Devine government. As funding fell, the demand for the service grew. Because of the economic slowdown, there was an increase in debt-related civil cases, and in cases reflecting financial strain, such as family disputes and marriage breakups, landlord-tenant disputes, and fights with the Social Services department over welfare payments.

The government responded by introducing user fees (a minimum of $60 to a maximum of $400) for legal aid clients deemed capable of paying them. After meeting with lawyers opposed to the fees, Grant Schmidt branded them "left-leaning" and in favour of "socialized law." In fact, many lawyers opposed the fees, including the executive of the Saskatchewan branch of the Canadian Bar Association, who represented about 80 percent of the lawyers in the province.

The federal government, as a partial funder of legal aid services, also had an interest in how well the system was working in Saskatchewan, and launched a thorough evaluation by a group of consultants under the supervision of the dean of law at the University of Saskatchewan. He reported that legal aid in the province was no longer fulfilling its original mandate. Whereas in former years it had provided a full range of services, including both criminal and civil cases, underfunding had led to a concentration on criminal and Family Services Act matters and on cases involving young offenders. The second major finding of the study was that the user fees created financial hardships for some clients. It recommended raising the ceiling on how much money an individual could earn before qualifying for legal aid.

Other law-related programs, such as the John Howard Society mediation services, had their funding entirely eliminated. The mediation service had given first-time offenders a chance to settle their case out of court by making amends to the victim of the crime, keeping an average of between 500 and 600 cases from going to court each year. A program to help ex-convicts readjust to society upon their release from prison was also cancelled, despite its effectiveness in keeping down the rate of repeat offences.

Even more damaging was the gutting of the native courtworker program. It had long been recognized that many native people in Saskatchewan had a hard time understanding and dealing with the justice system. With an uncertain grasp of English, many natives charged with a crime were too shy or intimidated to tell their side of the story to an all-white court. They often shook their heads when addressed by the judge and silently accepted verdicts and sentences based solely on the Crown's version of the facts. The native courtworkers spoke the native languages and were able to explain to their clients what was going on. This was appreciated by judges who felt more confident that justice was being done. As 65 percent of the inmates in provincial jails were native, the program was well-utilized.

In 1987, the provincial government withdrew its funding, which meant that the matching federal contribution was also lost. Expressions of regret by federal Justice Minister Ray Hnatyshyn failed to revive the program. The impact of the loss of the court-workers was brought home by NDP MLA Keith Goulet, the only native sitting in the Legislative Assembly. He recounted what happened to Joseph Morin of Sandy Bay, an illiterate 30-year-old Cree who made his living by chopping firewood, snaring rabbits, and hunting. Morin's first encounter with the justice system occurred when he tried to recover a stolen snowmobile. He was apprehended by the RCMP and charged with operating a motor vehicle while impaired. Morin had heard stories of the terrible things that happen to people in jail and was petrified of going there. He spoke very little English, and there was no native courtworker to explain to him that an impaired driving offence did not necessarily mean a jail term. Rather than face the possibility of going to prison, Morin committed suicide. The local RCMP officer suggested that Morin had personal problems, but there was little doubt that his terror of going to jail contributed to his death.[26]

Marlon Pippin was another native who died violently in a confrontation with the law. The Regina high school student shot himself after being chased, cornered, and fired upon by police. This incident led the Saskatchewan Coalition Against Racism to demand a government inquiry into the justice system's treatment of aboriginal people. Grant Schmidt rejected the request, maintaining that there was no evidence that natives were being mistreated by the police or the court system, and that it was irresponsible to suggest such a thing. Schmidt dismissed the Coalition as a front for the New Democratic Party: "I would say that those groups, while they may not be totally politically dominated, are predominantly offshoots of the NDP in some shape or form, and what you have here is a political dispute and not a genuine dispute about the concern for people."[27] When informed that churches, including congregations of the United Church, were among those calling for an inquiry, Schmidt said he doubted that the clergy involved had consulted their parishioners. In any case, it was Schmidt's opinion that the NDP had attempted to "take over" and "gain political control" of the United Church.[28]

Because of the new right's opposition to the welfare state, interventionist government agencies came under attack, even when the purpose of those agencies was to protect human rights. By its actions and funding policies, the Devine government showed that it had little use for the Ombudsman, the Human Rights Commission, the Legal Aid Commission, or special programs to help disadvantaged groups deal with the justice system. On the surface, this appeared to contradict neo-conservative ideology which stands for individual rights. The point was, however, that these agencies, inherited from previous NDP administrations, were expressions of the community's commitment to protect the rights of its weakest members. The new right believed it was up to individuals, be they rich or poor, to protect their own rights without government assistance.

In the same way, the new right expected families to look after themselves as private, independent units. The intrusions of the welfare state, the claims to expertise by social workers, and the demands of women for equality, were seen as attempts to deprive the family of its rightful role. Even when the need for assistance to families was acknowledged, the new right preferred privately run, profit-oriented child care agencies. Even when child abuse and wife battering were identified as problems, the government moved slowly to do anything about them. Ironically, the new right, while claiming to be for "the family", actually hurt families, especially those below the poverty line. Rather than threatening families in the manner alleged by the new right, the welfare state often gave families essential support.

Notes for Chapter 12

1. Philip Resnick, p. 135. 2. Margaret Thatcher, *Let Our Children Grow Tall* (London: Centre for Policy Studies, 1977), p. 97.

3. Kay Willson and Elizabeth Smillie, "The Conservatives' Recipe for Preserving the Family," *Briarpatch*, March 1984. 4. *Star-Phoenix*, 10 February 1986.

5. *Leader-Post*, 26 September 1986. 6. Willson and Smillie, *Briarpatch*, March 1984.

7. *Saskatchewan Family Facts*, New Democratic Party, July 1989. 8. Chantal Devine, address to national conference of REAL Women, Toronto, 22 April 1989, quoted in *Briarpatch*, June 1989. 9. *Leader-Post*, 15 July 1988. 10. *Star-Phoenix*, 10 May 1989. 11. *Leader-Post*, 23 June 1988. 12. *Star-Phoenix*, 17 May 1988. 13. *Leader-Post*, 29 September 1989.

14. *Ibid.*, 15 January 1987. 15. *Ibid.*, Eisler, 15 January 1987. 16. *Star-Phoenix*, 14 January 1987. 17. *Leader-Post*, 14 January 1987. 18. *Star-Phoenix*, 15 January 1987. 19. *Leader-Post*, 15 January 1987. 20. *Ibid.*, 30 April 1987. 21. *Saskatchewan Family Facts*, New Democratic Party, July 1989.

22. *Leader-Post*, 9 October 1987.

23. *Ibid.*, 22 April 1988. 24. *Ibid.*, 8 April 1989. 25. *Ibid.*, 10 November 1987. 26. *Ibid.*, 5 April 1989. 27. *Ibid.*, 19 April 1988. 28. *Ibid.*, 7 April 1988.

13

THE NEW RIGHT
AND THE WELFARE STATE

THE ASSAULT
ON UNIONS

> I caution the leadership of the unions in this
> country and in all the free world that when they
> go to bed with socialists, they are sleeping with
> a bear – a great big red bear.
> – GRANT SCHMIDT, *Hansard*,
> *21 March 1983, p. 94.*

One of the main reasons for the stability of the postwar welfare state was the consensus that had been worked out between business and labour. Both endorsed the role assumed by the state in smoothing out the business cycle and providing full employment. However, the economic crisis of the mid-1970s brought an end to this consensus when business endorsed the neo-conservative call for reforms to the welfare state, including a reduction of the power and influence of the labour movement.

The new right claims that labour unions obstruct the operation of the free market, and restrict the ability of individuals to make independent choices about their working lives. They blame trade unions for a wide variety of ills plaguing industrial nations in the 1970s and 1980s, accusing them of making aggressive wage demands which bring about competitive decline, of serving their own selfish interests at the expense of consumers, and of limiting individual liberty by dictating when people could work, whom they should support politically, and how their union dues would be used. But, at a more fundamental level, unions have come under fire because they are structured on the basis of collectivist values, values which the new right considers illegitimate in the context of the latter's supposed love of freedom and self-determination.

While unions in general are considered undesirable, public sector unions are subject to particular scorn. This animosity stems from the fact that public sector unions do not operate under market constraints such as profit or unemployment which could temper their demands. In contrast, private sector employees must live with the fear that excessive wage gains might hurl them into unemployment. The new right also charges that large wage gains in the public sector lead to labour unrest and militancy by private sector unions if their wages lag behind. The only remedy to "unfettered" collective bargaining in the public sector is thus the removal of government workers' right to strike as well as their ability to negotiate over pay.[1]

These attitudes pervaded the PC party at the time of the 1982 election. A well-entrenched hostility towards trade unions existed among the farmers, businessmen and small-town lawyers who made up the cabinet. None of them had any affiliation with the labour movement; nor were they sympathetic to labour's goals and aspirations. Much of their abhorrence of unions was, therefore, based not on any rational economic argument, but on sheer partisan instinct. The unions were despised as the close allies of the NDP and representatives of the same hated social democratic philosophy which produced the welfare state.

This intense partisanship continually clouded the Tories' dealings with the union movement. Union briefs were inevitably labelled by the government as "fanciful" or "politically motivated." Upon reading a union brief, Grant Schmidt summed up this attitude with the comment, "You would think it was written by the opposition."[2] No one expressed these sentiments more fully than did Lorne McLaren, Devine's initial choice as labour minister. McLaren was the former general manager of the Morris Rod Weeder Co., a Yorkton-based farm implement manufacturer that had been charged with numerous counts of unfair labour practices under the province's Trade Union Act. In December 1972, Morris Rod Weeder was found guilty of wrongfully dismissing an employee who was involved in a union organizing drive.[3] Similar incidents continued throughout the 1970s, resulting in company convictions for refusing to collect union dues and harassing employees during organizing drives. McLaren's appointment came as a shock to the labour movement, which interpreted it as an act of gross insensitivity or open hostility.[4]

McLaren's perspective has been described as a "unitary view,"[5] which holds that there should be a common point of view within any firm, that a single goal should animate the enterprise, and that everyone should share the rewards of a team effort. Unions are regarded as illegitimate, and their challenges to managerial authority are seen as counterproductive. This view tends to be strongest in small firms, especially old family firms like the Morris Rod Weeder Co., which take a paternalistic attitude towards their employees. Larger firms with greater organizational sophistication are more willing to accept unions, even viewing them as a useful tool in stabilizing the workforce. This approach was rejected by McLaren, who sought to impose his unitary view on labour relations in Saskatchewan.

The Tories were supported in their efforts by the Chamber of Commerce, with whom McLaren had close personal ties. The Chamber had longstanding complaints about the province's labour laws, which they regarded as biased in favour of unions. Over the years the Chamber's newsletter had published many anti-union articles, including one credited to the Morris Rod Weeder Company entitled "Compulsory Unionism – A Destructive Force in Saskatchewan?" The article endorsed the anti-union stance of the new right: "A person can no longer freely offer his labour and services to an employer, because a union now stands between the individual and the prospective employer . . . In essence, our entire democratic system of liberty and freedom is slowly being undermined by union ideology."[6] It was evident that the Chamber saw itself not as just another special interest group, like labour, but as a champion of democracy and freedom, while unions were portrayed as threats to these cherished values.

The war against 104

The Tory government accepted the small businessman's instinctive belief that unions held too much power, and were merely an extraparliamentary extension of the NDP. This led to a frontal assault on the province's Trade Union Act, which many considered the most advanced legislation of its kind in the country, if not the continent. One of the first pieces of legislation passed by the CCF government in 1944, it contained unequivocal guarantees of the right to form unions and engage in a variety of actions, including strikes, without fear of employer reprisals. The Act was patterned after the famous Wagner Act passed in the United States in 1935, which was based on the belief that there was a fundamental inequality between the power of corporations to intimidate and harass unions, and the unions' ability to effectively organize and bargain for the collective rights of workers. Saskatchewan's Trade Union Act, like the Wagner Act, was designed to restore an equality of bargaining power between employees and employers.

The Trade Union Act was seriously undermined during the Liberal regime of Premier Ross Thatcher (1964-71), whose government passed a number of amendments restricting the right of workers to organize. When the NDP returned to power in 1971 they restored the Act to its original form, and amendments were added broadening the definition of an employee to include professional employees as part of the bargaining unit, liberalizing the certification process, and taking away the right of an employer to initiate a second vote when a strike had lasted 30 days. These changes were welcomed by the labour movement, which felt that Saskatchewan had regained its position as having the most progressive labour legislation in the country.

Employers' organizations, including the Saskatchewan Mining Association, the Saskatchewan Chamber of Commerce, Federated Co-ops, and the Saskatchewan Construction Labour Relations Council argued that the Trade Union Act gave too much power to the unions. Upon Grant Devine's 1982 election victory they urged the new PC government to change the legislation, claiming that unions were interfering with business operations and the decision-making process. The amendments proposed by employers groups came in a series of briefs to the government which were made public in December 1982.[7] No labour groups were asked to submit briefs. Will Klein, executive vice-president of Canadian Pioneer Management, believed that the anti-union amendments "would do more in one fell swoop to bring business to Saskatchewan than any other single thing you could do."[8] The briefs focused on reducing the size of the unionized work force, limiting the ability of unions to bargain, and increasing employer control over union activity.[9]

Bill 104, passed in June 1983, implemented the employers' recommendations and shifted the balance of power from unions to business interests. The bill included provisions for excluding management personnel from unions, and allowed employers to define employees with marginal supervisory duties as management. Employers were also able to designate employees as independent contractors, and, as such, not part of the union. The bill allowed all employees, even those who were not union members, to participate in a strike vote, a provision enabling an employer to "rent-a-vote" a few days before balloting. Equally unsettling for the unions was an amendment which made them liable to lawsuits, which presented the possibility of employers bankrupting unions in lengthy legal battles.

The bill also featured a so-called "freedom of speech" amendment which gave employers the right to communicate with their employees during a union organizing drive, provided their anti-union message was presented in a manner that avoided intimidation, threat, or coercion. This amendment put employers' freedom of speech above the employees' freedom of association.[10] The unions' biggest concerns centered around the "30-day rule" which had been introduced by the Thatcher government and repealed by the NDP in 1971. Reinstituted by Bill 104, it empowered the Labour Relations Board to order a vote on the employer's last offer once a strike had gone on for 30 days. Many felt this would encourage employers to refuse negotiations in an attempt to force a vote, while they tried in the mean time to convince part of the workforce to accept the deal. The clause was seen as destroying the practice of good-faith bargaining.[11]

Bill 104's opponents, which included the labour movement as well as the NDP, argued that the government seemed more concerned with protecting employees from their unions than from their employers, and that the amendments represented a complete reversal of the original intent of the Trade Union Act. The Saskatchewan Federation of Labour organized a massive campaign under the slogan, "Join the War Against 104." It sponsored public meetings, collected signatures on petitions, presented video tapes and pamphlets, made lists of trade unionists available to speak against the bill, and held a huge protest rally on the grounds of the legislature, all to no avail. McLaren defended the bill with arguments based on economic necessity: it would encourage investor confidence, enhance labour peace, and increase and protect the rights of individual workers. In the legislature, he insisted that "the amendments before us are not anti-labour. They are not anti-anything. They are pro-labour, they are pro-management, and they are pro the people of Saskatchewan, and pro the future investors and job creators in Saskatchewan."[12] The government ignored the protests of the unions and passed the bill with virtually no changes.

Before Bill 104, unions in Saskatchewan had been bargaining for such progressive measures as pay equity, childcare provisions, paid paternity leave, affirmative action, career development, and the right to refuse dangerous work; now they had to fight anew the old battles for the simple and fundamental right to organize and engage in free collective bargaining. Concerns shifted back to the basic issues of wages and job security. The new right had succeeded in turning back the clock on more than ten years of advances by the labour movement.

Although Bill 104 was a major gain for the business community, many on the right believed the government had not gone far enough – they had hoped for some form of right-to-work legislation. The Tories were unwilling to go that far, not because of a lack of interest in the idea, but because of a pragmatic sense of how far the labour movement could be pushed. While they believed that reducing the power of unions would lead to labour stability and more investment, they also knew that labour was a powerful lobby in the province and could marshal a large and vocal opposition. The government feared that an all-out war with the union movement would have done more to sour the business climate than improve it.

The unions undermined

Bill 104 was just the first step in the Devine government's campaign to undermine the position of unions. Another example was the treatment accorded the construction trades, which were involved in a bitter four-month strike in 1982. The unions wanted to maintain wages at current levels, but the Construction Association, representing the employers, demanded wage cuts of as much as 25 percent. The Construction Association's problem was that they were being outbid by non-unionized contractors from outside the province; they would have to reduce wages to remain competitive. The unions naturally wanted none of this and asked the government to use only unionized contractors on publicly-funded construction projects, a request the government predictably rejected.

In fact, the Tories granted the employers' wishes by repealing the Construction Industry Labour Relations Act, which had been passed by the NDP in 1978 and had allowed for industry-wide bargaining for the province's 600 unionized tradesmen. Although the trade unions had been largely satisfied with the Act, the contractors were eager to have it repealed. From their point of view, the major problem was that it did not permit the creation of "spin-off" or "double-breasted" companies, whereby a union contractor created a non-union subsidiary. When the government did away with the Act, contractors almost immediately began setting up such subsidiaries. The effect of this was that union employees either had to accept lower wages or face the prospect of being laid off.

Before long, virtually every major construction job went to non-union firms, whose bids were as much as a third lower than those of union firms. Union workers stood around in union hiring halls without work or hid their union membership so that they could work on non-union jobs. In 1982, an estimated 70 percent of the building trades were unionized; by 1989 only 5 percent were. Tradesmen accepted wages with non-union contractors that were between 20 and 40 percent less than union rates.[13] Even more employer savings were realized because there were no longer jurisdictional disputes about who should do the work. Many jobs used only a minimum number of journeymen, with apprentices doing most of the work at wages that were 40 to 60 percent below the former going rate.

On another front, the government moved to undermine the influence of the labour movement by restricting its representation on numerous provincial boards and commissions.[14] While organized labour had in the past been represented on virtually every provincial board including those of Crown corporations, by 1989 it was represented only on the Workers' Compensation Board. When the Tories did make a rare "labour" appointment, it was usually someone with only a remote or vague connection to organized labour. Typically, they would appoint someone who was once a tradesman, but had long since traded in his overalls for a suit as the owner of a small business. Alternatively, they would select someone who, while nominally a union member, had never been active in the union and had no real responsibility to labour.

Over the years, the government continued to weaken both the union movement and the rights of unorganized workers. In 1986, the name of the Department of Labour was downgraded to the Department of Human Resources, Labour and Employment. More significantly, a new Employment Benefits Act was introduced in 1988 (Bill 73) to replace the old Labour Standards Act. Bill 73 would permit union contracts which denied workers the minimum wage, paid vacation, overtime pay, maternity leave and other benefits; the NDP sarcastically called it the Employer Benefits Act.

Bill 73 was also hard on non-unionized workers. It allowed employers to deduct alleged cash shortages or loss of property from an employee's wages, and reduced the notice period required before laying off workers.[15] It also drastically limited the powers of the Minimum Wage Board, a move that was seen by the NDP opposition as paving the way for the government's cherished idea of a "two-tier" minimum wage. Among the other "benefits" conferred by the Act was the right of retail employers to make their employees work two shifts back-to-back, with no overtime pay. At the same time, female employees were denied the right to paid transportation after midnight. Part-time workers were also treated badly because, while the Act would entitle them to fringe benefits proportional to the time they worked, they had to have had two or more years of continuous employment with one employer to qualify – a condition few part-time workers can meet. In addition, employers would have no obligation to provide fringe benefits to part-time employees unless they asked for them.

Even the Regina *Leader-Post* thought the government had gone too far this time, and called on the Minister of Labour, Grant Schmidt, to put aside his anti-labour feelings.[16] Responding to the pressure of public opinion, Schmidt retreated: "Seeing there is such opposition to the Employment Benefits Act, we'll leave it and keep the status quo."[17] By this time, the Tories were gearing up for an election and did not want a confrontation with labour to add to their woes.

The combined effect of the government's anti-union bias (which, in typical neo-conservative fashion, they called its "pro-worker" attitude), the passage of legislation that weakened and harassed the labour movement, the general reduction of employee rights, and the decline of labour representation on the province's boards and commissions had the desired result. Beginning in 1982, union membership as a percentage of the non-agricultural workforce steadily declined. Real wages also declined, with no increase in benefits as compensation. The government's attack on unions had weakened the position of both organized and unorganized workers.

Public sector unions: Patronage and privatization

While organized labour in general was unhappy about Tory labour policy, public sector unions had some added concerns. These unions, the Saskatchewan Government Employees Union (SGEU) in particular, had a more complicated task when dealing with the government because of their employer/employee relationship. If nothing else, the 1982 election taught the public sector unions that all governments, including the NDP, could be cynical and manipulative in the way they treated their employees. Yet, whatever the shortcomings of the NDP as an employer, they were minor compared with those of the Tories. The SGEU was soon drawn into almost continuous warfare with the new government over two issues – patronage and privatization.

Through patronage, the Tories sought to clean the "reds" out of the civil service and replace them with "blue" supporters. Patronage prevailed not only in the senior echelons, where it might be defensible, but also at the lower levels. The SGEU watched with horror as the Public Service Commission, which was supposed to be a professional hiring agency guaranteeing the merit principle, was politically intimidated and transformed into a partisan hiring body. Merit was slowly eclipsed by partisanship as the main criterion for employment in the public service.

The Devine administration ignored the spirit of the Civil Service Act and the collective agreement, which together had guaranteed the merit principle and public servants' political rights, formalized lay-off procedures and eligibility for promotions, and facilitated career moves into senior non-union positions. Typical of the government's tendency to ignore these acts was its decision to by-pass union members when hiring for positions outside the union's scope. The collective agreement clearly stated that out-of-scope positions "should be regularly bulletined" and that, merit and ability being equal, the job should go to an existing government employee. The Tories, however, ignored this clause and for the most part hired on the basis of partisan connection.

The union also watched helplessly as the government turned many civil service career positions into partisan appointments by removing them from the scope of the union contract. Many upper-level civil service jobs to which career civil servants aspired were converted into order-in-council positions and filled with patronage appointees. At the other end of the administrative hierarchy, permanent positions were reclassified as non-permanent and temporary, making it easier for the government to place Tories in jobs that now fell outside the union contract. The SGEU estimated that the use of casual employees jumped about

200 percent between 1985 and 1988. This created frustration and anger among managers who often had to make room for unqualified party hacks.

The "blueing" of the public service caused a severe decline in the morale of government workers.[18] Union officials noted that certain departments, most notably social services, attached blue cardboard flags to Tory-referred job applicants to indicate that they should get special treatment. This was replaced by a system of computer coding, which brought patronage into the high-tech age. Further, personnel officers and other officials involved in hiring were often told to pick a name off "must hire" lists provided by the minister.

Frustrated by rampant patronage, the SGEU faced other serious irritants as well. Hostility between the union and the government over the issue of wages surfaced shortly after the 1982 election, when Finance Minister Bob Andrew introduced a public sector wage restraint program that was supposed to help fight inflation. The announcement was made on 30 September 1982, the same day the SGEU contract expired. This restraint program, which limited wage increases in the public sector to the rate of inflation minus 1 percent, was seen as a negation of collective bargaining rights. There could be little good-faith negotiation if the settlement had been determined before negotiations even began.[19] Devine's government remained uncompromising on the wage issue in the years that followed. In 1984, the union was told to expect no increases for the next two years. The government held that since farmers were suffering a loss in income due to severe drought conditions, civil servants should suffer right along with them.

Another action that stung the union was the creation of the Saskatchewan Water Corporation. This corporation was made up of 100 or so employees who had been transferred from the Departments of Agriculture and Environment. The Act creating this Crown corporation was unique in containing a provision that exempted it from section 37 of the Trade Union Act, which guaranteed union members a continuation of their union protection and contract rights in an employer-initiated transfer from one workplace to another. By means of this exemption the government assured itself of a non-union workplace and further weakened the SGEU.

The backdrop to these irritants was government contract negotiations which dragged along for over a year after the union's contract expired in September 1984. The stumbling block was not wages, but rather the government's desire to introduce legislative changes aimed at formalizing patronage in the public service. The SGEU accused the government of having an "immature understanding of state power" and forgetting the traditional separation of political and administrative functions.[20] The union, which viewed the move as an attempt to give cabinet ministers more access to the levers of patronage, refused to negotiate any change in this aspect of their collective agreement and vowed to oppose any changes to the Civil Service Act.

Faced with continual attacks, whether in the form of patronage, reclassified jobs, or wage restraint, the union felt the need to assert itself, and called a series of rotating strikes between October 1985 and January 1986. The main issue in the dispute was the union's desire for reinstatement of fair hiring practices and job security, and a return to the old lay-off procedures which required that employees be transferred within government when a job came open. The government was willing to offer more money, but not to back down on its plan to decentralize hiring from the Public Service Commission. A conciliator's report, presented in January 1986, was unacceptable to the union because it failed to deal with the major issue of fair hiring and lay-off procedures. With no settlement in sight, the government legislated the union back to work.

In doing so, the government took the unprecedented step of invoking section 33 of the Charter of Rights and Freedoms, the constitutional override clause. This heavy-handed legal weapon took away the workers' constitutional guarantee of freedom of association. The action created a storm of controversy throughout the nation, and nearly all legal experts and civil libertarians agreed that it was a serious breach of the spirit of the Charter. By invoking section 33, the Devine government had pre-empted a full and open discussion of the issues, and had denied the courts an opportunity to make a decision on the nature of the government's actions. As Alan Borovoy, the general counsel for the Canadian Civil Liberties Association, explained, "The hearing in court can affect the political climate. This was the way the system was intended to operate. It increases the political flack [governments] have to take for invoking the override clause."[21]

While unprecedented at the time, this action was not out of character with the Tories' overall understanding of how political power should be exercised. They had the power and they were going to use it, regardless of constitutional subtleties. The government failed to appreciate the spirit in which section 33 had been included in the Charter, nor did they see how civil liberties could take precedence over their own partisan interests.

Another issue that focused public sector union opposition to the Devine government was privatization. As citizens and taxpayers, unionists opposed the dismantling of Crown corporations which had provided social and economic benefits to the people of the province. As members of public sector unions, they regarded privatization as synonymous with deunionization. By 1989, privatization had cost the SGEU 2,000 members. Both the boards and senior executives of privatized firms received substantial benefits from privatization, whereas union members were often left without union protection, or were forced to take wage cuts to make the firm "competitive." In addition, privatization usually resulted in the reduction in size of the overall staff. Well-paying, secure union jobs were replaced by low-paying jobs with no security. From the union's perspective, the private sector's profits came not from greater efficiency, but from the use of cheaper non-union labour. When the unions fought privatization, they felt they were fighting for their very survival.

The SGEU maintained that privatization was false economy. Forcing government workers into lower paying jobs in the private sector, or onto unemployment insurance, meant there would be less money circulating in the provincial economy, and fewer taxes would be paid. From the union's perspective, the government was creating unemployment by axing huge numbers of jobs, while at the same time spending millions on job creation through subsidies to private firms.[22] The whole array of arguments for privatization failed to impress the public sector unions, which saw themselves as double losers, as trade unionists and as taxpayers.

The SGEU felt the impact of privatization when 200 Highways Department employees were fired in the spring of 1984 so that contracts for road maintenance and construction could be given to private contractors. At about the same time, the government privatized court reporting, throwing fifteen SGEU members out of work. The privatization of provincial parks began in the summer of 1984. Golf courses, condos, cabins, ski-hills, restaurants and campgrounds were sold or leased to private operators on highly favourable terms. By 1989, more than 160 union jobs had been lost from the provincial parks system. Other government services which were privatized included the sale of auto insurance and the issuing of drivers' licenses, the sale of telephones, the sale of crop insurance, and the children's dental plan.

In eight years of battle with the government over privatization, the unions could only claim limited victory on two fronts. The first was over the government's plan to privatize the province's liquor stores. After the union ran a hard-hitting advertising campaign which suggested that privatized liquor stores would sell to minors and increase alcohol consumption, the government backed down. The other small triumph came when the government had to retreat on its plans for the privatization of support services in hospitals and nursing homes. When a private businessman who had received the contract to provide housekeeping, laundry and dietary services for a nursing home in Melville refused to recognize the union, the case went to the Labour Relations Board, which upheld the union's "successor rights" and forced the private employer to respect the union contract.

The advent of the new right also brought one unintended benefit to unions – a new-found independence. The election of the PCs in 1982 left organized labour without its traditional political representation and forced the labour movement, which had been very dependent upon the NDP, to become more autonomous, cohesive and self-reliant. It joined forces with other groups opposed to Tory policies, and while it continued to work in alliance with the NDP, it also carried on its own independent fight.

The strength of the new right forced labour unions to marshal their resources to defend their alternative vision of the future of the province.

Notes for Chapter 13

1. Sandra Christensen, *Unions and the Public Interest* (Vancouver: The Fraser Institute, 1980). 2. *Star-Phoenix*, 1 April 1986. 3. *Ibid.*, 15 June 1982. 4. "Lorne McLaren: The Right Man for the Job." *Briarpatch*, July/August 1983. 5. Robert Sass, "The Saskatchewan Trade Union Amendment Act, 1983: The Public Battle," *Relations Industrielles* Vol. 40, No. 3, 1985, pp. 591-621, 614. 6. "Compulsory Unionism – A Destructive Force in Saskatchewan?" *Saskatchewan Business Review*, Spring 1977, p. 5.

7. *Leader-Post*, 24 December 1982. 8. *Financial Post*, 1 April 1983. 9. Glen Makahonuk, "The Trade Union Act is Under Attack," *Briarpatch*, April 1983. 10. S. Muthuchidambaram, "Legislative Background to and an Examination of The Saskatchewan Trade Union Amendment Act: Bill 104," unpublished paper, 1984. 11. *Star-Phoenix*, 16 June 1983. 12. *Debates and Proceedings (Hansard)*, Legislative Assembly of Saskatchewan, 3 June 1983, p. 2933.

13. *Star-Phoenix*, 13 February 1989. 14. Interview, Barb Byers, 29 September 1989. 15. Glen Makahonuk, "Restricting Workers' Rights," *Briarpatch*, November 1988. 16. *Leader-Post*, 14 April 1989. 17. *Ibid.*, 3 November 1989.

18. *Star-Phoenix*, 25 June 1985. 19. Leo Panitch and Donald Swartz, *From Consent to Coercion: The Assault on Trade Union Freedoms* (Toronto: Garamond Press, 1985), p. 12. 20. *Star-Phoenix*, 6 June 1985. 21. *Globe and Mail*, 13 February 1986. 22. *Star-Phoenix*, 6 April 1984.

14

THE NEW RIGHT'S CONTEMPT
FOR GOVERNMENT

◇ ———————————————— ◇

THE LEGISLATURE
UNDERMINED

> The Saskatchewan government appears to regard
> the province's auditor as a kind of Peeping Tom,
> a prowler in the backyard of its fiscal business
> and a rude intruder on its private affairs.
> – GLOBE AND MAIL, *22 May 1989.*

The Devine government has consistently behaved as though utterly convinced of the rightness of its cause, a common occurrence with ideological movements of both the right and the left. Within the PC party there is a strong belief that the market provides all the answers, and this conviction goes a long way toward explaining the Tories' insensitivity to the requirements and practices of parliamentary government. They regard the legislative assembly not as a forum in which reasonable people can discuss political issues and reach reasonable compromises, but rather as a hindrance to their ability to manage the government – and in the long run, as something to be barely tolerated rather than deeply respected.

This hostility to the procedures and practices of parliamentary democracy contrasts noticeably with the older style of conservatism, which cherished parliamentary debate and the traditions associated with it. The conservatism of Sir John A. Macdonald and John Diefenbaker was synonymous with parliamentary procedure and eloquent debate. The new conservatives, however, view the legislature with derision precisely because it is "old fashioned" and characterized by too much talk and not enough action. Legislative procedure is seen as an encumbrance and a luxury, to be indulged only to the extent that constitutional law requires. The new right, enamoured with the private sector's ideas of management, has no use for a "talking-shop" like the legislature.

Parliamentary tradition ignored

This attitude was apparent even before Devine and company were elected in 1982. During the 1982 campaign, the Tories announced that they would remove the gas tax the day after the election, showing a remarkable disregard for the legislative process. The gas tax had been instituted by a statute, and the proper way to get rid of it was through a bill to repeal the statute. This would take at least a week or two as the election had to be finalized, the government sworn in, a cabinet named, and so on. The Tories' error might have been attributed to inexperience, were it not for the fact they continued to make the same mistakes. In 1985, the government again tried to bypass the legislature when it abolished property tax rebates. The government simply wanted to stop paying these rebates, seemingly unaware that the people of the province had a statutory right to them until such time as the legislation was repealed. By avoiding the legislature, the Tories hoped to escape criticism and debate on the issue.[1]

The Devine government also moved quickly in the area of public administration. Aside from ignoring the tradition of a nonpartisan, professional public service, the Tories wanted to change the relationship between the government and the province's various boards and agencies. In July 1982, the government passed a new appointments bill empowering the executive to appoint new people to boards, commissions and agencies without regard to any other government act, order, regulation or agreement. This action destroyed the autonomy of many boards, such as the Workers' Compensation Board, which exercised quasi-judicial authority and, like the judiciary, required independence if people were to respect its rulings. If the chairman of the WCB could be removed by any government because it disagreed with his decisions, then the independence of the office became questionable. The Tories appeared unconcerned about the need for boards and commissions to have an arm's-length relationship with the government if public confidence was to be preserved.

Another concept that the government ignored was the matter of legislative privilege. In particular, there was a lack of recognition of the importance of an MLA's freedom of speech and immunity from legal prosecution. In 1984 NDP MLA Ned Shillington was sued for comments he made in the legislature, arising out of the government's sale of the old Saskatchewan Government Insurance building in Regina. He asserted that there was conflict of interest in that SGI's former facilities manager, Gary Miller, became a vice-president with the property management firm Silver Developments on the day the building was sold to that company. Complicating the issue was the fact that Shillington produced evidence that higher bids for the property had been rejected. Gary Miller and Silver Developments laid charges against Shillington in provincial court.

The statement of claim against Shillington quoted the words he had spoken in the legislature. Under all circumstances, speeches in any legislative assembly in Canada are privileged and beyond the reach of the law. Shillington naturally assumed that a breach of parliamentary privilege had occurred and asked the Speaker of the Legislature to rule on the matter. The Speaker agreed with Shillington but suggested that it was up to the Legislative Assembly to decide what was to be done. Shillington then made a motion to send the matter to the Legislature's Standing Committee on Elections and Privileges, where the people who were suing him could explain their actions and defend themselves.

But Tory House Leader Bob Andrew refused to co-operate. He felt that all that was necessary was for those responsible for the breach of privilege to send a letter to the Speaker apologizing for their actions. He also believed that the case should go to court where it would be immediately rejected by the judge, who would understand the doctrine of legislative privilege. Andrew took the opportunity to snidely mention that MLAs have certain responsibilities that come with their privileges and should not hide behind the parliamentary privilege to make comments they would not repeat outside its walls.[2] For his part, Justice Minister Gary Lane felt that the whole question of legislative privilege should be decided by courts, forgetting that having the courts rule on the privileges of the legislature was itself a violation of the doctrine that requires that these two branches of government remain separate.

When the government refused to send the matter to a legislative committee and instead referred it to the court, the NDP walked out of the legislature on a point of privilege, provoking the province's first bell-ringing incident. The NDP got support for their position from the legislative law clerk, Merrilee Rasmussen, who took the view that an MLA should not have to go to court to defend comments made in the legislature and that forcing an MLA into court under such circumstances interfered with his ability to perform his duties.[3] The matter resolved itself four days later when the litigants withdrew the law suit. The NDP was no doubt pleased with the result, given that the concept of legislative privilege is not easy for the public to grasp.

The Tories' failure to understand the role parliamentary rules play in ensuring public accountability continued in the government's second term. A few months after the 1986 election, the government began to centralize power in cabinet and ignore the legislature to an even greater extent than it had in the first term. The most obvious example was Bill 5, which gave the executive sweeping powers to reorganize government without informing the Legislative Assembly. It allowed the cabinet to establish and eliminate government departments, as well as to determine their objectives and purposes, beyond the scrutiny of either the legislature or the press. Roy Romanow called this an "attack on the democratic parliamentary traditions of the legislative assembly of Saskatchewan."[4] Allan Blakeney pointed out that the bill gave the cabinet the power to make laws, taking it away from the legislature where it properly belonged.[5] Bill 5 came on the heels of an election that substantially reduced the Tory majority and gave the NDP a powerful 25-member opposition with the ability to make life uncomfortable for the government. In that context, the bill can be interpreted as an attempt to neutralize the opposition and limit the amount of public scrutiny the government would have to face.

The protest against Bill 5 came not only from the NDP but also from the press. In an editorial, the Regina *Leader-Post* urged the government to reconsider: "Streamline yes; reorganize yes; but do it in the open where it can be seen, dissected and clearly understood."[6] SGEU president Barb Byers denounced the bill as a "radical departure from Saskatchewan traditions in the organization of government."[7] Most observers saw the bill as being legally, morally and constitutionally wrong. The acts creating the existing departments and agencies of government had all been passed by the legislature, and any attempt to reorganize them should proceed through the legislature. Bill 5 was a serious attempt to reduce the accountability of the government to the people.

The government House Leader, Eric Berntson, downplayed these concerns. "The Act is simply an administrative mechanism to create new departments from old, to change the names of departments, to change functions, and so on," he claimed, adding that the measure was similar to one introduced by the Schreyer government in Manitoba in 1970.[8] But the difference between the two bills was clear to anyone who read them. The Saskatchewan bill had a clause, absent from the Manitoba bill, that gave the cabinet the power to establish departments and determine their objectives, and even to eliminate them. In Manitoba and every other jurisdiction in the country, the legislature had to approve such changes. With the passage of Bill 5, the Devine Tories displayed an unprecedented disregard for the rights of the legislative assembly.

Countless other incidents illustrated the Tories' lack of respect for parliamentary traditions and conventions. During the debate on privatizing the Potash Corporation of Saskatchewan, Devine invoked closure before most of the front-bench ministers had entered the debate. In 1987, the Tories refused to call the legislature into session even though the normal time to introduce a budget had passed. In order to pay for government spending, the cabinet resorted to the use of special warrants, a practice the legislative law clerk warned was possibly illegal.

The concept of ministerial responsibility meant little to the Tory government. Deputy Premier Eric Berntson initially promised to take full responsibility for the more than $5 million the government invested in the scandal-plagued GigaText company. When the business was finally shut down, Berntson failed to comply with his parliamentary obligation to resign. Question period became a farce when the premier and his ministers made no pretence of answering questions, but used them as opportunities to launch into irrelevant tirades. Devine made a habit of not bothering to be present when the leader of the opposition replied to the budget speech or the speech from the throne; former premiers had always extended this courtesy. As all these breaches of parliamentary tradition show, the Devine government has disdain for the rules and conventions of the legislature.

Democratic rights disregarded

The Tories' flouting of the legislature broadened into a more general attack on such democratic principles as the right of free speech. When the ombudsman criticized the government for its inadequate child protection program, he was accused by Social Services Minister Grant Schmidt of "sensationalism" and "indulging in politics."[9] When a provincial employee expressed doubts about the Rafferty dam project, he was suspended for two weeks.[10] Non-government organizations (NGOs) which were dependent on grants from the social services department were forced to sign a document agreeing "to treat as confidential any policy information provided by the Department of Social Services." This meant that an organization ran the risk of losing its funding if it spoke out against government policy. According to Schmidt, "These are service contracts – contracts for them [NGOs] to serve the people of Saskatchewan, not to get involved in politics."[11] Eventually he was forced to back down, but only after a determined effort to curb freedom of speech.

A respect for representative democracy was conspicuously absent from the Tories' redrawing of electoral boundaries. After Premier Ross Thatcher's outrageous gerrymander of 1971, the Blakeney government introduced a degree of fairness to the system. It established an Electoral Boundaries Commission made up of three people: one appointed by the speaker of the legislature and agreeable to both the government and the opposition, the clerk of the legislative assembly, and an individual nominated by the chief justice of Saskatchewan. The legislation called for constituencies with an average of 10,000 voters, and permitted only a 15 percent variance from that number. It also provided for an automatic review of constituency boundaries every eight years.

When the eight-year period elapsed, Devine refused to allow the already-existing Electoral Boundaries Commission to do its work. Instead, he brought in a new law changing the commission's make-up. The clerk of the legislature, a non-partisan officer, was replaced by the chief electoral officer, a political appointee. Even more significant, the Tories changed the rules to permit the number of voters in a constituency to vary by as much as 25 per cent from the average. This paved the way for a gerrymander whereby rural seats, where the Tories are traditionally strongest, had fewer voters than did urban seats. Twenty-one of the 26 NDP seats had their boundaries redrawn, causing considerable disruption to constituency organizations, while only ten of the 38 seats held by the government saw their boundaries change.

Even more serious were the Devine government's treatment of the judiciary. For years the province's judges had been stonewalled in their request for an independent commission to govern judicial appointments, salary levels, job security, court staffing and other matters related to the courts. Their $80,000 annual salaries were the second-lowest in the country, more than $24,000 less than what their colleagues in Ontario and Alberta were getting. But worst of all, some judges were, according to press reports, concerned they might be transferred to remote locations if they offended the government in a decision, and Bob Andrew, while he was justice minister, took it upon himself to advise judges not to interpret the Canadian Charter of Rights and Freedoms in too "literal" or "liberal" a manner.[12]

After years of complaining in private, the judges decided to make their grievances public. In 1989, the Provincial Court Judges' Association threatened to take legal action against the government after what one judge described as years of "frustration, disillusionment and demoralization" in dealing with Andrew and Gary Lane, his predecessor as justice minister.[13] At first Lane dared them to proceed with a lawsuit, but, hours before the judges were scheduled to hold a news conference at which they intended to announce their challenge, he backed down and agreed to consider a negotiated settlement. The whole sorry episode was typical of what University of Western Ontario law professor Robert Martin called the "incompetent, mean-spirited government of Premier Grant Devine."[14]

The attack on the provincial auditor

Of all the government's dubious actions, the dispute with the provincial auditor, Willard Lutz, was one of the most serious because it involved the entire scope of government operations. The auditor's job is to report to the legislature on how the government is managing taxpayers' money. His audit consists of three things: he gives an opinion on the control systems that are in place in each government department and Crown corporation to make sure that money is not mis-spent; he reports as to whether government has complied with the law in the raising, spending, borrowing and lending of money; and he checks to see whether the government's financial statements truthfully and accurately reflect what happened to the money. The relationship between the government and the auditor is not usually a cozy one, nor should it be. His job is to ferret out the instances where the government has erred, not to praise the government for following correct procedures. Since no government likes to have its dirty linen aired, governments and auditors view one another with wary suspicion. At the same time, as the watchdog on government spending the auditor has an important role to play in the political process.

In his auditor's report for the fiscal year 1985-86, Willard Lutz condemned the government's slowness in releasing the public accounts, which detail how the government has spent its money. From 1945 to 1981, the public accounts for the previous fiscal year were always made available by the start of the new fiscal year. That is, past practice dictated that the public accounts for the fiscal year ending 31 March 1986 should have been released before April 1, 1987. In fact, in most years they would have been released by February or even earlier. But the Devine government did not release the public accounts for the year 1985-86 until 29 June 1987, fifteen months after the end of the fiscal year.[15] The following year was not much better; public accounts for the year ending 31 March 1987 were not available to the Legislative Assembly until 19 May 1988. This meant that the assembly had to debate and approve the budget for 1989 without having a chance to see how the government had spent its money in either 1988 or 1987. Lutz thought these delays were unacceptable.

It was not just the lateness of the public accounts that bothered Lutz; he also censured the government's spending practices. In his 1985-86 report, he noted that the government had loaned more than $1 billion to farmers without ensuring those who received the money were eligible, or that the loans were adequately secured. He also criticized the Economic Development and Trade Department for spending more than $531,000 on its Hong Kong office without government authorization.

In his 1986-87 report Lutz observed that the government was trying to sidestep proper scrutiny of its spending by transforming the Department of Supply and Services, which was responsible for government buildings, vehicles, capital projects and purchasing, into a Crown corporation, the Property Management Corporation. Unlike government departments, Crown corporations do not report their spending in detail.[16] Lutz also accused the Devine government of mis-stating the size of the deficit by disguising $181.9 million of it as a "loan" to the Property Management Corporation. Lutz argued that this "loan," which appeared on the government's books as an asset, couldn't really be considered so because the Corporation was unable to pay it back – it had no independent revenue base, and any money it received had to come from the government. A loan that cannot be paid back, he explained, is no longer an asset but an expenditure.[17]

Justice Minister Bob Andrew responded to Lutz's criticisms by insulting Lutz's profession. Auditors, he said, are "people who bump against reality once a year. They live in that jungle-zoo and call themselves bureaucrats. They wear thick glasses because they are looking at the fine print to see if every 'i' is dotted."[18] More seriously, the government cut the budget of the auditor's office and curbed his authority. The budget fell from $3.6 million in 1984-85 to $3.2 million in 1987-88; with a reduced staff, Lutz found it harder to carry out proper audits. In 1987, the government introduced amendments to the Provincial Auditor's Act to allow Crown corporations to hire private-sector auditors. They would now be appointed by the boards of directors of the Crowns, which were in turn appointed by the cabinet. In other words, from now on the cabinet was going to pick its own watchdog. This did not necessarily mean the private auditors would do a poor job, but they had to consider the possibility that if they irritated the government, they might not be rehired. The provincial auditor, by contrast, was appointed not by the cabinet but by the legislature, and his responsibility was to the people of the province through their elected representatives, not to the executive of the government.

Even though the 1987 amendments allowed for the appointment of private auditors for the Crowns, the law stated that the provincial auditor retained overall responsibility for approving all financial statements. That meant that Lutz retained the right to decide whether or not he wanted to rely on the work done by the private auditors. If he was not satisfied with the job they were doing, he could conduct his own audit – provided he had enough staff. Equally important, the auditor continued to have the authority – and this was a crucial point – to see any financial information that he wanted to see. It did not matter whether the information pertained to a government department or a Crown corporation, the auditor was legally entitled to see it.

All of this was the background to the provincial auditor's report for 1987-88. Rarely has a government been so severely chastised. "I cannot effectively carry out my role to watch over the public purse for my client, the Legislative Assembly," Lutz wrote. "Also, there were a number of cases where I could not get information that, by law, I was entitled to receive."[19] He cited specific instances where he had been denied access to the minutes of the boards of directors of the Crown Investments Corporation, the Potash Corporation, and SaskTel. When he sought information from the Property Management Corporation about the travel expenses of cabinet ministers, his inquiry was rebuffed. Overall, the auditor estimated that he was able to see only 50 percent of expenditures from the public purse, compared with about 90 percent in 1987. Opposition Leader Roy Romanow summed up the situation: "Something is very rotten in the state of Saskatchewan."[20]

Lutz found that he could not rely upon the appointed private auditors for the answers to important questions. For example, he could not determine what had become of the proceeds from the sale of $2.2 million worth of dental equipment that followed the abolition of the province's school-based dental health plan for children. When the program was abolished, the equipment was sent to the Property Management Corporation, but Lutz was unable to find out how much of the equipment had been sold and what had become of the money. This example, among others, forced the auditor to conclude that the financial statements of the Property Management Corporation contained significant departures from generally-accepted accounting principles.

The government's characteristic reaction was attack. Rather than admitting fault or apologizing, Bob Andrew told reporters that Lutz was "a hard guy to complain about working together. Jesus Christ, he can't work with anybody."[21] Then, in the legislature where he enjoyed immunity from prosecution for slander, Andrew read selected portions of a letter written by Lutz's lawyer on 20 April 1989. The selections left the impression that Lutz had offered to amend his harshly critical report if the government would give him a more attractive retirement package. Andrew implied that Lutz had tried to make a sleazy deal.

In his own defence, Lutz issued a special report containing all the relevant documents. They showed that the lawyer for the Crown Investments Corporation, acting on behalf of the government, had approached Lutz's lawyer to see if some resolution could be found for Lutz's disagreements with the government.

Lutz, who was 65 and due to retire, did not raise the matter of his retirement during these discussions; the issue was brought up by the government's lawyer. Lutz simply responded that all he wanted in the way of a retirement package was what he was legally entitled to, which, according to the Provincial Auditor's Act, is the same package as a deputy minister receives upon retirement.

Andrew twisted this into an accusation that Lutz had been willing to alter his report for personal gain. The Justice Minister tried to leave the impression that the auditor had compromised his professional ethics. But the strategy of trying to discredit the auditor's report by discrediting the auditor, backfired; the media came down hard on Andrew and the government. Regina *Leader-Post* commentator Dale Eisler said that Andrew was not worthy of the title of justice minister, and the Saskatoon *Star-Phoenix* said Andrew should either apologize to Lutz for his personal attacks, or resign.[22] Even the *Globe and Mail*, a friend of right-of-centre governments, was uncharacteristically stern: "The Saskatchewan government appears to regard the province's auditor as a kind of Peeping Tom, a prowler in the backyard of its fiscal business and a rude intruder on its private affairs...the image that emerges is of a shabby, almost furtive government."[23]

When the furor over Andrew's remarks died down, Devine announced that he had sent a directive to the heads of all Crown corporations, government agencies and provincial departments to stop interfering with the provincial auditor: "I insist that all departments and agencies provide the provincial auditor with all necessary co-operation."[24] Devine's statement was an admission that the auditor's complaints had substance; his government was revealed as sloppy in its spending, and unwilling to let the public know what it was doing with their money. When called to account for its wrongdoing, the government responded by smearing the reputation of the auditor, a man who had served the province with integrity for more than 30 years. Only when it became clear that this attack was not working did the government take action to mend its ways.

The Devine government clearly overstepped its bounds, but the treatment of the auditor was entirely predictable from the way the Tories treated the legislature in general. From 1982 onward, they were constantly bending or breaking the rules. This was only to be expected from a party whose ideology was based on a deeply ingrained hostility to the institution of government itself.

Notes for Chapter 14

1. Interview, Merrilee Rasmussen, 5 October 1989.   2. *Leader-Post*, 27 April 1984.   3. *Ibid.*, 1 May 1984.   4. *Ibid.*, 16 December 1986.   5. *Debates and Proceedings (Hansard)*, Legislative Assembly of Saskatchewan, 22 December 1986, p. 449.   6. *Leader-Post*, 18 December 1986.   7. *Ibid.*, 19 December 1986.   8. *Hansard*, 22 December 1986, p. 453.

9. *Leader-Post*, 14 May 1988.   10. *Ibid.*   11. *Ibid.*   12. *Leader-Post*, 3 November 1989.   13. *Globe and Mail*, 28 October 1989.   14. *Ibid.*

15. *Ibid.*, 21 April 1988.   16. *Ibid.*, 11 June 1988.   17. *Ibid.*, 27 May 1988.   18. *Star-Phoenix*, 25 June 1988.   19. Government of Saskatchewan, *Report of the Provincial Auditor, 1988.*   20. *Hansard*, 19 May 1989, p. 1269.   21. *Leader-Post*, 18 May 1989.   22. *Hansard*, 25 May 1989, p. 1363.   23. *Globe and Mail*, 22 May 1989.   24. *Leader-Post*, 14 June 1989.

15

THE NEW RIGHT'S CONTEMPT FOR GOVERNMENT

◇ ────────────────────────────── ◇

INCOMPETENCE AND CORRUPTION

> George Hill is my friend, and Dennis Ball is my
> friend. Al Woods is my friend; Eli Fluter is my
> friend; Cliff Wright is my friend; Wally Nelson
> is my friend; Herb Pinder is my friend...I don't
> apologize for hiring our friends.
> — ERIC BERNTSON, *Hansard*,
> *22 November 1983, p. 90.*

The new right has no vested interest in striving for competence and integrity in government. Government inefficiency is not only to be expected, it provides the justification for the transfer of enterprises and services from the public to the private sector. The Saskatchewan Tories, embracing this ideology, did not deliberately set out to mismanage the affairs of the province, but they did fail to place a high priority on competent public administration. Their goal was to downgrade the role of government, not to make it a more effective instrument.

In addition, because the new right attaches relatively little importance to community, as opposed to individual, values, it fails to see government as the servant of the common good. The common good is viewed as nothing more than the net result of allowing individuals the freedom to pursue their private interests. This emphasis on the private over the public leads to contempt for government. It is not regarded as an honourable and worthwhile means to build a better society, but as an unfriendly taxer and source of harassment. This attitude becomes the justification for extracting as much private benefit as possible out of the public purse, and the door is opened to corruption. Our argument is not that any one political party has a monopoly on virtue – obviously, the complete range of ethical and unethical behaviour will be found in all parties – but that neo-conservative ideology, by undermining collectivist values, lowers esteem for the institution of government, which in turn encourages such practices as vote buying, patronage, influence peddling, and misuse of public funds.

Patronage

Patronage is one of the classic forms of government corruption. It is so deeply entrenched in our political system that it is not a question of whether it exists, but to what degree. The Tories have played the patronage game to the hilt. Numerous stories can be recounted: from the premier's brother-in-law getting a consultant's job in the Department of Education[1] to a defeated PC candidate installing without tender $10,000 worth of water purifiers in the legislature building.[2] Defeated Tory candidates, MLAs, and cabinet ministers, the very people who extolled opportunity in the private sector, made soft landings into well-paying government jobs. Paul Schoenhals was made full-time chairman of the Potash Corporation; Gordon Dirks was paid $30,000 to do a study of private school issues; Sid Dutchak was appointed to a management position with the Saskatchewan Housing Corporation; and Tim Embury received a lucrative government consulting contract. The list goes on almost indefinitely.

Tory patronage extended across the border into Manitoba where Sterling Lyon's Conservative government was defeated in 1981. Don Craik, Manitoba's former finance minister, was hired to do a consultant's report on the Saskatchewan Crown Investment Corporation; a contract to carry out an administrative review of the Saskatchewan Department of Health was awarded to Bud Sherman, the former Minister of Health in Manitoba; and Derek Bedson, the former principal secretary to Lyon's cabinet, was hired to fill a similar role for Devine. Bedson, as it turned out, was too much of a traditional Tory and had too much respect for the procedures and practices of parliamentary government to suit the Saskatchewan PCs, so he was later shifted to the new Vienna office of Agdevco, the international agricultural marketing corporation established by the NDP.

The Devine government excelled in looking after its friends. The SaskPower building in Moose Jaw was sold to a well-known PC party supporter on unusual terms. The sale price was $280,000, but SaskPower agreed to lease back half the building for $37,000 a year for ten years as well as pay 50 percent of the building's operating costs. The real estate agency which sold the building on behalf of the provincial government was run by the wife of the man who bought it.[3] Another deal involved the construction of the Ramada Renaissance Hotel in Regina by Remai Investments, controlled by John Remai. The government first commissioned Remai to do a study of the project's feasibility, then on the basis of a favourable report, allowed Remai to build it. To make the project viable, the government agreed to lease most of the building, and ended up paying rent for several months on 500,000 square feet of empty office space.[4] Remai expressed its gratitude by donating more than $12,000 to the Conservative party in 1988. The Tories' policy of leasing, rather than owning, government buildings was a boon to private real estate developers. Meanwhile, those in the construction industry who did not support the Tories found government contracts hard to come by; what better way of showing support than to make financial contributions to the PC party?

Patronage and government advertising went hand in hand. A letter written by Bruce Cameron, a member of the committee that organized the PC convention in November 1987, to PC party president Peter Matthews, shed light on the relationship between the Tories and advertising agencies. Cameron was objecting to the fact that Dome Advertising, which had provided the PCs with services, was pressing the party for payment of its invoice. He noted that by comparison, a smaller advertising agency, Smail Communications, had donated services worth $15,000 to the Tory convention. Cameron wrote, "Perhaps Dome Advertising with its far greater share of the provincial advertising budget should be expected to donate the cost of this particular bill to the party."[5] In other words, an advertising firm receiving government business was expected to pay a toll to the Conservative party.

Another unsavoury case arose when Carl Shiels, an assistant vice-president in charge of the traffic safety services branch of Saskatchewan Government Insurance, questioned the payment of invoices in the amount of $81,000 to Dome Advertising.[6] He could not find that the services to which the invoices referred had been rendered. After Shiels made this complaint, Dome Advertising discontinued billing SGI for consulting fees and agreed to charge the corporation at a regular hourly rate. Shiels later informed the press that when he first raised the issue of Dome's billing practices with his superior, he was told it was "a very delicate matter," that "we have to be very careful how we handle that," that the invoices he was questioning were "only the tip of the iceberg," and that large amounts of SGI money were being funnelled through Dome into the Conservative party campaign fund.[7]

Shiels first raised the issue on 3 July 1986, a few months before the 20 October 1986 provincial election. On 28 October 1986 he was summarily dismissed from his position at SGI on charges of sexual harassment.[8] Shiels sued for wrongful dismissal and won the case. In his judgment, Justice R.A. MacLean rejected the idea that Shiels had been guilty of sexual harassment. The judge went on to state: "I think it likely, too, that a contributing factor in the plaintiff's dismissal was the attitude he adopted with respect to the accounts of Dome Advertising Ltd. . . . The plaintiff testified, and I accept his evidence, that his superior was upset with the way he handled the matter, and perhaps too, because the superior himself had approved payment of similar invoices when perhaps he should not have."[9]

In February 1990 a new scandal for the Devine administration, this time involving the Saskatchewan Transportation Company, the Crown-owned bus line, eerily recalled the earlier Dome/SGI story. STC president Don Castle and vice-president Darrell Lowry were charged with felony offences under the American Foreign Corrupt Practices Act for allegedly demanding and receiving a kickback of $50,000 on the purchase of eleven buses from Eagle Bus Company of Brownsville, Texas. The FBI presented evidence indicating that the bribe money may have been headed for Progressive Conservative party coffers, but this was denied by party officials.

The Devine government also got into trouble over the issue of cabinet ministers' use of government aircraft for private travel. Highways Minister Jim Garner was forced to resign from the cabinet over this issue, and Bob Andrew was criticized when he and his family used a government airplane to attend a wedding in Calgary. At first, when questioned in the legislature about the flight, Andrew said he had gone to Calgary to meet with potential Saskatchewan investors, but outside the legislature he admitted the wedding was the main purpose of the trip.[10] While the "Bridal Bob" affair quickly blew over, it was in keeping with the government's casual attitude to public expenditures.

Pioneer Trust

A major controversy erupted in early 1985 with the collapse of Pioneer Trust, a financial institution that had an intimate relationship with the PCs. Indeed, the entire scandal was precipitated by the close ties between the top executives of Pioneer Trust and the Tory political hierarchy. The event exposed the tight, mutually supportive relationship between the Tories and elements in the provincial business elite.

Canadian Pioneer Management (CPM) was an aggressive Saskatchewan-based holding company whose main assets included Pioneer Life, Pioneer Trust, and Pioneer Securities. It had been founded in 1971 by Ross Sneath and Will Klein, free-enterprisers who loved to preach the virtues of business individualism. Both Sneath and Klein had close ties with the Tory party; Klein in particular was a key backroom figure, credited by some for having saved the 1982 election by helping the Tories secure a line of credit that allowed them to run a credible campaign.

After a decade of spectacular growth, CPM began to experience serious difficulties in the early eighties. Pioneer Securities was the first venture to experience trouble, when an investigation

by the Saskatchewan Securities Commission found it to be in violation of numerous regulations, including improper reporting
procedures, insufficient free capital, and poor record-keeping for
financial transactions. Most serious was the Commission's allegations of "unethical conduct" involving the trading of shares in
Pioneer Securities' parent company, CPM. As a consequence of
this investigation, Pioneer Securities was put on probation and
ordered to make numerous administrative changes.

Similar examples of poor management were soon to appear in
another CPM company, Pioneer Trust, but the ramifications this
time would reach up to the provincial cabinet. Like many financial institutions in the west, Pioneer Trust had much of its capital
tied up in the booming real estate market. But when the land
boom of the 1970s began to fizzle in the early 1980s, land prices
dropped as much as 50 percent. When that happened, some
investors simply walked away from their land holdings, leaving
mortgagers like Pioneer Trust to foreclose on property whose value was only a fraction of what it had been mortgaged for. Interest
rates were also an unbelievable 22 percent, virtually snuffing out
the demand for new housing. This situation caused problems for
numerous trust companies, including the infamous Principal
Group in Alberta – a company whose close connections to the
Tory party in that province and whose collapse were foreshad-
owed by Pioneer Trust's demise.

Faced with many bad debts and a severe shortfall in operating
cash, Pioneer Trust approached the provincial government in
November 1984 in the hope of gaining a guarantee for a share
issue that would allow the company to raise $25 to $30 million
and help it survive the crisis. Given the ties between CPM and
the Tories, it was not surprising that the company quickly
received a letter from Bob Andrew stating that "the government
of Saskatchewan will guarantee the 27.5 million preferred share
offering of Canadian Pioneer Management Ltd. Details of the
guarantee are now being reviewed by officials."[11] Bob Andrew was
soon to regret his hasty signature on this letter and his "absent-
mindedness" in not sending the letter to the federal government
which, as the regulator of financial institutions, needed to be
informed if one of these institutions was in difficulty.

Despite later regrets, in late 1984 the Tories thought that supporting the institution was the correct decision. Not only was it owned by some of the best friends the Tories had, it also represented the kind of entrepreneurial company the government had promised would thrive in the new "open for business" environment in Saskatchewan. Even though Pioneer was greedy, had overextended itself, and had not given itself adequate protection from bad loans, the government believed it needed to be saved. There were thousands of Saskatchewan residents who had their savings invested in the company, and they would be angered if the government did nothing. This, at least, was the excuse offered by the government.

The Tories tried arguing that propping up Pioneer Trust was consistent with government policy. The government had previously protected homeowners and farmers from the effects of fluctuating interest rates; why not protect real estate speculators too? The problems faced by Pioneer Trust were similar, having been caused by "rising interest rates and a collapse in real estate values."[12] Devine even took a page out of the NDP policy book and said that he was worried about Pioneer's head office moving out of the province if the government didn't act swiftly. The Tories were equally worried about the effect of the collapse of a financial institution on the new positive investment climate they were trying to build.

Naturally, the NDP was extremely critical of the decision to bail out a firm that provided few jobs and whose only purpose was to make money for investors, most of whom were protected in the event of a collapse by the Canadian Deposit Insurance Corporation. The NDP also complained that the decision to prop up the company was inconsistent with the tough Tory talk about the need for risk takers and the entrepreneurial spirit. The Saskatoon *Star-Phoenix* echoed these sentiments when it asked, "Why is a private company which has prided itself on its independence turning to the public for credit guarantees? By its own creed, this firm should rise or fall on the merits of its abilities and/or fortune in the marketplace."[13]

Yet the government was stubborn. The Tories believed that by guaranteeing an issue of preferred shares, they would save the company and have an easy political victory, while simultaneously helping out their friends. However, new problems soon revealed themselves. The government had generously agreed to support Pioneer Trust, but when Finance Department officials tried to get a better picture of the company's financial position, Pioneer officials were less than forthcoming. A top Pioneer official left the country, and lower-level officials proved unwilling or unable to answer questions about the company's financial situation. The company remained a closed book to government officials. This behaviour began to spook Andrew and the rest of the cabinet. What did Pioneer Trust have to hide?

The government began to fear that the company was in much worse shape than it had indicated when Andrew agreed to guarantee their share issue. To learn the facts, the government appointed a respected financial investigator (and, incidentally, a defeated Tory candidate in the last election), Al Wagar, to examine the books of Pioneer Trust. Upon receiving Wagar's report, the Tories decided that it would cost much more than $35 million to keep the troubled financial institution afloat, and they withdrew the offer to guarantee Pioneer's proposed share release. At 11 p.m. on 6 February, 1985 Bob Andrew phoned Will Klein to inform him that the government had changed its mind. The next day, Pioneer Trust closed its eleven branch offices and went into receivership.

In a few short weeks, the Tories had done an about-face on the question of saving Pioneer Trust. From arguing that it was an essential institution that must not be allowed to fail, they moved to the position that "the risks were too high financially for the people of Saskatchewan."[14] Yet the fact that the government was willing to support Pioneer Trust in the first place, without having looked at the books, showed the extent to which the Tories were willing to help political allies in the business community. Had the government even scratched the surface, it would have discovered a level of mismanagement throughout the company which would have given the most reckless investor pause. Pioneer Trust had made loans against the advice of some of the most respected real estate developers in the nation and had engaged in the questionable, though not illegal, practice of loaning money to its top officials on very favourable terms. So extensive was the mismanagement that CBC's *Fifth Estate* devoted an entire hour-long program to chronicling the incompetence and unsound business practices that abounded in the company. Even if only half of what the CBC documentary alleged were true, any investor would have been foolhardy to invest in it.

But the controversy did not end with the collapse of Pioneer Trust; there was still the question of what to do about the uninsured depositors. The Canadian Deposit Insurance Corporation, a federal Crown agency, insured individuals' deposits up to $60,000, but amounts over $60,000 were not covered. The Pioneer Trust collapse left $38.6 million in uninsured deposits, belonging to 1,800 depositors. While the NDP and others sought an investigation into the collapse, the federal and provincial governments entered into quiet negotiations about a settlement package.

While the Tories were able to stonewall and avoid a public inquiry, they were less fortunate in their dealings with the federal government. At the conclusion of negotiations, it was agreed that the provincial government would be responsible for $28.4 million and the federal government would pick up $10.2 million. This was unusual given that Pioneer Trust was a federally regulated institution, but Ottawa felt that the province, through its haste in agreeing to support the share offering only to withdraw the support later, was partially responsible for its collapse. If Pioneer Trust had informed the federal government of its financial difficulties in November 1984, some stop-gap financing might have been arranged. Instead, Pioneer went to the provincial government, which promised assistance which, four months later, turned out to be worthless. The immediate cause of the company's bankruptcy was the provincial government's failure to keep its word. If the Devine government had not interfered, the onus would have been on the federal government, and the province would not have faced such a huge bill to compensate the uninsured depositors.

Surprisingly, there were no major repercussions from this fiasco. No resignations resulted, although the pressure on Bob Andrew was intense as the debacle unfolded. Andrew admitted that he had made a serious error in judgment in agreeing to bail the company out, but he steadfastly refused to resign, and Devine likewise refused to fire him. While the provincial treasury was some $30 million poorer as a result of Tory meddling in the affairs of their friends, the government nonetheless managed to weather this storm. Unfortunately, the Tories did not absorb the lesson of the dire results that can flow from the abuse of power, and were soon enmeshed in fresh scandals.

The Rafferty-Alameda dams

The government's handling of the Pioneer Trust affair mingled cronyism with incompetence. In the case of the Rafferty-Alameda dams, controversy resulted from the government's disregard for proper procedures. The self-confessed provincial strategy was to create so much momentum for the project that all opposition would be crushed. The government's cavalier attitude and its failure to take seriously all of the environmental concerns led to court actions and a huge waste of public funds.

The idea of building a dam on the Souris River in southeastern Saskatchewan was an old one. It had been proposed as early as 1932, and was endorsed by the International Joint Commission in 1940 as a "long-range means of regulating the flow on this unusually variable stream." A joint study carried out by the governments of Saskatchewan, Manitoba, and Canada in 1975-76 pointed out that the only way the Rafferty Dam could be made economically feasible would be to link it to a major industrial project. The Devine government found such a project when it decided to increase the power-generating capacity of SaskPower by building a coal-fired power plant near Estevan; the resulting Shand plant would be cooled with water from the reservoir created by the dam. The project looked even more appealing when the United States government agreed in 1985 to contribute $41.1 million U.S. toward the dam's $140 million cost. The Souris flows into North Dakota after it leaves Saskatchewan, and the Americans were anxious to purchase some flood protection.[15]

The government established the Souris Basin Development Authority (SBDA) to oversee the construction of the Rafferty

Dam on the Souris and the Alameda Dam on nearby Moose Mountain Creek. Appointed head of the SBDA was SaskPower president George Hill, whose political ties to the Tories were well-known. A further political consideration was that the premier's riding of Estevan would be the main beneficiary of the economic spin-offs from the project. Second in line to benefit was the neighbouring constituency of Souris-Cannington, represented by the Deputy Premier Eric Berntson. All of these circumstances make it difficult to sort out politics from economics when discussing Shand, Rafferty or Alameda.

Provincial law required carrying out an environmental impact assessment before work could proceed on a project of this scale. The 1,800-page report, released to the public in August 1987, listed as the major benefits of the project 12,000 acres of new irrigated farm land, enhanced tourism as a result of the reservoirs, and better flood control and water conservation. The report admitted some ignorance about the impact of the dams on wildlife, but gave the assurance that $3.8 million would be set aside for further studies and habitat preservation.[16] Members of the public were invited to give their opinions before a government-appointed board of inquiry. At the conclusion of the hearings, Environment Minister Herb Swan announced that he was satisfied almost all environmental damage could be "mitigated, compensated, or avoided through careful planning," and gave his go-ahead to the project.

One of the many concerns of opponents of the project was that there would not be enough water from the Souris River to fill up the huge 57-kilometer-long Rafferty reservoir. The river, which springs from snowdrifts and the odd torrential rain, often has little water in it and, in fact, ran completely dry during the 1930s, the 1960s and the 1980s. Environment Canada hydrologists, who based their research on Souris water flow statistics collected over the past 50 years, concluded that 75 percent of the annual runoff, when collected above the Rafferty Dam, would simply evaporate. This led to fears that surrounding marshes and wetlands would be drained or that groundwater would have to be pumped to provide sufficient water. To allay this concern, the board of inquiry recommended that drainage of wetlands not be allowed.

However, when Swan gave his approval for the project, he ignored this recommendation.[17]

Since the Souris River was not confined to Saskatchewan, but flowed into North Dakota and then looped north into Manitoba, a federal government license had to be obtained before the dams could be built. The Devine government did not bother waiting for this formality. Instead, unlicensed construction began at the Rafferty site in the early spring of 1988. The Canadian Wildlife Federation denounced this action as a flagrant violation of federal law. According to CWF lawyer Stephen Hazell, "The Saskatchewan government is guessing that [federal Environment Minister] Tom McMillan won't have the nerve to pursue charges... They seem to think the federal government will not do anything to jeopardize Devine's support of free trade and the Meech Lake Accord."[18]

In June 1988, when the federal government finally issued the license, opponents of the dams cried foul. Rod MacDonald, lawyer for the anti-dam coalition called SCRAP (Stop Construction of the Rafferty-Alameda Projects), said the decision was a triumph of "politics over procedure." The Canadian Wildlife Federation was so upset that it took the federal government to court. Their lawsuit alleged that the federal government had failed to follow its own Environmental Assessment Review Procedures (EARP) guidelines. The federal government argued in its own defence that the guidelines were not mandatory and that it was up to the federal environment minister to decide whether Ottawa should conduct its own environmental study, or rely on the study done by the provincial government.

The evidence suggests that lawyers in the Saskatchewan Department of Justice realized that a federal environmental assessment was required. A leaked memo from the Justice Department to the SBDA in 1986 warned that since 4,100 acres of federally owned community pasture land would be flooded, the federal government would have to conduct a study.[19] Federal environment officials lamely replied that although the federal government did own the land, the pasture would not be lost because the province was providing compensation for it.[20]

The attempt to cut corners backfired because on 10 April 1989

Federal Court Justice Bud Cullen decided in favour of the Canadian Wildlife Federation and quashed the license to build the dams. The decision distressed the provincial government. More than $34 million had already been spent on construction, 400,000 cubic meters of dam fill had been moved to the site, and four out of every five farmers in the flood plain had already reached deals to sell their land.[21] Eric Berntson furiously accused the CWF of "fiddling with the very future of the province"[22] and blamed the debacle on "a couple of wingies out of Central Canada" and the Saskatchewan NDP caucus which had been "aiding and abetting" them.[23] NDP leader Roy Romanow calmly reminded Berntson: "We didn't fund Rafferty. We didn't start the lawsuit. We didn't make the judgment."[24] The government's own haste and indiscretion had been responsible for the setback.

Rod MacDonald, spokesperson for SCRAP, said the court's decision vindicated the stance taken by his group, and called upon Devine to apologize for his attacks: "We've suffered a lot of personal abuse and threats."[25] Devine, however, was unapologetic and said of the court's decision: "It may be legally correct, but it makes no sense at all."[26] He made light of environmental concerns, suggesting the reservoir that would be created by the project would be good for the family life of ducks, and thus for the environment. "Evidently, one third of all ducks in North America do their thing in Saskatchewan. They can't hug very well if there isn't any water. They need water to hug in. They like that – they come up and wrap their wings around each other and smack away in the water."[27]

In accordance with the court ruling, the federal government undertook its own environmental review of the dam project. The initial evaluation identified ten significant "information deficiencies" where insufficient information made it difficult to predict Rafferty's impact. This directly contradicted the Saskatchewan government's claim that the dam had been "studied to death." Federal environmental review guidelines required the government to appoint an independent panel to review the project where there was significant public concern about its effects. This was the course of action recommended by the Tory government in Manitoba, which was worried about the downstream water quality of the Souris River. The federal government ignored this advice and on 31 August 1989 issued a new license for the construction of Rafferty. It attached 22 "stringent conditions" on Saskatchewan, including the replacement of lost habitats for waterfowl and fish, adherence to international water quality objectives, and a prohibition against pumping groundwater or draining nearby wetlands to fill the reservoir.

Thus, after a five-month delay, construction resumed. The delay was estimated to add another $20 million to the cost, an extra expense that was entirely due to the Devine government's arrogant and inept handling of the project.

The Canadian Wildlife Federation did not give up. They went to court again in an effort to force the federal government to set up an independent review panel. On 28 December 1989 the federal court ruled that if such a panel were not set up within a month, the Rafferty project license would be void. Four days before the court-imposed deadline, federal Environment Minister Lucien Bouchard appointed the panel. Construction on the dams was suspended for at least a year while the panel completed its work.

As the Regina *Leader-Post* editorialized, if the provincial and federal governments had followed proper procedures in the first place, all of these difficulties could have been avoided.[28] Certainly, there had been ample warning that the SBDA's study was inadequate. The Saskatchewan Wildlife Federation, the Canadian Wildlife Federation, the National Wildlife Federation in the United States, the U.S. Environmental Protection Agency, the U.S. Corps of Army Engineers, and the North Dakota Wildlife Society had all called attention to its shortcomings. Even more revealing, federal environmental officials expressed serious reservations about the SBDA study before the initial federal license was granted. According to Elizabeth May, an adviser to federal Environment Minister Tom McMillan, Saskatchewan's Tories had put political pressure on their federal counterparts to override the advice of the experts and get the license issued. If the Canadian Wildlife Federation had not taken the federal government to court, the Saskatchewan government would have gotten away with its illegal behaviour.

The essence of the Devine government's strategy was to conceal facts and ram the project through. When a civil servant suggested that water might have to be drained from the South Saskatchewan River Basin, Lake Diefenbaker, and the Qu'Appelle lakes to help fill the Rafferty reservoir, he was suspended from his job for two weeks without pay.[29] An officer of the Saskatchewan Water Corporation was fired after he released a consultant's report that stated the Rafferty-Alameda project was probably not economically feasible.[30] But perhaps the most damning indictment of provincial government policy was contained in a document written by the director of planning and operations for the SBDA, which revealed that the government's strategy was to keep people in the dark as long as possible: "[We should take] the project as far as we possibly can on our own and build up as much momentum behind it before we open the process up to other governments...I do not think it advisable for us to initiate an 'open-minded' consultation process with either the Canadian federal government or the government of the province of Manitoba."[31]

GigaText

Of all the Keystone Kops misadventures of the Devine government, none surpassed the GigaText affair. The trouble started when the government got mixed up with high-tech entrepreneur Guy Montpetit. Montpetit himself gave the best description of his style of operating: "You know, I've never had a damned cent in my life, but I've always travelled in a Mercedes."[32] With $39 million borrowed from a Japanese businessman named Takayuki Tsuru, Montpetit embarked on a number of ventures, including a plan to manufacture computer chips in an abandoned tranquilizer factory near Montreal. The project required $45 million in federal and provincial government grants. To obtain them, Montpetit secured the services of Michel Cogger, a close friend of, and campaign chairman for, Brian Mulroney. Cogger, whom Mulroney would later appoint to the senate, put pressure on federal civil servants to help Montpetit, but the bureaucrats took one look at the latter's history of financial failure and closed the door.

Saskatchewan officials, unfortunately, gave Montpetit a hearing. At Cogger's behest, Ken Waschuk, a Conservative party pollster in Saskatchewan, introduced the supposed high-tech wizard to Deputy Premier Eric Berntson. The Quebec entrepreneur claimed that his company, GigaText, had the computer technology to translate English into French. For Berntson, Montpetit's appearance must have seemed providential because the provincial government, prompted by a Supreme Court ruling, had just undertaken to translate some of its laws into French. The Devine government quickly invested $4 million in GigaText for 25 percent of the shares. Montpetit and his business partner, Douglas Young, a Winnipeg university professor, invested no money, but received 75 percent of the shares.

GigaText used the money to purchase twenty computers from another Montpetit-owned company, Lisp, which in turn had obtained the computers from GigaMos Systems, Inc., yet another Montpetit company. GigaMos had obtained the computers from a bankrupt U.S. computer company a few months earlier. They were part of the U.S. company's inventory and, according to an independent court-appointed auditor, had a value of $39,000.[33] However, GigaMos billed Lisp $1.5 million for the computers; an invoice was sent, but no money changed hands. In other words, Lisp didn't pay anything for the computers. For these same computers, GigaText (that is, the government of Saskatchewan, the sole financial backer of GigaText) paid $2.9 million.

When questioned about these transactions, Deputy Premier Eric Berntson claimed that the province "got value for the dollar when GigaText bought the computers."[34] If Berntson actually believed that, he was one of the few who did. What happened to the $2.9 million? According to the evidence that came to light when Japanese businessman Tsuru took Montpetit to court, $1.25 million of it made its way into Montpetit's personal bank account, via his two Bermuda holding companies; $100,000 of this was used to pay off a personal loan and to make various purchases, including two luxury boats.[35]

Montpetit, who had sole cheque-signing authority for Giga-Text, also wrote himself a cheque for $300,000. On top of this, he collected an annual salary of $60,000, a monthly expense account of $18,000, and a monthly payment of $35,000 to rent an executive jet, which, incidentally, was owned by another of his companies. He used the jet to fly around the continent, including a weekend trip with a female companion to San Francisco, at a cost of $41,500. He also flew Eric Berntson, Berntson's chief political aide Terry Leier, and Ken Waschuk to various destinations. Leier, as a GigaText board member, received a $5,000 cash advance, while Waschuk was given a $150,000 interest-free loan. The loan was casually requested and immediately granted while the two men were golfing. Montpetit saw nothing irregular about this. "After all, he [Waschuk] had rendered us a good service, he had negotiated for us," he said. "He was after all my representative or the one used with respect to the government of Saskatchewan."[36] Montpetit's partner, Douglas Young, hinted at similar payments of this kind, stating that Montpetit had spoken of spending "hundreds of thousands of dollars paying considerations" to people who helped arrange the Saskatchewan government's investment in GigaText.[37]

The government first noticed that not all was well with its GigaText investment in the fall of 1988. Five months had passed since the start-up of the company, $4 million had been spent, but not one sentence had been translated into French. Douglas Young tried to sound the alarm that something was terribly wrong, but he had difficulty getting through to the senior people in the government. "When it became clear to me that the four million dollars was apparently nearly expended, I began to try to talk with Eric Berntson on the matter," he later told a reporter. "Rumour already had it that there was to be yet another ten machines acquired, which to me was quite insane. But despite several attempts through Otto Cutts [president of the Saskatchewan Property Management Corporation] and one visit to Regina just in an attempt to see Eric on this and other matters of major concern. . . I failed to be able to convey to anyone the seriousness of the whole situation, because no one except Otto would even listen to what I had to say."[38] When the government finally realized that there was a problem, it responded by loaning GigaText another $1.25 million to keep the company afloat while it struggled to make the technology work. Strangely enough, Montpetit

still retained sole cheque-signing authority, a right he did not relinquish until March 1989, when the government took over complete control of the company.[39]

The government set 17 June 1989 as the deadline for GigaText
to prove that its technology worked. The deadline passed, however, with no evidence of any translation being done. The media
was called in to observe the GigaText computer translate a 21-
word sentence, but when the reporters asked to submit a sentence
of their own, they were refused. Finally, in mid-November 1989,
the government, after having invested another $75,000 in addi-
tion to the $5.25 million it had previously sunk into the com-
pany, closed down GigaText. It was then revealed that Jean-
Pierre Paillet, who had been induced to come to Regina to
become GigaText's operations manager with the offer of a 1988
Mercedes Benz and a $137,000 condominium paid for by the gov-
ernment of Saskatchewan, had made no serious attempt after June
1989 to make the translation system work. After telling reporters
on 26 June that translations would be possible by the end of summer, Paillet privately advised employees to look for other work,
then left for a six-week overseas vacation.

It was not just the loss of more than $5 million of taxpayers'
money that made GigaText such a blot on the government's
record. It was the way the money was lost: computers worth
$39,000 being purchased for $2.9 million; public funds being
squandered to support the luxurious lifestyle of an operator lacking both competence and integrity; government money finding its
way into Bermuda bank accounts and being doled out in a
$150,000 interest-free loan to a prominent Saskatchewan Tory.
The GigaText affair exposed many of the Devine government's
failings – carelessness with public money, patronage at high levels, administrative incompetence, and the inability to distinguish
between an entrepreneur and a crook.

"A shabby, almost furtive government" was the way the *Globe
and Mail* summed up the performance of the PCs in Saskatchewan. A government that was tending to its business in an orderly
and capable manner would not have invested in GigaText, would
not have run roughshod over environmental review procedures
before beginning construction on the Rafferty Dam, would not

have bungled the bail-out of Pioneer Trust, and would not have indulged in unrestrained patronage. The incompetence of the Devine government sprang partly from the hostility of the new right toward the public sector and the institution of government itself. Private interests were placed ahead of the public interest. This helps explain the dismal record of the Devine government.

Notes for Chapter 15

1. *Leader-Post*, 7 October 1982. 2. *Ibid.*, 25 August 1982. 3. *Ibid.*, 2 April 1988. 4. *Ibid.*, 26 January 1988. 5. *Ibid.*, 28 April 1988. 6. *Star-Phoenix*, 9 July 1988. 7. *Leader-Post*, 28 June 1988. 8. *Ibid.* 9. *Ibid.*, Eisler, 28 June 1988; *Shiels v. Saskatchewan Government Insurance*, Saskatchewan Court of Queen's Bench, 6 April 1988. 10. *Star-Phoenix*, 21 July 1987.

11. *Leader-Post*, 17 May 1985. 12. *Ibid.*, 11 January 1985. 13. *Star-Phoenix*, 12 January 1985. 14. *Ibid.*, 8 February 1985.

15. *Leader-Post*, Eisler, 13 April 1989. 16. *Ibid.*, 12 August 1987. 17. *Ibid.*, 16 February 1988. 18. *Ibid.*, 19 February 1988. 19. *Ibid.*, 14 April 1989. 20. *Globe and Mail*, 23 March 1989. 21. *Leader-Post*, 12 April 1989. 22. *Ibid.*, 13 April 1989. 23. *Ibid.* 24. *Ibid.*, 14 April 1989. 25. *Ibid.*, 23 June 1989. 26. *Ibid.*, 14 April 1989. 27. *Ibid.*, 10 May 1989. 28. *Leader-Post*, 30 January 1990. 29. *Ibid.*, 13 May 1988. 30. *Ibid.*, 16 June 1989. 31. *Commonwealth*, March 1989.

32. *Leader-Post*, 10 October 1989. 33. *Globe and Mail*, 22 June 1989. 34. *Leader-Post*, 23 June 1989. 35. *Globe and Mail*, 22 June 1989. 36. *Leader-Post*, 3 June 1989. 37. *Globe and Mail*, 9 August 1989. 38. *Leader-Post*, 3 June 1989. 39. *Ibid.*

PERMANENT REVOLUTION?

Saskatchewan was the first jurisdiction in North America to elect a social democratic government, and has ever since led the way in health care, labour law, human rights, and public enterprise. Under the leadership of Tommy Douglas, Woodrow Lloyd, and Allan Blakeney, Saskatchewan has been the stronghold of social democracy in Canada. In 1982, this tradition was challenged by the rise to power of the new right under Grant Devine. The Tories embody a neo-conservative ideology which defies the pattern of Saskatchewan politics since the election of the CCF in 1944, and just as 1944 changed the direction of the province in a fundamental way, 1982 could yet turn out to do the same.

The central goal of the new right is to reduce the role of government and to strengthen the private sector, and this has been the main theme of the Tory bid to bring about a neo-conservative revolution in Saskatchewan. Whereas social democrats believe that Crown corporations have an important role to play in the provincial economy, the new right favours privatization so the free market can prevail. Whereas social democrats endorse the programs of the welfare state to advance the cause of social justice, the new right is cutting back the welfare state to force individuals to become more self-reliant. Whereas social democrats support trade unions to protect the rights of workers, the new right opposes unions because they interfere with private enterprise. And whereas social democrats value government institutions as expressions of collective ideals, the new right holds government in low esteem because it supposedly limits individual liberty.

While Grant Devine and the Tories are ideologues with a mission, they are also practical politicians who want to win and retain power. This has obliged them to offer their program in a manner acceptable to the electorate. In the 1982 election, Devine portrayed himself more as a populist than as an ideological extremist in the mould of Margaret Thatcher or Ronald Reagan. Once elected, the Tories did not immediately move to sell the Crown corporations, the symbols of the NDP approach to economic development. Devine, in 1982, expressed admiration for government-owned companies, saying they could do a "very, very effective job if they are run properly." The new government's economic policy was summed up in their advertising slogan, "open for business." The main element of this strategy was the promotion of Saskatchewan as a safe haven for private business investment. At the same time, the Crown corporations were prevented from expanding in the hope that the private sector would take up the slack. As a further incentive to the business community, the government launched an attack on organized labour, froze the minimum wage, and cut welfare payments.

It was soon apparent from the pitifully few examples of new businesses coming to the province that this strategy had failed. The government gradually became aware of the limitations of a free market philosophy for Saskatchewan, and began to increase spending on economic development. To this end, they made extensive use of tax incentives, cash grants, low interest loans, and direct partnerships. The government's strategy in essence was not free enterprise, but government-supported free enterprise.

Yet even with generous government handouts to private companies, the Saskatchewan economy sank further into recession. From 1982 to 1986, the unemployment rate increased from 6 percent to 9.5 percent, and the number of manufacturing jobs declined by 2,000. In the same period, the provincial treasury moved from a modest surplus to a $1.7 billion debt, while the debt of the Crown corporations increased from $3.4 billion to more than $5.2 billion.

Heading into the 1986 election, the Tories decided to conceal the true extent of this fiscal crisis from the electorate. The pre-election budget understated the deficit by close to a billion dollars, and money flowed freely for election promises. As in 1982, the Tories played down ideological issues; privatization was not even mentioned. The key to the narrow PC victory was the timely intervention of the Mulroney government with a half-billion dollar farm deficiency payment, which enabled the Tories to hold on to their rural base.

After the 1986 election, the political climate changed dramatically. When the true size of the public debt was revealed, the government began to preach restraint and the need for good management. This led to a harsh series of budget reductions including the abolition of the school-based children's dental plan, reduced coverage under the prescription drug plan, and many other hurtful cutbacks. Faced with sagging popularity, an economic policy in tatters, low morale at the grassroots level, and a rapidly escalating debt, the government grasped privatization as the solution to Saskatchewan's economic woes. An elaborate and expensive educational campaign was mounted to promote the idea.

Borrowing arguments and advisors from Margaret Thatcher's Britain, Devine sold privatization as a means to reduce government debt, facilitate "public participation" in the economy, bring about greater economic efficiency, and develop a new entrepreneurial culture. But unloading income-earning assets at a discount enriched private shareholders without improving the government's financial position. Far from encouraging public participation, privatization led to the loss of ownership and control of significant portions of the Saskatchewan economy to central Canadian and foreign interests. The argument that privatization induces efficiency by bringing market discipline to bear on publicly owned companies was also bogus: some of the Crown corporations, including Saskoil and the Potash Corporation, were already competing with private companies, while others, like SaskPower and SaskTel, were natural monopolies. Finally, the notion that privatization would create an "entrepreneurial culture" ignores the fact that economic development in Saskatchewan requires defying, rather than succumbing to, free market forces.

Despite the intellectual poverty of the arguments for privatization and their inapplicability to Saskatchewan, the government spent millions of dollars promoting its ideological cause. Bonds and shares were sold on financially irresistible terms. But while residents and non-residents took advantage of the deals, the government had a harder time persuading the general public that privatization was in their interest, and a growing opposition coalesced around the battle to stop the government from selling off the natural gas utility. Subdued but unrepentant, the Tories postponed some of their privatization plans, while they waited for public opinion to "catch up" with them.

Another component of the new right agenda is the attack on the welfare state, especially the programs benefiting lower income groups. The Devine government cut social assistance on the grounds that it destroyed the incentive to work. The outcome of so-called "welfare reform" was the breakdown of the public welfare system, more people below the poverty line, and the imposition of the work test on those stigmatized as undeserving. Action by workers to improve wages and conditions were frustrated by concerted government efforts to undermine the labour movement. The new right, cherishing the free market and private enterprise, rejects the collective values inherent in trade unions and the welfare state.

In addition, the attack on the welfare state contained a moralistic dimension contributed by the new Christian right. Devine presents himself as a staunch defender of the family, the social unit which the new right holds responsible for inculcating moral values in youth. Big government and social programs are said to weaken family responsibility and interfere with the rights and duties of parents. By pitting the welfare state against the family, the Tories have created great hardship. As social assistance payments and job opportunities declined, more families sank below the poverty line. As funds for transition houses, family counselling, and other support services failed to keep pace with the demand, more families suffered. Once again, as with most of the policies of the new right, ideology and reality are miles apart.

A basic premise of new right philosophy is that government is at best a necessary evil. There is little understanding of the need for a strong public sector co-existing with a strong private sector in a civilized society that gives due recognition to both the values of community and the values of individual freedom. The Devine government's dislike for the public sector sometimes bordered on contempt. It led to a flouting of parliamentary traditions and conventions, including an unprecedented attack on the provincial auditor. It led also to patronage excesses, disregard for the merit principle in the civil service, careless spending, and inept decision-making. A used-car tax and a lottery tax were introduced, only to be withdrawn a few months later; improper procedures to push through the Rafferty Dam landed the government in court; the bail-out of Pioneer Trust was badly bungled; and millions of dollars were wasted in Joytec, Supercart, Giga-Text, and other fiascos.

Although it is too early to make a definitive statement about the impact and historical significance of the new right in Saskatchewan, some preliminary conclusions are possible. In the 1980s, a major rightward shift occurred in political discourse in the province. The NDP stopped talking about bringing new enterprises under public ownership; it concentrated instead on trying to save those Crowns that had not yet been privatized. It is doubtful that Saskatchewan will in the near future see a level of public enterprise comparable to what existed in the 1970s. Under the Tories, the province incurred so much debt that major investments, even if politically acceptable, will not be affordable. The cuts to the welfare state will be easier to restore, but even here lack of money is a limiting factor.

Although the new right has left its imprint upon Saskatchewan, its impact has been modified by the province's political culture and economy. The residual strength of social democracy forced the Tories to proceed with caution. This accounted for Devine's down-playing of ideological issues during the 1982 and 1986 elections and his decision to unveil privatization slowly. On the one occasion in 1987 when he boldly proclaimed the neo-conservative revolution, declaring his intention to privatize almost everything, he suffered a severe setback. The other factor limiting the full expression of neo-conservatism was the hinterland nature of the provincial economy. The new right believes in the free market, but the free market judges Saskatchewan harshly. When Devine discovered this, his government, in a major contradiction of neo-conservative theory, began to give handouts to private enterprise. Instead of reducing the role of the state, the Tories, at least in this respect, increased it.

Saskatchewan's resource-based, agricultural economy makes it vulnerable both to adverse climatic conditions and to price swings in the international marketplace. Drought and weak prices for wheat, potash, uranium and other exports created economic hardship in the 1980s. In 1988, Saskatchewan's per capita gross domestic product was 22 percent below the national average, the worst performance of the economy since 1970. Out-migration statistics reflect the severity of the depression: during the first nine months of 1989, people left Saskatchewan at the rate of one every 23 minutes. Meanwhile, provincial debt on ordinary government expenditures passed the $4 billion mark, more than $4,000 for every man, woman, and child. By the spring of 1990 the heavy debt load forced Devine to re-impose the gasoline tax, something he had promised never to do as long as he was premier, and to cancel home improvement grants and loans. Thus, Devine reneged on the major commitments he had made to the electorate in the 1982 and 1986 elections. The grim economic situation cast a pall over the government and its neo-conservative projects.

Will the new right succeed in its goal of shifting Saskatchewan from its social democratic base and altering the fundamental orientation of the province? Will the neo-conservative revolution be permanent? Or will the Conservative government elected in 1982 be viewed in hindsight as an aberration from the mainstream Saskatchewan political tradition, much like the Conservative-led coalition government of 1929-1934? Although this question cannot yet be answered, one thing is clear from the record of the Devine government and the impact of the new right since 1982. The Saskatchewan Tories, while motivated by the same survival instincts as most other political movements, are true revolutionaries. As long as they hold office, they will continue to privatize, to attack the welfare state, and to do all in their power to make the neo-conservative revolution permanent.

INDEX

As almost every page of this book contains a reference to Grant Devine, the Progressive Conservative Party, the Devine government's privatization efforts, and Crown corporations, index entries have been dispensed with for these topics (although there is an entry for Chantal Devine, as well as individual Crowns such as the Potash Corporation of Saskatchewan). Similarly, there is no entry for the New Democratic Party, which has opposed the Devine government's activities at every step (although Allan Blakeney, Roy Romanow, and the Co-operative Commonwealth Federation do get their own entries).

288

Printed in Canada